Iran and Saudi Arabia

For the victims of an enmity they played no role in creating

This is a thorough account of one of the most important interstate rivalries in recent decades, one that has done much damage in the wider Middle East and Islamic World. This book stands out for not only providing a lucid analysis of the drivers of conflict between Saudi Arabia and Iran, but also for offering concrete suggestions for reducing tensions between those two regional powers.

Toby Matthiesen, University of Oxford

In this eminently fair and balanced assessment of the intractable conflict between Iran and Saudi Arabia, Ibrahim Fraihat is in the unenviable position of trying to make sense of a nonsensical hostility between two ruling regimes that are wasting their respective nations' resources and endangering an entire volatile region. By modestly subtitling his deeply informed and balanced intervention just 'Taming a Chaotic Conflict', Fraihat signals the working of a judicious mind that has wisely abandoned the search for 'root causes' and gently teaches us to be humble and human in our expectations. A superb strategic intervention on how to prevent a colossal calamity from happening.

Hamid Dabashi, Columbia University

This is exactly the book we need right now! Whereas much has been already been written about the causes and developments of the Iran–Saudi Arabia rivalry, we have precious little knowledge about how this conflict can be peacefully managed and ultimately resolved. Fraihat combines his own personal experiences of participation in dialogue efforts over the years with the scholarly insights of the large body of research on conflict resolution, in order to shed light on this. The book gives us a solid basis for analysing the prospects and challenges for how to transform the current destructive relationship between these two regional powers into more constructive interactions, a transformation that would radically change the Middle East region, and thereby the world.

**Isak Svensson, Department of Peace and
Conflict Research, Uppsala University**

Remarkable for its lucidity, fieldwork and command of the literature, this is a timely and authoritative study of the Middle East's most consequential bilateral relationship. Ibrahim Fraihat wisely jettisons timeworn primordialist tropes about the intractability and immutability of the Saudi–Iranian rivalry and focuses instead on how tensions between the two powers can be regulated and managed through wiser statecraft, grassroots activism and domestic reforms. What sets this magisterial book apart from others on this topic is that it moves beyond diagnosis and analysis to propose creative policy recommendations.

Frederic Wehrey, Carnegie Endowment for International Peace

In a climate of rising hostility across the Persian Gulf where diplomatic engagement appears distant, Ibrahim Fraihat's book is a welcome and timely contribution and, more importantly, offers a degree of hope. While many see the rivalry between Saudi Arabia and Iran in zero-sum ways, Fraihat argues that rapprochement is possible, in a radical and welcome departure from other literature on the topic. Drawing on first-hand attempts to facilitate conflict reconciliation, this rich and insightful tome is essential reading for policy makers, peace-builders, academics and anyone wishing to better understand the politics of the region.

Simon Mabon, Lancaster University

Ibrahim Fraihat is not a newcomer to the field and has already distinguished himself with a strong body of work on Saudi Arabia, Iran and also KSA–IRI relations, so it is very good news to see him distil his considerable contributions in a new project on managing the conflict between Tehran and Riyadh. It is clear in this book that Fraihat comes closest to shining light on the way forward. I think we all need to take note of this outstanding research and learn from it, for both scholarly and practical reasons.

Anoush Ehteshami, Durham University

A timely and well-informed analysis of one of the Middle East's most enduring and consequential rivalries. Fraihat offers an insider's perspective into the Iran–Saudi conflict along with practical suggestions for de-escalation through the lens of conflict resolution. A must for anyone seeking to understand the origins and manifestations of the regional 'cold war' between Saudi Arabia and Iran – and potential strategies for ending it.

**Justin Gengler – Social and Economic Survey
Research Institute, Qatar University**

Iran and Saudi Arabia

Taming a Chaotic Conflict

Ibrahim Fraihat

EDINBURGH
University Press

Edinburgh University Press is one of the leading university presses in the UK. We publish academic books and journals in our selected subject areas across the humanities and social sciences, combining cutting-edge scholarship with high editorial and production values to produce academic works of lasting importance. For more information visit our website: edinburghuniversitypress.com

Edinburgh University Press Ltd
The Tun – Holyrood Road
12(2f) Jackson's Entry
Edinburgh EH8 8PJ

Typeset in 11/15 Adobe Garamond by
IDSUK (DataConnection) Ltd, and
printed and bound in Great Britain

A CIP record for this book is available from the British Library

ISBN 978 1 4744 6618 9 (hardback)
ISBN 978 1 4744 6620 2 (webready PDF)
ISBN 978 1 4744 6619 6 (paperback)
ISBN 978 1 4744 6621 9 (epub)

Contents

Preface

When my Omani friend Abdullah Baabood, former Gulf Studies Professor at the University of Cambridge and Qatar University, expressed his very balanced and well-informed scholarly views of the Iran–Saudi conflict in a track two workshop held in Doha, he was told by a Saudi participant that he was 'betraying the Gulf cause and supporting Iran'. When the workshop ended, an Iranian participant came to him and said, 'I did not know you work for an American agenda.' That one statement could elicit such opposite reactions demonstrates the extent to which the Iran–Saudi relationship remains a hotly contested issue in the Gulf.

Researching the tension between Iran and Saudi Arabia, with a commitment to taking a critical, objective and constructive approach, has therefore proven to be particularly challenging. Because this book is focused on objective analysis of the conflict and finding constructive solutions to it, it will likely be challenged by both parties, since this approach does not tend to be promoted by governments or media in the region. Indeed, such divergence in opinions is a common phenomenon in conflicts of deep polarisation, which lead in turn to assertions that one is 'either with us or against us'. Though critical of both the policies of the two parties that propagated the conflict and of its recent escalation, I make every effort to provide alternative and constructive solutions to the destructive polices both parties are promoting for their own countries as well as for the entire region.

At first, I struggled with how to label the Iran–Saudi relationship, whether it is a conflict, dispute, rivalry, or, as my friend Gregory Gause likes to call it, a cold war. Ultimately, I have decided primarily to use the term 'conflict', given particularly that diplomatic relations were severed between the two countries in 2016 and that the relationship has only worsened since the

Donald Trump administration fuelled the conflict after the Riyadh summit in May 2017. Despite our primary use of this term, others are occasionally employed depending on the context.

I next had to decide which country's name to use first, since this is such a sensitive topic. I resolved this by using an alphabetical order, 'Iran–Saudi', for simplicity. However, it should be noted that this order changes when I use the names of capital cities, as it then becomes the 'Riyadh–Tehran' conflict.

Another semantic issue, which has often inflamed passions, is whether to label the Gulf Arabian or Persian. Indeed, the Iranian government would discredit a scholar's argument simply for using the term 'Arabian Gulf', regardless of the content of the monograph. Similarly, Saudi Arabia would treat a monograph as biased for the use of 'Persian Gulf'. Therefore, I use the term 'the Gulf' consistently throughout the entire book to refer to the Arabian/Persian Gulf.

I tell my conflict resolution students that the first step in resolving any conflict is to accurately define the main issues of that conflict. However, when I tried to do this in the track two workshops held over a span of three years in Doha, it became clear that that was easier said than done. I tried to press both Iranians and participants from the Arab side of the Gulf to agree at least on what the core issues of the conflict are (i.e. security, Sunni–Shia sectarianism, Arab–Persian nationalism, leadership of the Muslim *Ummah*), but both parties strongly resisted, insisting instead on their own versions of the conflict narrative. For this reason, I dedicate the first part of this book mainly to discussion of the conflict issues to understand how they affect the conflict and the potential for its resolution.

As is the case with most conflicts, defining the starting point of the Iran–Saudi Arabia conflict was an additional challenge. It became clear to me that parties politicise the starting points of the conflict to suit their agendas and support their narratives. President Obama, for example, clearly framed the conflict as essentially primordial to distance his administration from any role in exacerbating it. Saudi interlocutors, on the other hand, often consider the Islamic revolution in Tehran in 1979, and along with it the goal of exporting the revolution, the starting point of this conflict. However, Iran proactively acted on expanding its influence in the region mainly after the US invasion of Iraq in 2003, after the balance of power in the region had decidedly changed. I had to take into account all of these starting points, giving them the importance they deserve, yet assess them away from politicisations or instrumentalisation of certain timelines.

Acknowledgements

I was extremely fortunate to be invited by numerous organisations to serve as participant, speaker and co-organiser in over a dozen track two workshops dedicated to discussing the conflict between Iran and its Gulf neighbours and exploring approaches to its resolution. I am very grateful to the organisations that made this possible, including but not limited to Georgetown University's Center for Regional and International Studies in Qatar, the Gulf Studies Program at Qatar University, the European Iran Research Group, the Arab Center for Research and Policy Studies, the International Institute for Strategic Studies (IISS) and the Center of Applied Research in Partnership with the Orient (CAPRO).

These workshops included, among others, former policymakers, regional and international scholars, opinion leaders and political activists. Held in different parts of the world, all workshops took place under the Chatham House Rule, which means that information can be used in publications with no attribution to participants. These workshops therefore gave me a unique opportunity to have access to high-quality analysis of conflict dynamics and the potential for its resolution. The primary data that I gathered over the past four years from these workshops became the backbone of this research, as it helped me shape my arguments, analysis and conclusions. Extraordinary interactions with former policymakers, scholars and activists happened in these meetings that contributed to uncovering important dynamics affecting our understanding of this conflict.

The experience of bringing participants from Iran, the Gulf and other parts of the world spurred a three-layer process of learning for me. First, what participants say in the media is said mainly for the media and the public, rather than to convince the other party to engage in a meaningful resolution approach to the conflict. Second, what is said in these workshops is delivered not only to the other party in the conflict, but, equally importantly, to their compatriots who return with them to Iran or the other Gulf states. As a result, participants want to show their peers that they were very tough on their adversaries, especially since some participants were linked to senior policymakers. But there is the third layer of learning, which is what I call the 'pure and innocent analysis', and that is what is learned during lunch time, coffee breaks and other one-on-one conversations. Analysis of these conversations, which tend to be far from being politicised or intended to send messages to adversaries or to peers, is extremely useful. In these fora, participants share what they really think could affect the conflict in terms of exacerbation or resolution.

There are many people to thank for their generous support which made this book possible. I owe much to my friend Jamal Khashoggi – may his soul rest in peace – for educating me immensely about this conflict and also about his track two activities with Iranians. He was a fierce critique of Iranian foreign policy in the Arab world, but believed that peace with Iran could be achieved if built on justice, mutual respect and non-interference in domestic affairs. Jamal and I shared panels, debated on TV shows and discussed tough subjects one-on-one. He loved his country, Saudi Arabia, with no limits, but refused to appease political authorities, considering himself an 'honest advisor' who told policymakers what he thought was right for them and their country rather than relaying what they wanted to hear. Sadly, however, he ended up paying with his life for his free and honest speech. I hope publishing his quotes in this book will contribute to his vision of achieving a just peace in this region. I am sure Jamal would have been happy to receive an autographed copy of this book.

My heartfelt appreciation goes to all scholars, former policymakers and activists from Iran, the Gulf region, and from Europe and the United States who gave me ample time to discuss the conflict with them. Their views were essential for me to make sense of a very chaotic conflict, where the causes, issues and dynamics are all interrelated. I would not have been able to synthesise and draw conclusions without their thorough understanding of the conflict. I list all their names in the Bibliography of this book, hoping they take this message as a special thank you to each one of them for their generosity of time and analysis.

I owe my deep gratitude to the Doha Institute for Graduate Studies (DI) for being an ideal place for the production of scholarly, original and local knowledge. Supported by its sister research centre, the Arab Center for Research and Policy Studies (ACRPS), the Institute has built a vibrant environment that nurtures intellectual debate and advanced scholarly research. I particularly appreciate DI and ACRPS continuously running scholarly activities throughout the year in order to advance their emphasis on interdisciplinary social sciences and Arab contribution of knowledge production. I am also grateful to the DI research office and its director, Raed Habayeb, for continuous support and for making this research possible.

I cannot begin to express my thanks to Courtney Freer for helping with copy-editing and research support. She gave illuminating feedback and challenged me to further research and develop certain areas of the book. It has been a great pleasure to work with her and for that I am deeply grateful. I appreciate the feedback offered by Shahram Akbarzadeh, convener of the Middle East Studies Forum at Deakin University, Australia, who read the first draft and gave insightful comments and suggestions to improve certain areas of the book.

I am extremely grateful to Adela Rauchova, Commissioning Editor at Edinburgh University Press, for her leadership and sound management. In particular, I would like to sincerely thank her for her unwavering guidance and persistent support that made the publication of this book possible.

I am also thankful to my good friends Abu Ali Bourini, Basem Ezbidi, Khaled Hroub and Ahmed Azem whose very long and thought-provoking conversations on Middle East politics have always inspired me to research more.

Finally, I owe a very important debt to my lovely family. My wife, Abeer, and my children, Lana, Leena, Dina and Tayem, were very patient, supportive and caring throughout the process of drafting this book. I would not have been able to complete this research without their generous support. I am blessed to have them in my life. I particularly enjoyed the enabling educational environment my children created, with them reading and preparing for their schools while I was writing this book. My nine-year-old son, Tayem, would always tell me that he and I should author a book together. I hope that by acknowledging his words, inspiration and encouragement here this will satisfy his great ambitions.

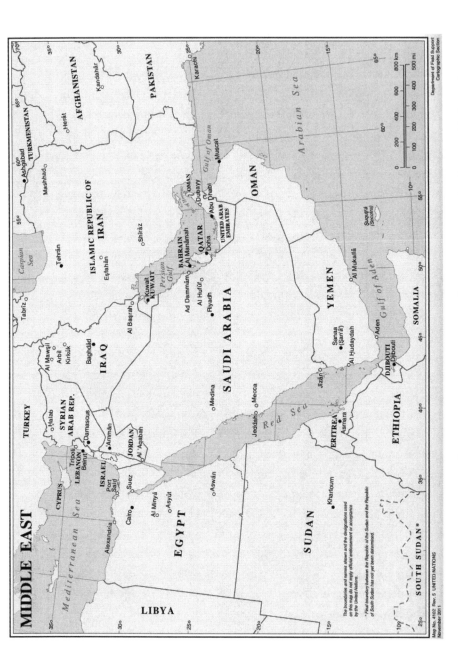

Figure I.1 Map of the Persian Gulf, Map No. 4102 Rev. 5, November 2011. Source: UN Geospatial Information Section, http://www.un.org/Depts/Cartographic/map/profile/mideastr.pdf. Accessed on 25 July 2019. The boundaries and names on this map do not imply endorsement or acceptance by the author or the publisher

Introduction

'If the conflict between Iran and Saudi Arabia is resolved, then half of the Middle East conflicts will disappear,'[1] said one participant in a track two dialogue workshop organised to discuss the Iran–Saudi conflict and the prospects for its resolution. These comments motivated me to further research scholarly literature to learn what types of solutions are offered to effectively move this conflict towards a resolution. My research revealed a plethora of excellent books and articles that thoroughly analyse this conflict, its history, driving mechanisms, dynamics, and its impact on the overall region.[2] Nonetheless, scholarly literature that rigorously assesses potential solutions is notably absent and, where such material exists, it looks solely at what governments can do to resolve the conflict, or the track one approach. Furthermore, the existing literature tends to examine this conflict from an area studies perspective, rather than through the lens of conflict resolution, the approach this book is taking.

This book attempts to fill a gap in the literature by doing three things: first, unlike the majority of the available literature that focuses on an understanding of the conflict, this book takes a conflict resolution approach in order to assess how the conflict can be managed and effectively resolved, rather than simply examining what actions the two countries are currently undertaking. Second, while discussion generally revolves around what each government can do to resolve the conflict – also known as track one – this book takes an integrated approach to the resolution, arguing that effective peacebuilding in this conflict needs to be applied on three levels: government, track two and grassroots. Third, while the conflict between Iran and Saudi Arabia is generally treated in the literature as a subject for area studies, this book takes an interdisciplinary approach by bringing area studies together with conflict resolution and peace studies to present a coherent understanding of the drivers of the conflict and how it could be effectively resolved.

With these three goals in mind, the book's main argument is that the conflict between Iran and Saudi Arabia is resolvable yet must be properly managed first; indeed, better managed and regulated conflicts are better suited for resolution. At present, the Iran–Saudi conflict is a zero-sum chaotic conflict that is heavily burdened by deep mistrust, lack of communication and clear ground rules, confusion about driving issues, and uncertainty about each party's decision-making process. Under such circumstances, resolution becomes particularly elusive and the build-up of a conflict management strategy is a necessity.

Why is it a chaotic conflict? The Iran–Saudi rivalry started decades ago and has reached an unprecedented level of escalation, although policymakers and the scholarly community remain divided about the core drivers of this conflict. Sectarianism, security, competition over global leadership, geopolitics and even nationalism all appear to affect the conflict, with little distinction as to what ultimately drives the patterns of engagement and confrontation. Furthermore, Saudi Arabia is confused about the proper strategy to respond to Iran, resorting on one hand to a regional proxy conflict approach in Syria, Lebanon, Yemen and Bahrain, and on the other to an overarching alliance with the United States and several other players. Iran's opaque decision-making process further fuels this confusion about the correct approach for resolving conflict. As Robert Mason puts it, 'factionalism has been a part of Iranian politics from the birth of the Islamic Republic of Iran'.[3] Certainly, it is difficult to know who makes the decisions on the conflict with Saudi Arabia, whether conservatives, moderates, the Supreme Leader, Revolutionary Guard, or the President, and it is therefore unclear with whom third-party intervention teams could engage to change the course of action. The mixed messages coming from both parties (sometimes offering an olive branch and dialogue while at other times talking about controlling four Arab capitals) only add to the chaos of the conflict. Actions like cutting diplomatic relations, refusing to engage through other channels of communications, and an absence of clear ground rules to regulate engagement make this conflict deeply chaotic, and resolution increasingly elusive.

Contrary to the zero-sum approach currently being propagated by both parties of the conflict, this book takes a critical but constructive approach in explaining how each party can reform its conflict strategies and reach an outcome that corresponds with critical needs, interests and concerns. To do

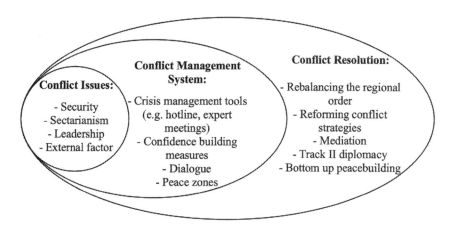

Figure I.2   A conflict resolution model for Iran and Saudi Arabia

so, the book proposes a model built on three pillars: accurate definition of the real issues of this conflict; installation of a conflict management system that aims to contain escalation and regulate conflict; and institution of an integrated resolution approach of track one, track two and grassroot that addresses the underlying causes and conditions of the conflict. Figure I.2 explains this model.

Pillar 1: Issues Driving the Conflict

It is first critical to understand what the driving issues are behind the Iran–Saudi conflict. Indeed,

> [o]ne notable feature of many disputes is that the parties involved often disagree on what the conflict is 'really' about, one side defining the issues as being a set of (to them) salient problems, the other claiming the actual core issues are something completely different.[4]

In addition to their own biases, each party defines the main issues of the conflict based on its own perception, interest and needs. Different understandings of the real issues driving a rift become a major hindrance to the parties' engagement in meaningful conflict management and resolution strategies and thus makes escalation more likely. Indeed, the lack of an accurate understanding of the real issues driving a conflict leads to the reproduction of poor resolution strategies.

After decades, the primary parties of the Iran–Saudi conflict still disagree about what is fundamentally driving their conflict. While Saudi Arabia claims that sectarianism is the key factor, Iran promotes the narrative that the conflict essentially concerns the preservation of its national and regional security. Nevertheless, what both parties refuse to acknowledge is that this conflict is, at least in part, about regime legitimacy and the desire of governments of both states to take a leading role in the Muslim world. When I asked the participants in a joint Iran–Gulf track two workshop about the fundamental issues of the conflict, I received answers ranging from national and regional security, Iran's hegemonic behaviour in the region, Sunni–Shia sectarianism, Arab–Persian nationalism, American–Israeli alliance against Iran, and geopolitics and leadership in the Muslim world. The first pillar, therefore, will critically identify the key issues driving this conflict and what role each plays, as well as how each affects conflict management and resolution efforts.

This book takes the view that the major issue driving the Iran–Saudi conflict is security. Security is of course of critical importance for both parties, and, if both feel that their security is guaranteed, the conflict will be substantially downgraded. What makes this conflict particularly complex is the clash of security needs and perceived 'encirclement' of both parties. Iran feels constantly threatened by the United States and Israel, as well as encircled by American military bases and areas of influence in, for example, Iraq, Saudi Arabia, Bahrain, Qatar, the UAE, Turkey and Afghanistan. Iran responds, in turn, by expanding its own areas of influence in Arab countries and in the process leads Saudi Arabia to feel encircled – as Iran's primary rival and ally of the United States – in Iraq, Syria, Lebanon and Yemen. Both Iran and Saudi Arabia are caught up in this security dilemma and mistakenly have adopted a strategy of escalation to resolve it.

A key factor exacerbating this dilemma is the drive for security and survival of the two regimes in Tehran and Riyadh. That is, escalation conveniently serves the agendas of both regimes, and thus they feel no rush to change the course of action. By standing up to the 'Great Satan', Iran's regime is internally legitimising its revolutionary rhetoric, distracting the attention of the Iranian people from its inability to deliver on the economic level, and validating its expansionist foreign policy in the neighbouring Arab countries.

Meanwhile, standing up to the 'expansionist Shia aggressor, Iran', is serving the Saudi regime by silencing any domestic calls for political reform and keeping a united internal front under the regime's reign.

Many of the other conflict issues, including sectarianism, leadership and influence, are rooted in this security dilemma. They will continue to thrive in the absence of a suitable security scheme that addresses the needs of both parties. Contrary to President Obama's sectarian characterisation of this conflict as rooted in antagonisms that 'date back millennia', this conflict is not originally or essentially sectarian. Indeed, Shia-majority Iran supported Sunni-Palestinian Hamas and sided with Christian Armenia against Shia-majority Azerbaijan. By the same token, Sunni-majority Saudi Arabia supported the Shia Imamate in the 1960s in Yemen and the predominantly Christian March 14th alliance in Lebanon. However, the politicisation of sectarianism by both parties to mobilise support for their political agendas has served as a reinforcing mechanism for Iranian–Saudi animosity, thus furthering conflict escalation. In this case, sectarianism is an enabling factor rather than a cause of the rivalry. Nonetheless, the extensive and varied use of sectarianism by the governments, the mainstream media, major figures on social media, the clergy and even think tanks on both sides has turned sectarianism into a cause for further escalation of the conflict.

Resulting from the politicisation of sectarianism, both sides of the conflict have come to stand for their own sect. Iran appointed itself as the leader of the Shia world by assuming responsibility for protecting the Shia in Iraq, Yemen and Lebanon. Likewise, Saudi Arabia appointed itself as the leader of the Sunni world that would stand up to Iran and prevent the 'Shia-isation' in the Arab and Muslim majority countries.

Pillar 2: Conflict Management

One of this book's major arguments is that better-managed and regulated conflicts are better suited for resolution. Conflict regulation 'refers to the rules that govern the contending parties' conduct in a dispute'.[5] Unilaterally imposing certain rules cannot be considered regulating the conflict, however. Instead, the goal is to establish what Louis Kriesberg calls authentic regulations that 'exists insofar as the contending parties recognize each other's legitimacy and regard the rules governing their conflict as legitimate'.[6]

A dangerous aspect of the Iran–Saudi conflict is its lack of an effective conflict management system that clearly outlines the 'rules of the game' and regulates the parties' conflict behaviour. Allowing the conflict to continue without a restraining mechanism will cause deeper damage through the sustained use of proxies in the region, which could potentially lead to a direct war between Riyadh and Tehran in the future. An effective conflict management system should include the following four components.

First, crisis management tools. Such tools would entail responding to the evolving tension by taking actions like establishing a Riyadh–Tehran hotline, exchanging senior government visits, and forming technical committees to research win-win resolutions to the primary issues at hand. One important factor that prevented the escalation of the US–USSR Cold War into an actual war was the crisis management system that involved, for instance, a direct hotline between Moscow and Washington, DC and regular exchange of senior government visits.

Second, dialogue. There is deep mistrust as well as a lack of political will to build relations across the conflict, combined with barely concealed hatred and even violence (though still carried out via proxies in the region) between both sides. Only through open dialogue can these escalatory dynamics be altered. Dialogue is not meant to necessarily resolve a conflict, but instead should serve as a mechanism to remove misperceptions, develop certain understandings, build a working trust, and open channels of communication between Riyadh and Tehran. Unfortunately, in January 2016, Saudi Arabia formally severed diplomatic relations with Iran and thus shut down the official communication channels that could help in a better management of the conflict.

Third, confidence-building measures. The goal of such measures is not to make Iran and Saudi Arabia like each other or address the underlying causes and conditions of this conflict. Rather, it is meant to take a series of small actions that will help build confidence and prepare Iran and Saudi Arabia to engage in formal negotiations that address the causes and issues of the conflict. While both dialogue and confidence-building measures aim to build a working relationship, the first is mostly about talking and clearing perceptions, while the latter is about taking action.

Fourth, peace zones or a Middle East non-aligned movement in a reversed conflict resolution process. When Iran and Saudi Arabia disagree on means of resolving the core conflict issues (e.g. security and sectarianism), they can engage in conflict management exercises that aim to isolate certain issues (e.g. oil prices, Gulf maritime trade) and even countries (e.g. Oman, Bahrain) from the conflict. Riyadh and Tehran agreeing to avoid escalation in these domains would be an effective conflict-management strategy, which could help in a later formal resolution process. Regional players may choose to take things into their own hands and distance themselves from the conflict if Riyadh and Tehran fail to agree on a containment strategy, and in this case, may resort to establishing a non-aligned movement for this conflict.

In fact, the seeds for this movement exist already. Oman has historically resisted pressure from both sides to join the conflict. Especially after the May 2017 Gulf crisis, Kuwait and Qatar started to demonstrate signals of avoiding being polarised by either of the parties. Jordan occasionally expresses similar interests, such as its Foreign Minister Nasser Judeh making calls from Tehran for dialogue. Tired of historically being a battleground for two powerful rivals, Lebanon is constantly raising slogans like 'self-distancing' (*al-naa'i be-nafs*).

Pillar 3: Conflict Resolution

Building on the establishment of clear regulations and sound management of the conflict, this book makes the argument that an effective resolution strategy should meet two requirements: addressing the underlying causes and conditions of the conflict; and taking an integrated approach to resolution by supplementing official (track one) peacemaking efforts with the activation of the currently unused but hugely potential track two and grassroots levels.

Addressing the underlying causes of the conflict

Solutions should stem from conflict causes, though they rarely drive international peacemaking efforts, as mediators are generally lured by promises of deals, concessions and compromises while often leaving the underlying causes that produced conflicts intact. Both Iran and Saudi Arabia, like many others, understand that addressing the underlying causes of the conflict will improve their relationship, yet the more difficult challenge is defining what these causes are (security, sectarianisms, leadership, etc.), and it is even more difficult to determine how to satisfy them. Hence, the major cause of the aggressive Iran–Saudi rivalry could be seen in the imbalance of power created as a result of the American invasion of Iraq in 2003. This imbalance had enormous security implications not only for the two parties but also for the entire Middle East.

A sustainable balance of regional order must be restored in order for the rivalry to come to an end; neither party seems aware of how best to do this, however. Instead, both sides have sought to restore the balance by engaging in an aggressive arms race and the spread of civil and proxy wars in the region that will only worsen affairs. This conflict started in Iraq and can be resolved from Iraq as well. Because Iraq was considered to have shifted its position from the Arab side to that of Iran, Saudi Arabia was left in a vulnerable position and triggered Iran's appetite for regional expansion. The solution to the imbalance in the regional order is a democratic, independent, sovereign Iraq, free from the influence of Iran, Saudi Arabia and the United States. Iraq must take a neutral position in this conflict to preserve its own national interest since it could otherwise risk becoming a battleground for regional and international conflicts. Iraq's inability to detach from the Iran–Saudi rivalry has been one reason for its prolonged civil strife since 2003. Given its ethnic and religious mosaic, Iraq can become a uniting rather than a dividing force. Iraq becoming the meeting point will be the core interest of all parties and most importantly Baghdad itself.

Saudi Arabia seeking to rebalance regional power by strengthening its alliance with the United States is not a sustainable strategy, although Riyadh felt abandoned and vulnerable under the Obama administration. The Trump administration has made matters worse, as the entire region, not just Saudi Arabia and Iran, has slid into probably the most acute security crisis in decades. The national security of Saudi Arabia, for example, has become a bargaining chip for President Trump, who frequently and publicly asks Riyadh to pay for its protection from Iran and to help stem the tide of Iranian expansionism. Of course, the United States is a key player that can become a stabilising force, but if Saudi Arabia continues to leave its national security subject to the changes in American administrations and different policies that Washington may embrace (e.g. the pivot to Asia), it would be a strategic mistake.

Another approach to rebalancing the regional order is through the creation of a security framework that involves West Asia and North Africa (WANA). Involving key players like Turkey and Pakistan, which have vital national interest, in regional stability and the region's security architecture can create a more balanced regional order that prevents one party from becoming hegemonic.

Meanwhile, strategies employed by Iran and Saudi Arabia to rebalance the region have in fact exacerbated the crisis of imbalance of the regional order. The strategies are counterproductive and must be substantially reformed if the objectives of either side are to be achieved. Neither running an aggressive arms race nor turning this conflict into a sectarian issue will give Saudi Arabia the security it needs. By the same token, expansionism and building militias throughout the region will not give Iran the security and acceptance in the Middle East that it seeks. As has been said, 'Iran has legitimate needs in the region that it is pursuing in illegitimate ways.' The way to achieve these objectives and others is by instead instituting new policies in three main areas: domestic politics, sectarian policies and soft power strategies.

The current political system of Saudi Arabia does not support the country playing a powerful role to strategically balance the regional order with Iran. Deep political and constitutional reforms thus must be introduced. Building hard power to balance with Iran can always help in the short-term but ultimately cannot guarantee Riyadh's security. For example, Israel is generally believed to possess nuclear capabilities and the unquestionable support of the United States, yet it remains insecure in the region; the cause of its security problem is not a lack of advanced military might but its occupation of the Palestinian territories. To feel secure, Israel will have to end its occupation and resolve its conflict with the Palestinians. Likewise, what will make Riyadh feel secure, however, is not purchasing additional arms, but a new social contract that fixes the relationship between the society and state. A new social contract that will enable Saudi Arabia to counter Iranian expansion should be built on a partnership between state and society where accountability and transparency are protected, along with fighting corruption, instituting acceptable levels of power sharing, and ensuring that citizenship is the basis for individuals' access to the Kingdom's resources. As Jamal Khashoggi[7] often stated, Saudi Arabia missed an opportunity to support the political reform in the region that the Arab Spring demanded, and instead resorted to leading and supporting counter-revolutions that maintained old regime structures. Reformed Arab political systems, however, would have provided a viable and sustainable means to stop Iranian expansion in the region; certainly,

Arab youth did not revolt against their corrupt political systems to embrace Iranian theocracy.

Iran is also ripe for domestic reform and, perhaps most urgently, economic reform. To win its cold war with Saudi Arabia, Iran is using a similar strategy that led to the collapse of the USSR in its cold war with the United States. That is, Iran is heavily investing in building its hard power (mainly its missiles programme and nuclear projects) and arming militias abroad, while ignoring what the ordinary Iranian citizen needs: a strong economy that delivers jobs and caters to their livelihoods. Driven by economic factors, the 2017–18 protests in dozens of Iranian cities that turned to raising slogans against the regime and its interventionist foreign policy sends a reliable signal to the Iranian leadership that domestic reform is long overdue.

Politicisation of sectarianism by both Iran and Saudi Arabia must be changed. Iran should refrain from appointing itself the representative of the Shia community in the Arab world, as these Shia are citizens of their own countries rather than part of a transnational coherent Shia whole. Iran's policy of 'supporting the oppressed' remains unconvincing, since it has supported revolutions in Yemen and Bahrain yet continued to back Syria's Shia Alawite regime, dubbing the revolution an 'external conspiracy'. As Shahram Akbarzadeh has argued, Iran's patronage of Shia groups in the region has turned Iran into a 'reluctant Shia Power'.[8] Using Arab Shias as a 'sandbag defence' – in the words of one Iraqi Shia leader – is in fact exacerbating their plight and deepening their grievances. Such a contradiction in Iran's foreign policy only serves its rival Saudi Arabia's propaganda campaign – that conflict is essentially sectarian, a narrative which has led to recruitment to Sunni extremist groups like ISIS that Iran claims it is fighting in the region. In this case, Iran's misuse of its sectarian foreign policy is actually multiplying the enemies that it claims to be fighting.

Saudi Arabia, on the other hand, should be careful of the potential 'self-fulfilling prophecy' in terms of the treatment of its own Shia minority. Perceiving Shia Saudis as a fifth column loyal to Iran has led to their unequal treatment, a policy that may lead segments of this population to become truly loyal to Iran or at least sympathetic to its message. In particular, the Wahhabi Saudi clergy has seriously alienated their fellow Shia citizens when 'every week during Friday prayers we are being called infidels', as one Shia

Saudi told me. By the same token, the alienation is exacerbated when Shia students are expected to learn a Sunni Hanbali curriculum, with its strict interpretation against Shia Muslims, in order to pass their classes. The problem with being Shia in Saudi Arabia is not just about political economy or identity politics, but also about religious belief, as Toby Matthiesen explains.[9] Alienation of the Shia population significantly weakens Saudi Arabia's domestic political front as it pushes a segment of its society to identify with Iran or its message. A solidly built Saudi internal political system is as important as its arms race strategy in confronting Iran, if not even more so.

In their pursuit of hard power to impact the regional order, Iran and Saudi Arabia have ignored the strength of soft power. Iran's image in the Arab countries has never been worse. One major reason for the deterioration of its soft power in Arab countries is its association with the brutal civil war in Syria. Iran gained the world's sympathy when Saddam Hussein used chemical weapons against them during the 1980–8 war. Iran's backing of the Assad regime, which allegedly used the same chemical weapons that Iran suffered from against his own people, has left little sympathy for Tehran as a 'victim of chemical weapons', at least in many Arab countries. Iran must understand that it cannot pursue partnerships with the Arab world by force and with this type of image; thus, fundamental reform of its soft power is needed for it to be accepted in the region as a partner.

Saudi Arabia is equally in need of reforming its soft power strategy if it wants to contain Iranian intervention and find a constructive resolution to the conflict. To develop soft power effectively, Saudi Arabia needs to rid itself of the enormous burden of being associated with the brand of Wahhabism, especially since this has been (at least to a certain extent) associated with jihadi Salafi terrorism worldwide. Saudi Arabia cannot win the battle of global public opinion with this type of image. Another factor that has seriously damaged Saudi Arabia's image is its war in Yemen, which has caused one of the world's worst man-made humanitarian disasters in recent history. Saudi Arabia will have to work for decades to repair the damage to its image caused by this war. Moreover, genuinely reforming Saudi Arabia's soft power requires the Kingdom to crack down on rampant corruption that has seriously damaged its bureaucratic system, deepened mistrust between the public and their government, and made it difficult for Riyadh to market itself abroad. The Saudi campaign to 'fight corruption' that resulted in the arrest of dozens of shaykhs and former ministers – in what came to be known as the Ritz-Carlton hotel-prison – and forcing them to surrender major parts of their wealth to the state increased suspicions about the way the Kingdom is being run.

Integrating official peacemaking, track two intervention, and bottom-up grassroots peacebuilding

Though track two and grassroots efforts remain of critical importance to achieving peace in the Gulf region, government-led peacemaking can be more effective in terms of sustainability, especially if aided by what is called track two intervention as well as a bottom-up grassroots-exercised peacebuilding.

As both parties have been unable to resolve the conflict on their own, third party intervention is both necessary and timely for Riyadh and Tehran to engage in peacemaking. Theoretically, powerful party mediation would be most effective in resolving this and other conflicts. As one Saudi official explained to me, 'We need a powerful mediator who can oversee the dialogue and guarantee the implementation of the results if mediation is to work with Iran.' In this case, countries like the United States, United Kingdom and France would fit the criteria to mediate and 'guarantee implementation'. The problem, however, is that these 'powerful countries' are parties to the conflict as well, especially the United States, and it is in the American interest, at least under the Trump administration, to keep the conflict unresolved so as to continue to build an alliance with Saudi Arabia and other Gulf States to counter Iranian influence, and make additional gains, whether arms sales or general geopolitical gains, in the Middle East and North Africa.

A third-party approach to mediating this conflict is represented by regional powers like Turkey and Pakistan. A peaceful resolution to this conflict is in the strategic interest of these regional powers. Historically, Turks, Arabs and Iranians have shaped the politics and stability of the region. Resolving the conflict would save Turkey the risk of proxy wars escalating on its southern borders. The biggest security challenge to Turkey in its contemporary history has been the Syria war, where Iran and Saudi Arabia indirectly clash. With intervention, Turkey can contribute to rebalancing the regional order, whose disorder was a key cause of this conflict in the first place. Likewise, a nuclear Pakistan can help restore balance with serious intervention in the peacebuilding between

Iran and Saudi Arabia. A sectarian conflict between Riyadh and Tehran poses a serious structural security threat to Pakistan, as the country has historically suffered from sectarian tensions. Rising sectarianism between Iran and Saudi Arabia could reflect on various levels in Pakistan, including through its army, which contains both Sunni and Shia generals. Pakistan has strategic interests with both countries, and the most difficult decision that Islamabad will have to make is to be forced to choose between them. Therefore, investing in peace between its two powerful rivals is undoubtedly in its strategic security interest.

Since official peacemaking efforts have not yet yielded tangible outcomes, the track two approach should be used, particularly because it can play a complementary role to track one processes and often do what governments cannot. Track two is generally led by what John Paul Lederach calls 'middle-range actors', who are positioned in such a way that 'they are connected to, and often have the trust of, both top-level and grassroots actors'.[10] As Jamal Khashoggi, who conducted numerous track two activities with Iranian counterparts, told me,

> there is something to be said about the potential benefits of track two diplomacy between the two countries. Track two is great for public relations and won't cost the government anything. Who knows, it might sow the seeds for some real change in the future.[11]

Track two peacebuilding can provide a variety of benefits when governments are unable or unwilling to come to the negotiating table. Government officials are constantly under media pressure, especially as the rivalry has become increasingly public. This environment is not conducive to creative thinking and innovative conflict resolution. However,

> among the varied goals of track two are to provide a safe, off-the-record venue for dialogue; to create the conditions necessary for formal agreements to 'take hold'; increase communication, understanding and trust among polarized groups; break-down the stereotypes and dehumanizing cognitions that permit the partisans to wage the conflict destructively; and to develop consensus-based proposals that can be transferred to the track one processes.[12]

Particularly because Iran and Saudi Arabia officially severed diplomatic relations in January 2016, leaving only unofficial communications in place, channels of communications like those offered by track two negotiations become particularly relevant. Unfortunately, track two efforts have not reached their full potential in the Gulf due to the centrality of the political systems of both Iran and Saudi Arabia. Put simply, socially influential individuals are not allowed to freely engage in conflict resolution with the other side. However, the present situation provides an opportunity for the two governments to use unconventional approaches and ease their tight control on what non-official prominent society leaders can do. The potential for track two participants to have an impact on the situation is real and can be seen on multiple levels, including in developing personal relationships among participants themselves, returning home and changing the contours of the debate in their societies (especially through their writings), and even influencing their own governments since they are known by them.

Historically, decisions about war and peace in the Gulf have been made by leaders with a top-down approach, without the involvement of their own people. A bottom-up approach to peacebuilding in the Gulf, however, must be incorporated into governments' planning and overall handling of their conflicts. There is a huge trust deficit between the people of Iran and their neighbours in the Gulf as people-to-people interaction is almost non-existent. For example, there are no student and faculty exchange programmes, no joint institutions, and even tourism is extremely limited. The media is playing a destructive role on both sides. It is very rare to find Saudis who speak the Persian language and vice versa. Stereotypes and the dynamics of polarisation and mistrust guide the formation of perceptions on both sides. Under these circumstances, governments will find it difficult to proceed with peace and reconciliation between the two countries even if they want to do so, simply because their populations are not supportive. Bottom-up peacebuilding in the Gulf will help address the change and transformation needed in the relationship between the two peoples. Successful people-to-people programmes will form a kind of social incubator for any future government-brokered solutions as peace agreements need support on the ground to survive. Peace between Iran and its Gulf neighbours will begin with people themselves living this peace, not with governments whose actions are more constrained.

Rapprochement is Possible

Despite what seems to be a bleak situation with slim prospects for resolution, rapprochement between Iran and Saudi Arabia remains a possibility. By 'rapprochement' we refer to scaling back on levels of hostilities, disengagement from escalation and destructive policies in the region, and co-existence between the two states despite their continued differences. Rapprochement does not necessarily imply full reconciliation or elimination of competitive behaviour; instead, it aims primarily to reform relationships from hostilities to co-existence. As Gregory Gause puts it,

> the recent past tells us that it is not impossible to imagine a Saudi–Iranian rapprochement. This would not be an alliance. The two sides have too many contrary interests. It would not even be the shotgun marriage that characterized relations during the time of the Shah, when Cold War dynamics and a common antipathy toward leftist Arab nationalism brought Riyadh and Tehran together. A rapprochement would simply be an agreement to lower the temperature of their mutual condemnations and to act with self-restraint in order to limit the regional spillover consequences of the Syrian and Iraqi domestic conflicts.[13]

Achieving a reasonable level of rapprochement between Riyadh and Tehran depends first on the political will of both parties. Unless both parties are convinced that rapprochement will yield better outcomes for their security and national interests, it will be difficult to force them to reconcile; rapprochement requires initial concessions on both sides so that they can reap fruitful outcomes later. Political will thus becomes necessary. As Frederic Wehrey argues,

> Saudi Arabia and Iran are capable of dialling back and tempering sectarianism. We saw this play out in Lebanon in the aftermath of the 2006 war. We are seeing it again now in Bahrain, where Iran (and Hezbollah) have lowered the tenor of their criticism of Saudi policies.[14]

Furthermore, 'both countries pursued détente in the 1990s after the Iran-Iraq War and Saddam Hussein's invasion of Kuwait, culminating in the signing of a security pact in 2001'.[15] If political will does not exist, it is geography that will ultimately force the parties to reconcile. The parties can procrastinate, manoeuvre and manipulate for the foreseeable future, but the fact that they are living in one area and will remain neighbours with mutual needs and common interests necessitates at least a degree of cooperation.

History also tells us that rapprochement between Riyadh and Tehran is theoretically possible. In fact, the two countries have a history of friendlier relations: 'As recently as the early 2000s their bilateral relationship was not nearly as conflictual, as both Tehran and Riyadh pursued more normal diplomatic relations with each other even as they jostled for influence in the region.'[16] It is true that their ancient history had crisis and tensions, but for most of that history they managed to co-exist and collaborate, damaging arguments that the rivalry is essentially sectarian and therefore primordial in nature.

History and geography also tell us that countries like Germany and France had worse relationships yet eventually managed to work together, at least for a limited period, through one uniting framework, the European Union. It is unrealistic to expect Iran to join the Gulf Cooperation Council (GCC), but the expectation of Germany and France cooperating would have likewise been low a few decades ago.

Another reason that makes rapprochement possible is that both Iran and Saudi Arabia have reached what Zartman calls the 'mutually hurting stalemate'.[17] The conflict has most likely ripened and, since 2003, both parties have invested in the conflict with no achievable outcomes in sight. Yemen has become for Saudi Arabia what Vietnam was for the United States and Afghanistan for the former USSR. The Saudi challenge in Yemen is not solely in winning the war militarily but also ensuring post-war stability and neutralising the security threat on its southern borders. By the same token, Iran has bled for many years in Syria and Iraq, which continues to exert tremendous pressure on its economy.

Domestic pressure in both Iran and Saudi Arabia has also contributed to the stalemate that Riyadh and Tehran are currently experiencing, and this situation may force both countries to scale back or avoid antagonism. In this regard, Iran has survived two uprisings in the last decade, in 2009 and 2017–18, which should serve as credible indicators regarding domestic pressure in the country, while also raising questions about its long-term ability to continue to fund armed militias in the Arab countries. It is no coincidence that the protesters in 2017–18 raised economic demands first before turning to political slogans against the regime, and even against the Supreme Leader, as well as condemning intervention in regional crises and civil wars. This pressure has led some voices in Iran to come to terms with the need to prioritise domestic demands. As Rouzbeh Parsi argues, 'the political elite in Tehran is slowly and reluctantly coming to grips with being a post-revolutionary state. The society has been way ahead of it for quite some time.'[18]

Saudi Arabia's domestic economic challenges are equally threatening to the survival of the regime; in 2017, dozens of princes, former ministers and other business tycoons were arrested in what they called a fighting corruption campaign, and forced to surrender significant amounts of their wealth to the state. Furthermore, dozens of clerics and intellectuals were arrested in September 2017 to neutralise dissent from the Islamic sphere. Despite these measures, domestic political pressure and demands for reform are mounting, leading the state to engage in what would have been seen as taboo only a couple of years before, including, but not limited to, lifting the ban on women driving and diminishing the state-linked clergy's influence on politics. Coupling the current damaging stalemate that the two countries experience with a way out or an 'enticing opportunity'[19] may help them confidently proceed to rapprochement.

Finally, the conflict behaviour of the parties tells us that both of them are willing to make compromises and reach agreements even with their worst enemies. Iran was able to reach a nuclear deal with what it calls the 'Great Satan' – the United States – on its nuclear project, which has always been defined as part of its national pride, national security and sovereignty. By the same token, in 2002, Saudi Arabia presented the Arab Peace Initiative to Israel – for a century considered the Arabs' central enemy – for a comprehensive solution and full normalisation. It would be ironic if the two parties are willing to engage in 'deals' and 'normalization' with their distant enemies yet remain unwilling to reconcile as neighbours with shared vital needs and interests in the Gulf region.

Notes

1. Workshop organised by Georgetown University's Center for Regional and International Studies in Qatar as part of a series of Iran–GCC dialogue activities. Workshop held under Chatham House Rule where information can be shared but identities of speakers are undisclosed. Doha, January 2016.

2. See Simon Mabon, *Saudi Arabia and Iran: Soft Power Rivalry in the Middle East* (London: I. B. Tauris, 2013); Toby Matthiesen, *The Other Saudis: Shiism, Dissent and Sectarianism* (Cambridge: Cambridge University Press, 2014); Banafsheh Keynoush, *Saudi Arabia and Iran: Friends or Foes?* (London: Palgrave Macmillan, 2016); Frederic Wehrey (ed.), *Beyond Sunni and Shia: The Roots of Sectarianism in a Changing Middle East* (London: C. Hurst & Co., 2017); Farzad Cyrus Sharifi-Yazdi, *Arab–Iranian Rivalry in the Persian Gulf: Territorial Disputes and the Balance of Power in the Middle East* (London: I. B. Tauris, 2015).
3. Robert Mason, *Foreign Policy in Iran and Saudi Arabia, Economics and Diplomacy in the Middle East* (London: I. B. Tauris, 2015), p. 86.
4. Christopher Mitchell, *The Structure of International Conflict* (London: Palgrave Macmillan, 1981), p. 44.
5. Louis Kriesberg, *Constructive Conflicts, from Escalation to Resolution* (Lanham: Rowman & Littlefield, 2007), p. 104.
6. Ibid. p. 104.
7. Saudi journalist, author, opinion leader and *Washington Post* columnist, Jamal paid with his life for continuing to speak out; he was cruelly murdered at the Saudi Arabian consulate in Istanbul on 2 October 2018 by agents of the government of Saudi Arabia.
8. Shahram Akbarzadeh, 'Iran and Daesh: the case of a reluctant Shia power', *Middle East Policy* XXII, 3 (Fall 2015): 44–54.
9. Matthiesen, *The Other Saudis*, p. 8.
10. John Paul Lederach, *Building Peace, Sustainable Reconciliation in Divided Societies* (Washington: United States Institute of Peace, 1997), p. 94.
11. Author's interview and discussion, Doha, November 2015.
12. Esra Çuhadar and Bruce Dayton, 'The social psychology of identity and intergroup conflict: from theory to practice', *International Studies Perspectives* 12 (2011): 273–93, p. 282.
13. F. Gregory Gause III, 'Saudi–Iranian rapprochement? The incentives and the obstacles', *Brookings Institution*, March 2014, http://www.brookings.edu/research/articles/2014/03/17-iran-ksa-rapprochement-gause.
14. Frederic Wehrey, 'The roots and future of sectarianism in the Gulf', *Project on Middle East Political Science*, 21 March 2014, http://pomeps.org/2014/03/21/the-roots-and-future-of-sectarianism-in-the-gulf/, p. 28.
15. Seyed Hossein Mousavian, 'Saudi Arabia is Iran's new national security threat', *Huffington Post*, 3 June 2016, https://www.huffingtonpost.com/seyed-hossein-mousavian/saudi-arabia-iran-threat_b_10282296.html.

16. Gause, 'Saudi–Iranian rapprochement?', p. 7.

17. William Zartman, 'Ripening conflict, ripe moment, formula, and mediation', in Diane B. Bendahmane and John W. McDonald (eds), *Perspectives on Negotiation* (Washington: Center for the Study of Foreign Affairs, Foreign Service Institute, US Department of State, 1986).

18. Rouzbeh Parsi, 'The elusive project of common security in the Persian Gulf', *Project on Middle East Political Science*, 17 March 2014, https://pomeps.org/2014/03/24/the-elusive-project-of-common-security-in-the-persian-gulf/, p. 13.

19. Zartman, 'Ripening conflict'.

I

History of Iran–Saudi Arabian Rivalry and Peacemaking Efforts

The current rivalry between Iran and Saudi Arabia is the result of a history of tense relations over the past four decades, although both have invested in serious peacemaking efforts to manage and/or resolve the conflict between them.

A History of Rivalry

As is usually the case with international conflicts, the starting point of the Iran–Saudi rivalry is hotly contested. While some analysts use contemporary history, citing the Islamic revolution of 1979 as the starting point of this conflict, others trace it back to ancient history, using arguments about Arab versus Persian nationalism[1] and the prevalence of primordial Shia–Sunni sectarianism. No matter what approach one takes to studying this conflict, however, two major developments in the conflict's contemporary history are never ignored: the 1979 Islamic revolution and the 2003 American invasion of Iraq. Ancient history, whether the prevalence of nationalism or sectarianism, could have played a role in the conflict, but these two more recent developments provided the driving mechanisms that contributed to the start-up and sustainment of the conflict over the past few decades. In particular, the 1979 Islamic revolution fuelled the 'export of the revolution' that is still seen, at least by Saudi Arabia, as the ultimate objective of Tehran, while the 2003 American invasion of Iraq structurally upset the balance of the regional order and therefore opened the door for aggressive intervention by the two rivals to fill the resulting vacuum.

Scholarly debates about the Iran–Saudi Arabian rivalry tend to echo the literature on sectarianism more broadly and, as such, are often divided between the camp that sees the split as ideologically or religiously driven, and those who view the rivalry as the result of geopolitical conditions. For their part, Shahram Chubin and Charles Tripp cite 'structural factors' as driving the Iran–Saudi rivalry.[2] They identify such factors as geopolitical differences, particularly differences in demography and geography, as driving decision making when it comes to regional affairs. In addition to these issues, as well as the aspiration of each state to lead the Gulf, sectarian, cultural and ethnic differences have exacerbated a latent competition. Furthermore, the emergence of a revolutionary Iran post-1979 is considered a fundamental and 'direct' threat to the Gulf and others in the region, since the Iranian government claims to speak on behalf of Islamic authority, which directly threatens Saudi Arabia as the home of the Two Holy Mosques.[3]

Simon Mabon describes Iran–Saudi competition as encompassing two areas: the ideological and the geopolitical.[4] The first, in his words, 'is driven by competing identities, in particular, ethno-national and religious identities'.[5] Indeed, both Arab and Persian leaders have long competed over dominance of the region, and religious competition occurs as well, particularly due to the fact that Saudi Arabia houses the Two Holy Mosques.[6] Mabon explains:

> The notion of being the guardian of Mecca and Medina is an integral aspect of the Al Saud's legitimacy, both internally and across the Islamic world. As such, the emergence of Iran as a major power within the Islamic world adhering to a diametrically opposed interpretation of Islam offered a further source of entanglement in relations between the two.[7]

Events over the course of the twentieth century have changed the dynamics of this relationship as well. Mabon outlines the two areas of competition, the ideological and geopolitical, as being 'separate entities' that 'feed into each other'.[8] Of course, the emergence of the Islamic Republic of Iran in 1979 increased competition in both spheres, and the rivalry has been further influenced by the shift in Tehran's alignment towards the United States, which changed drastically following the removal of the Shah in 1979 and has been altered more recently by the Joint Comprehensive Plan of Action and then by the Trump administration.[9]

Before World War II, Iran and Saudi Arabia had a relationship mainly concerned with regulation of the hajj, which also 'encouraged small-scale trade of Persian goods, mainly carpets, and the settlement of a small Persian community in Jeddah'.[10] Although boundary disputes persisted, especially over joint oil-fields, these did not spur larger cross-border tensions, since domestic concerns during that period were more urgent, particularly after the withdrawal of the British Residency, which both countries had relied upon to 'ensure stability along their borders'.[11] Prior to that, however, Mabon explains that

> [t]he relationship was initially characterised by suspicion between the royal families of the Al Saud and the Pahvalis. This suspicion stemmed predominantly from competition over regional dominance and prior to 1958, was in part due to the involvement of the Hashemites in Baghdad, whose presence complicated relations within the regional order.[12]

Indeed, after World War II, Iran under the Shah was a very close United States ally, with which Saudi Arabia could not compete due to its smaller military and population.[13] Although Saudi Aramco had been founded in the early 1930s, cooperation between the US and Saudi Arabia in the oil sector only flourished after World War II and led to enhanced military ties between the two, who were both committed to fighting Soviet influence abroad, countering the threat of Nasserist Egypt, and maintaining a steady flow of oil.[14] After the departure of British forces from the Gulf was announced in 1968, the Iran–Saudi relationship became more strained due to competition over regional leadership, control of the Organization of Petroleum Exporting Countries (OPEC), and a multilateral approach to Gulf security.[15]

After British power waned, American financial support aided both countries that suffered after World War II. During the Cold War, American arms imports to both countries increased and the Twin Pillars policy, developed under the Nixon Doctrine in 1971, emerged, with the US hoping to use Iran and Saudi Arabia to stop the spread of communism.[16] As Keynoush notes, however, 'Iran's larger economy and well-trained army compared to Saudi Arabia, and proximity to the Soviet Union, made its role central to the success of the policy.'[17] Though it was considered the West's 'regional policeman', Saudi Arabia, along with its Gulf neighbours,

> did not view Iran as an enemy, but they also did not see it as an ally, either. Despite a concerted effort by Tehran to charm the Arab monarchs after the Bahrain issue was settled, Saudi Arabia and the smaller states resisted Iranian efforts to formalize security cooperation in an explicit Gulf security pact.[18]

Saudi Arabia worried about Iran's closeness to the United States under the leadership of Shah Mohammad Reza Pahlavi. Indeed, Shah Pahlavi had a close personal relationship with President Richard Nixon, which helped to secure arms deals and the partnership.[19] The Americans knew that the Shah eventually hoped to diminish foreign presence in the Gulf, however. Under President Gerald Ford, the Shah began 'losing US backing on account of disagreements over his drive for higher oil prices, became vulnerable to domestic opposition, frequent strikes, and high inflation rates of 30–40 percent'.[20] When Jimmy Carter became president in January 1977, the Shah tried to stop protests by pushing up oil prices, while Saudi Arabia used its supply to stabilise the market and thus aid the United States during a period of global recession.[21] During this time, 'Saudi Arabia distanced itself slightly from Iran as it improved relations with Iraq.'[22]

Mabon describes how, following British withdrawal from the Gulf in 1968 and the emergence of independent states in the lower Gulf, Iran had an opportunity to assert dominance over the region and indeed revived historic Persian claims to control Shia-dominated Bahrain, which put it into direct conflict with Saudi interests.[23] Indeed, the issue of Bahrain is one that undoubtedly predated the 1979 revolution and continues to this day. In an effort to resolve the issue, in 1970 the Shah proposed a United Nations-led poll in Bahrain, which proved the overwhelming desire among residents of Bahrain for independence.[24]

After the revolution overthrew the Pahlavi dynasty in 1979, the balance of power between the so-called Twin Pillars shifted, and Iranian and Saudi interests diverged as Ayatollah Ruhollah Khomeini called for the overthrow of Arab rulers allied with the United States.[25] Ehteshami, for his part, opines that the tensions between the countries 'are of a contemporary nature, derived from the Iranian revolution'.[26] Certainly, Utaybi Juhayman's takeover of the Grand Mosque and Shia uprisings in the Eastern Province took place shortly after the revolution, spurring even more fear about the role of the region's new revolutionary state and its role in destabilising its neighbours.

Terrill describes the Saudi leadership as fundamentally anti-revolutionary due to its ultra conservative leadership.[27] In November 1979, shortly after the success of the Iranian revolution, unrest emerged in Saudi Arabia's Shia-dominated Eastern Province, with the performance of an illegal religious procession to celebrate the holiday of Ashura; some in the crowd carried pictures of Iran's revolutionary leader Ayatollah Ruhollah Khomeini in addition to anti-Saudi and anti-United States slogans.[28] Riots resulted after Saudi authorities tried to disperse the crowds, leading to substantial property damage and a number of civilian casualties, all of which Saudi Arabia blamed on Iran.[29]

As a result, then, the Soviet invasion of Afghanistan in 1979 provided Saudi Arabia with a valuable opportunity to demonstrate its Islamic legitimacy at home and abroad after the discord caused by the revolution in Iran.[30] To that end, the Saudi government subsidised travel and training, as well as recruitment of jihadi fighters from around the world, in addition to sponsoring anti-Iranian and anti-Shia tracts meant 'to highlight the narrowly ethnic and sectarian aspirations of the Khomeinist regime and mitigate its more universal appeal throughout the region and the world'.[31] Indeed, after 1979,

> neither Riyadh nor Tehran were anxious to cast their rivalry in ideological terms, and more so because the former had never felt at ease with the shah . . . When Tehran insisted on spreading its revolution, for example, the kingdom charged it of exporting terrorism, and questioned whether revolution should be Iran's aim, or the construction of a model Islamic state.[32]

Throughout the 1980s, tensions between the newly revolutionary Iran and Saudi Arabia persisted. The war between Iran and Iraq (1980–8), also known in Iran as the 'imposed war',[33] had huge security implications for the entire Gulf region, including Iran–Saudi relations. Six Gulf states – Saudi Arabia, the United Arab Emirates, Qatar, Kuwait, Oman and Bahrain – formed the Gulf Cooperation Council in 1981, in part as a security response to the Iranian revolution and the Iran–Iraq war. In 1982, Saudi Arabia reportedly supplied Iraq with $1 billion per month in aid.[34] Furthermore, Saudi and Bahraini authorities uncovered a plot to overthrow Bahrain's government shortly after the war. Iran was blamed and may have been involved.[35] In 1987, violence emerged again at the hajj after Iranian pilgrims began protesting, leading to 450 deaths. Iran blamed Saudi Arabia for this event and even suggested that custody of the Two Holy Mosques should go to Iran; Riyadh responded in turn by drastically decreasing the number of Iranians allowed at the hajj.[36]

Following Khomeini's death in 1989, Iran—Saudi relations appeared to improve slightly, with President Ali Akbar Hashemi Rafsanjani (r. 1989–97) and later President Mohammad Khatami (r. 1997–2005) more open to cooperation. Khatami was particularly focused on improving the relationship with Saudi Arabia, especially by ending covert actions by Iran inside the Kingdom. In June 1991, Iran and Saudi Arabia resumed diplomatic relations, and a large number of official visits to Riyadh followed from the foreign minister, and elements of the intelligence, judiciary and military sectors.[37]

King Abdullah, who had come to power in 1995 in Saudi Arabia, met with President Rafsanjani on the sidelines of the Organization of Islamic Cooperation (OIC) in Pakistan in 1997. He also supported Iran's presidency and aimed to assuage Iranian fears by stating that American troops would not be in the region long-term to contain Iran; Rafsanjani said that Iranian pilgrims would not incite issues during the hajj.[38] Relations improved so much that in 1999, Khatami became the first sitting Iranian president to visit Riyadh on an official state visit.[39] Neither Rafsanjani nor Khatami, however, could control the demands of hard-liners, and, more problematically, the Islamic Revolutionary Guard Corps (IRGC) were still able to conduct covert actions abroad without consulting the President, since the Supreme Leader manages the group.[40] Ayatollah Ali Khamenei has served as Supreme Leader since Khomeini's death and remains 'conservative and suspicious of reform'.[41]

Further, despite the détente, fundamental tensions persisted over the course of the 1990s. The United States in 1994 announced its new dual containment policy aimed at Iraq and Iran, which increased Saudi importance to the Americans whilst increasingly isolating Iran.[42] Most importantly, though, after the fall of the Soviet Union spurred newly independent republics in the Caucasus and Central Asia, fears were stirred among Iranian and Saudi leaderships that their own ethnic populations would also demand independence.[43] In addition, Tehran hoped to expand its sphere of influence into Central Asia, since it had lost power in the Gulf.[44] Saudi Arabia, on the other hand,

> indirectly supported the United States' efforts to counter Iranian influence by backing Turkey's appeal to pan-Turkism in the region. But Riyadh also saw the area as ripe for the spread of Salafism among the predominately Sunni populations of the Central Asian republics as a means to 'out-Islamicize' Tehran's similar efforts [Afghanistan, Tajikistan].[45]

There was, at least outwardly, a shift in tone, however, after the 9/11 attacks. During this period, Iran and Saudi Arabia signed security and regional agreements in 2001 and 2002 on terrorism, money laundering, drug trafficking and illegal immigration, largely because both hoped to fight Al Qaeda and opposed the US invasion of Iraq.[46]

The role of the United States is very important when it comes to sustaining the rivalry: indeed, revolutionary Tehran resents Riyadh as 'America's principal local proxy against Iran taking what it feels is its rightful place as the region's preeminent power'.[47] Iran also hopes to eventually remove foreign presence from the region and sees Saudi Arabia as standing in the way of achieving that goal. From the Saudi point of view, the 1979 revolution and resulting call to overturn the Saudi monarchy has bred mistrust.[48] It is important to note, though, that 'even before this ideological challenge, Riyadh long perceived a stark asymmetry between its own national power and that of Iran, in terms of demography, industrial capacity, and military strength'.[49]

Geopolitical competition, in Mabon's view, has been enhanced after the decline of Iraq post-2003, which is perhaps most clearly demonstrated by the considerable debate about the nomenclature of the Gulf separating Iran and Saudi Arabia.[50] Further, as Wehrey *et al.* posit, 'a weak Iraq can arguably be said to increase rivalry between Saudi Arabia and Iran, whereas a strong Iraq can stabilize or moderate the tensions'.[51] Logically, then, the downfall of Iraq in 2003 led to considerable angst among Saudi authorities, particularly since Iran revived claims of itself being 'a natural state' dating back to 700 BC, as opposed to others that have experienced periods under colonial power.[52]

The post-2003 resurgence of Shia power in Iraq and Tehran's pursuit of nuclear power is seen in Riyadh's eyes as fundamentally upsetting the regional power balance that has in the past favoured Saudi Arabia, meaning that the prospect of a rapprochement between Iran and the United States was particularly frightening to the Saudi leadership.[53] Indeed, 'Iran's Khomeinist ideology is vehemently anti-monarchical, formalizes clerical authority in politics and – especially under President Mahmoud Ahmadinejad – trumpets an explicitly populist line.'[54]

Regardless of causes of increased sectarianism in recent years, events in the 2000s undoubtedly spurred religious violence. The 2003 toppling of Saddam Hussein in Iraq has recently been cited as a critical turning point for sectarianism in the Middle East as it disturbed the equilibrium of Sunni and Shia states in the Gulf.[55] Mabon summarises:

> From the Gulf perspective, the fall of the Iraqi dictator raised the specter of a Shi'a-dominated Iraq that would form linkages with coreligionists in Iran and, more ominously, might inspire the Shi'a in Saudi Arabia, Bahrain, and Kuwait toward greater agitation and even militancy. In conjunction, Iranian foreign policy took a sharply activist and nationalistic turn with the rise of the so-called new conservatives led by President Mahmud Ahmadinejad.[56]

Notably, these changes coincided with the rise of international social media, which have since that time been used to diffuse sectarian messages from both sides.

The 2006 Hezbollah–Israel war in Lebanon again stoked sectarian tensions.[57] Sunni states which had prided themselves on supporting the Palestinian cause felt threatened as Hezbollah, supported by rival Iran, took the lead in the fight against Israel.[58] Hezbollah's actions, supported by Iran, were considered to threaten the delicate balance between Shia and Sunni power in the region.

Iran has further threatened Saudi interests and position abroad through what Wehrey *et al.* dub its

> 'Arab street' strategy of speaking directly over the heads of Arab rulers to their publics, undermining the rulers' legitimacy by portraying them as sclerotic lackeys of Washington, and upstaging them on the Palestinian question through provocative rhetoric and support to such groups as Hamas and Hizballah.[59]

Indeed, following Ahmadinejad's election in 2005, Iran became increasingly active in the Middle East; 'hyperactivism on pan-Arab issues is not necessarily proof of its influence, but rather just the opposite – an effort to overcompensate for its fundamental isolation from the rest of the region'.[60] Iran's support for Hezbollah in 2006 was seen as a turning point, as it gave Iran the upper hand in terms of popularity, and this policy has again been pursued in the post-Arab Spring era.[61]

Most recently, the Arab Spring in 2011 jeopardised the sectarian balance in the Middle East, as it led Shias in Bahrain and Saudi Arabia to rise up against their governments as pro-democracy movements were revived around the Middle East. Vali Nasr concludes:

> The Arab Spring has allowed it [sectarianism] to resurface by weakening states that have long kept sectarian divisions in place, and brutally suppressed popular grievances. Today, Shias clamor for greater rights in Lebanon, Bahrain and Saudi Arabia, while Sunnis are restless in Iraq and Syria.[62]

This most recent outbreak of political sectarianism can be differentiated, according to Nasr, by the fact that each side (Shia and Sunni) is backed by a regional superpower, namely Iran for the Shias and Saudi Arabia for the Sunnis.

The imprint of this rivalry was evident in regional conflicts before the Arab Spring. Saudis saw Iran's hand behind a rebellion among Yemen's Houthi tribe – who are Zaydis, an offshoot of Shiism – that started in 2004. Iran blamed Arab financing for its own decade-long revolt by Sunni Baluchis along its southeastern border with Pakistan. And since 2005, when Shia Hezbollah was implicated in the assassination of Rafik Hariri, a popular Sunni prime minister who was close to the Saudis, a wide rift has divided Lebanon's Sunni and Shia communities, and prompted Saudi fury against Hezbollah. The sectarian divide in Lebanon shows no sign of narrowing, and now the turmoil in Syria next door has brought Lebanon to a knife's edge.[63]

When the Arab Spring emerged, both Iran and Saudi Arabia acted to protect their interests: for Saudi Arabia this meant aiding allies facing protests yet aiding opposition movements active in adversarial countries.[64] Most importantly, when it came to the protest movement in Shia-dominated Bahrain, Iran backed the protests, while in Syria, Tehran stands with Assad; Saudi Arabia's interests, meanwhile, have been the opposite.[65]

The relationship between Iran and Saudi Arabia has passed through four escalatory phases since 2003:

1. Phase I: increased tension (2003). This resulted from the imbalance in the regional order that was created after the US invasion of Iraq.
2. Phase II: proxy wars and the Arab Spring (2011). Especially in Syria, Iran has invested highly in the Assad regime, while Saudi Arabia

supported the revolution with the hope that Iran would lose its influential presence there.

3. Phase III: direct one-party involvement and the war in Yemen (2015).[66] On 21 September 2014, Iran's primary ally in Yemen, the Houthi movement, with help from former President Ali Saleh, orchestrated a coup against the Saudi-backed government in Yemen, overthrew Riyadh's ally President Abed Rabbu Mansour Hadi, and took over state institutions. On 25 March 2015, the Iran–Saudi regional rivalry took a new turn with Saudi Arabia launching Operation Decisive Storm (ODS) against what it perceived to be the Iranian presence in Yemen, represented by the Houthis.

4. Phase IV: direct two-party confrontation (2016). After the Saudi execution of its influential Shia cleric Nimr al-Nimr[67] in January 2016 on charges related to 'terrorism', the confrontation escalated directly between Tehran and Riyadh, rather than through a third party. The battleground now is Tehran, where the Saudi embassy was attacked and set on fire, and Riyadh, where Iranian diplomats have been expelled from the Saudi capital. Diplomatic relations between the two countries were severed and political tension has prevailed since that time.

The Riyadh summit in May 2017 and the American–Saudi alliance that emerged from it further signalled a strategy of facing down Iran. The involvement of the Trump administration – needing little convincing to act against Tehran – indicated a further entrenchment of the rivalry. Indeed, the involvement of additional and powerful new parties, like the United States, sends more alarming messages than ever before in an acute security environment, signalling that this conflict could intensify if no serious actions are taken to de-escalate the situation.

The Peacemaking Effort since the US Invasion of Iraq in 2003

There have been some serious peacemaking efforts made by the two countries since the US invasion of Iraq, though mostly on the government level, also known as track one. Little effort has been invested at the community and domestic level to address the rivalry that has become encompassing to almost all levels of both states.

Track one peacemaking

The 2003 US invasion of Iraq unsettled the existing sectarian balance in the Gulf, after much of the Muslim world had been briefly united following the 11 September 2001 attacks. An unstable Iraq stoked Saudi fears that it could become a Shia – and by extension, Iranian – stronghold in the Gulf. Until that time, 'the door wasn't really open [for Iran to challenge the regional order], except in limited ways like supporting Hezbollah and Hamas'.[68] Iraq offered an opportunity for Iran to gain a foothold inside the Gulf, in particular if a Shia government came to power, a terrifying prospect for the Saudis who hoped to maintain the Sunni hegemony of the region.

Since the invasion, however, and in particular during Ahmadinejad's tenure, the primary Saudi grievance with Iranian foreign policy has not centred on sectarianism, making it more difficult to assess how to lessen conflict between the states. In fact,

> Iran's policy outlook has been marked by a sense of triumphalism and an activist embrace of pan-Arab causes, most notably the Israeli–Palestinian issue. Combined with its defiance of the West on the nuclear issue, Iran has acquired an appeal that has on occasion transcended sectarian differences. This appeal represents an indirect critique of the al-Saud, who are perceived by regional and domestic opponents as being too cautious and deferential to the West.[69]

Iran's outlook has thus been 'aggressively non-sectarian', as it aims to appeal to Arab populations beyond Shias.[70] One official in Hezbollah's research wing cited two issues at the centre of Iran's foreign policy: the Palestinian cause and facing down the Western presence in the Middle East.[71] Notably, '[t]here is nothing particularly Shia about the two issues'.[72] In pushing universal causes, Iran aims to overcome its isolation from the wider Middle East.[73] Iran's leadership on such issues has not only threatened the Kingdom's position as the primary player in the region, but has also undermined its stance in the Arab world more broadly by criticising Saudi Arabia's connections to the United States in particular.

In the face of Iran's non-sectarian foreign policy, Saudi Arabia has criticised the state's 'policy behaviour and regional ambitions, not Shiasm per se'.[74] Between 2005 and 2007, Saudi Arabia took three approaches to dealing with Iran.[75] First, officials tried to appease the new Ahmadinejad administration to diminish sources of tension, through acts like offering to support Iran's nuclear programme on the condition that it allowed International Atomic Energy Agency (IAEA) inspections.[76] Second, when that approach proved unproductive, the Saudis began strategic talks in 2006 and 2007, which

> were designed to engage directly with Iran's supreme leader and his aides to bypass the Iranian president's tough stance. This approach did achieve moderate – and somewhat temporary – results in Lebanon, but at the final stages it hit a dead end as the supreme leader's aids – especially the Supreme National Security Council (SNSC) – indicated that any agreement with the Saudi government should include the Ahmadinejad administration.[77]

As a result, taking a third approach, the Saudi government tried to build up international pressure to urge a softening of Iran's stances, with Prince Bandar bin Sultan travelling around the world to urge other states to pressure Iran.[78]

The Kingdom has endeavoured to stem the tide of sectarianism in certain instances, such as preventing Saudi volunteers from fighting in Iraq by silencing clerical appeals for Sunnis to fight jihad in that state.[79] Another sign of progress was King Abdullah's meeting with Shia cleric Muqtada al-Sadr in January 2006.[80] Furthermore, in October 2006, the Saudi government hosted a meeting of Sunni and Shia clerics in Makkah, which ended with 'a statement condemning sectarian violence in Iraq'.[81] Also in 2006, the GCC announced that it would create a joint nuclear research programme, primarily due to Iranian developments, though reaffirming support for an Iranian nuclear deal.[82] Suspicion remained, however. During a visit to Washington, DC in December 2006, Saudi Foreign Minister Saud al-Faisal expressed concern about Iran's role in assisting Iraqi Shia groups.[83] Nonetheless, the states still managed to work together, with Iraqi National Security Advisor Muwaffaq al-Ruba'i announcing in July 2007 that he had reached an agreement with the Saudi Interior Minister that both states would 'monitor sectarian *fatawa*'.[84] In December 2007, in a major effort at reconciliation, President Ahmadinejad was invited to the GCC summit in Doha, where he

> proposed cooperation in economic, political and security fields. He emphasized that peace and security in the region could be ensured without any external interference and proposed that a mutual security agreement be signed between Iran and the GCC.[85]

Although the proposal itself was promising, GCC states remained suspicious of Iran, suspecting that the proposition could be 'another Iranian ploy to undermine them'.[86] Further, and most troubling to Gulf governments, the tenth point of the proposal involved requesting that foreign forces leave the region, which they feared could allow Iran to become the primary political player in the Gulf.[87]

Still, 'the Iranian proposal offering to produce joint nuclear energy with the GCC countries is really a commendable move to build confidence among its Gulf neighbours'.[88] Nonetheless, Iran's lingering refusal to accept the presence of foreign, and in particular American, troops in the Gulf has remained a major source of contention: 'While the presence of the U.S. is necessary for GCC security, Iran views it as a primary security threat. Thus for the GCC the U.S. presence is necessary while for Iran it is an evil.'[89] Though the ten-point programme was ultimately rejected, ties between Iran and Saudi Arabia persisted. In 2008, GCC Secretary General Abdul Rahman al-Attiyah visited Iran where he 'focused primarily on expanding economic cooperation with Iran, as a precondition for broader cooperation. He also announced the formation of a committee for working on the possibility of setting up a joint security mechanism with Iran.'[90]

Efforts at rapprochement became more difficult in 2008, however, due to growing Saudi concern about Iran's nuclear programme after it refused the Kingdom's proposal to assist Iran if it complied with IAEA inspections.[91] Hezbollah's invasion of Beirut in May 2008 added tension to the relationship, as the Saudi government 'considered the act as an Iranian-Syrian plot to oust the 14 March Lebanese government – composed of Sunni and Christian parties – and aimed at undermining Arab interests'.[92] Diplomatic and economic ties remained, though were strained.

In August 2012, King Abdullah and President Ahmadinejad met in Mecca at an emergency session of the Organization of Islamic Cooperation wherein Syria's membership was suspended. This was seen as serious progress in the relationship between the two countries, given that Ahmadinejad previously visited Riyad back in 2005 and 2007. Furthermore, King Abdullah seated President Ahmadinejad at his side, 'an apparent conciliatory gesture'.[93] Considering that Syria is an ally of Iran, the move was likely an effort to reassure Iran that efforts against Syria were pointed at that country alone.[94] For his part, Ahmadinejad's speech proposed creating a centre for dialogue between the different Muslim sects.[95]

The election of Hassan Rouhani in August 2013 came with promises of ending Iran's isolation from the rest of the region, yet conflict in Syria continued harming the Iran–Saudi relationship, as both sides were accused of backing different militias inside the country. At a 2013 press conference, Saudi Foreign Minister Prince Saud al-Faisal went so far as to say that he 'consider[s] Syria an occupied land', due to Iranian presence there.[96] Following Hezbollah's public declarations in April and May 2013 that its members were fighting with Assad's troops inside Syria, anti-Shiism was renewed, considering the Iranian support of that group.[97] Nonetheless, the overthrow of the Mursi government in Egypt, and general regional paranoia about the power of Sunni Islamist parties, in particular the Muslim Brotherhood, appeared to momentarily distract the Kingdom from its feud with Iran.[98]

A number of positive developments took place afterwards. In May 2014, Saudi Foreign Minister Saud al-Faisal said that he had invited his Iranian counterpart to 'visit the kingdom at any time he saw fit'.[99] Furthermore, in April 2014, the Saudi government removed Intelligence Chief Prince Bandar bin Sultan (who was in charge of the Syria file) from his post. His removal was 'seen as part of a shift in policy of the Gulf state towards Syria'.[100] Prince Bandar had hawkish views against the Assad regime and in fact reached out specially to Russia to end its support for him. However, these gestures towards Iran did not succeed in bringing about a positive change in the relationship between the two countries.

The nuclear deal agreement between Iran and the United Nations Security Council (P5+1) in July 2015 had a serious negative impact on the relationship between Iran and Saudi Arabia. Agreeing with Tehran on its nuclear activities without linking this to Iran's foreign policy in the Middle East, Saudi Arabia perceived the agreement as a betrayal by the West. The nuclear deal made Saudi Arabia feel less secure because it believed Iran's agreement with the West would allow it to devote its resources to supporting Iran's proxies in the region, like the Houthis in Yemen and the Assad regime.

The Saudi strikes in Yemen against the Shia Houthi rebels in 2015 significantly intensified tension with Tehran. In April 2015, Supreme Leader Ayatollah Ali Khamenei severely criticised Saudi Arabia's airstrikes into

Yemen to quell the Houthi rebellion, comparing the campaign to Israeli actions in the Gaza Strip.[101]

> By invading Yemen, Saudis are making a mistake, setting a bad precedent in the region . . . It's a huge crime to kill children, destroy houses and obliterate a country's infrastructure . . . This is a crime and genocide which can be prosecuted internationally.[102]

President Rouhani also disproved of the campaign, calling for a ceasefire to be brokered solely among Yemeni parties.[103] For their part, the Saudis, along with their GCC allies and the United States, accused Iran of meddling in the crisis in Yemen. In fact, in an effort to cripple Iranian action in Yemen, Saudi Arabia intercepted two Iranian airplanes on 24 April, which were said to be carrying humanitarian aid.[104] Iran's Foreign Ministry summoned the Saudi chargé d'affaires to discuss the matter.[105]

Iranian–Saudi tensions have also contributed to anti-Saudi Arabian, and perhaps anti-Sunni, stances within Iraq. In early April, thousands of Iraqi Shias gathered in Baghdad's Firdous Square to protest Saudi actions in Yemen.[106] One MP from the Shia Badr bloc went so far as to say that he, along with other Iraqis, would be willing to fight to defend Yemen if Houthi leaders requested their help.[107] Iraqi Prime Minister Haider al-Abadi also decried Saudi actions in Yemen, stating

> [t]he dangerous thing is we don't know what the Saudis want to do after this. Is Iraq within their radar? That's very, very dangerous. The idea that you intervene in another state unprovoked just for regional ambition is wrong. Saddam has done it before. See what it has done to the country.[108]

Aside from the Syrian crisis, continued instability in Iraq and war in Yemen, which provide further opportunities for proxy warfare, other potential spoilers for reconciliation between the two include

> the decades of antagonism and mistrust (memories of the Iran–Iraq war remain strong); Israel's pugilistic foreign policy towards Iran, with which the Gulf itself often quietly colludes; the legacy of President Mahmoud Ahmadinejad's populist-driven hostility; and an ever more conservative religious establishment in Saudi Arabia.[109]

Furthermore, Iran's demonstrated preference for Islamist political forces, regardless of sects such as Hamas, has troubled Saudi Arabia as it has tried to suppress Sunni Islamist actors which it considers threatening to its rule.[110] While Saudi Arabia aims to dismantle such groups, Iran considers them to be a means of securing a region free of Western influence.[111] Also, the more Iran de-emphasises Shiism, the more difficult it will be for Saudi Arabia to isolate it from the Sunni world.[112] Even in discussing its support for Hezbollah, Iran has emphasised the organisation's role as undermining Israeli hegemony rather than aiding Shias:

> for Iran, by and large, the only available alliances are and have been with marginalised constituencies that happen to overwhelmingly be fellow Shias who are themselves victims of domestic power dynamics (to some extent reinforced by the foreign alliances of ruling elites).[113]

Local efforts at diminishing sectarianism

In 2003, King Abdullah launched a series of high-level National Dialogue meetings which 'focused on recognizing and bridging the gap with the internal "other" – fostering dialogue among Sufis, Salafis, Shias, and other sects within Saudi Arabia'.[114] Such a development was remarkable in a state which has such a strict institutionalised Salafi *ulama*. Such sessions, however, were little more than 'hollow debating societies', in the words of one reformer, as they did not influence the Salafi religious establishment.[115] By the end of 2006, the regime was doing little to rescind or counter anti-Shia *fatawa* that were being issued by popular Salafi clerics.

Certainly,

> despite King Abdullah's overtures to the Shias at a national level, the regime has consistently pursued what one interviewee termed a 'shut-eye policy' on anti-Shia abuse at the local level – tolerating or not cracking down sufficiently on instances of discrimination. The opening of official channels for reform was seen as a ploy to keep the Shias engaged in 'talking', rather than 'acting'.[116]

Another important by-product of Saudi–Iran tensions has been the fraying of reform cooperation among Sunni and Shia activists inside Saudi Arabia.[117] Also, Salafi clerics within Saudi Arabia, both inside and outside the religious bureaucracy, have pressured the government to take anti-Shia positions regarding Iran.[118]

In one sign of progress, in early 2013, the Saudi Interior Ministry instructed the media 'to avoid singling out Saudi Shias when discussing political issues involving Iran and Syria'.[119] Furthermore, the appointments of Prince Saud bin Nayef as governor of the Eastern Province and Khaled al-Sufayan as governor of the Qatif subregion 'were also welcomed by Shia community leaders who have acted as a conduit for dialogue with the authorities'.[120] However, no formal talks have been scheduled between Shia leaders and the government since 2011.[121] As for the domestic environment of Iran, rhetoric has been less extreme. Certainly,

> political and religious elites have by and large displayed no interest in fuelling the flames of sectarianism, despite Iran's considerable financial and military support for the Assad regime. Indeed, no major cleric in Qom has issued any fatwa authorizing travel to Syria for jihad.[122]

Anti-Shia sentiment in the Gulf often centres on the issue of whether Shias are loyal to their nation or to external *maraja' al-taqlid* – literally, 'sources of emulation' – senior clerics who exert influence over Shia social, cultural and, in the case of Iran, political affairs. Because these figures reside in Iran, Iraq and Lebanon, Saudi Salafis often accuse Shias in that country of acting as a fifth column for Iran.[123] In efforts to enhance national bona fides, some Shia scholars have advocated for the establishment of a Saudi-based *hawza* (seminary) to train Shia clerics, with the aim of creating an indigenous *marja'*.[124] Such a move could 'expedite the national integration of Shias and remove any basis for accusing them of loyalty to foreign authority'.[125] Nonetheless, some Shias oppose such a measure, contending that the authority of the *marja'* should be reduced as a means of fuelling national integration and reforming Shiism more broadly.[126]

> Since 2003, the Wahhabi view of Shiasm as being outside Islam has found resonance beyond the borders of Saudi Arabia. Accompanying this development has been a shift in the language often used to refer to Shias: long labeled *'ajam* (non-Arab, Persian) to indicate their 'outsider' status, they are now being described as *raafida*, or rejectionists.[127]

Despite the fact that sectarian differences complicate the Iranian–Saudi relationship, for each, 'ideology and religion have a certain instrumentality and utility – regimes in Tehran and Riyadh can emphasize, highlight, or minimize differences to serve broader geopolitical aims.'[128] The actions of these two states, however, undoubtedly have an 'echo effect' on the rest of the region, often fuelling purely sectarian conflict.[129]

Notes

1. Fred Halliday explains the rivalry in terms of a rise in nationalism. Fred Halliday, *Nation and Religion in the Middle East* (Boulder: Lynne Rienner, 2000).
2. Shahram Chubin and Charles Tripp, *Iran–Saudi Relations and Regional Order* (Oxford: Oxford University Press for the International Institute for Strategic Studies, 1996), p. 4.
3. Ibid. p. 4.
4. Mabon, *Saudi Arabia and Iran*, p. 4.
5. Ibid. p. 4.
6. Ibid. p. 4.
7. Ibid. p. 5.
8. Ibid. p. 42.
9. Ibid. p. 42.
10. Keynoush, *Saudi Arabia and Iran*, p. 9.
11. Ibid. p. 9.
12. Mabon, *Saudi Arabia and Iran*, p. 3.
13. Ibid. p. 3.
14. Ibid. p. 3.
15. Frederic Wehrey, Theodore W. Karasik, Alireza Nader, Jeremy Ghez, Lydia Hansell and Robert A. Guffey, *Saudi–Iranian Relations Since the Fall of Saddam: Rivalry, Cooperation, and Implications for U.S. Policy* (Santa Monica: RAND Corporation, 2009), pp. 12–13.
16. Keynoush, *Saudi Arabia and Iran*, p. 9.
17. Ibid. p. 9.
18. F. Gregory Gause III, *The International Relations of the Persian Gulf* (Cambridge: Cambridge University Press, 2010), p. 25.
19. Keynoush, *Saudi Arabia and Iran*, p. 10.
20. Ibid. p. 10.
21. Ibid. p. 10.

22. Gause, *The International Relations of the Persian Gulf*, p. 39.

23. Mabon, *Saudi Arabia and Iran*, p. 4.

24. Ibid. p. 4.

25. Keynoush, *Saudi Arabia and Iran*, p. 10.

26. Mabon, *Saudi Arabia and Iran*, p. 41.

27. W. Andrew Terrill, 'The Saudi–Iranian rivalry and the future of Middle East security', *Current Politics and Economics of the Middle East* 3, 4 (2011), p. 515.

28. Ibid. p. 519.

29. Ibid. p. 519.

30. Wehrey *et al.*, *Saudi–Iranian Relations*, p. 14.

31. Ibid. p. 14.

32. Keynoush, *Saudi Arabia and Iran*, p. 110.

33. Mason, *Foreign Policy in Iran and Saudi Arabia*, p. 20.

34. John Bulloch and Harvey Morris, *The Gulf War: Its Origins, History and Consequences* (London: Methuen, 1989).

35. Gause, *The International Relations of the Persian Gulf*, p. 72.

36. Terrill, 'The Saudi–Iranian rivalry', pp. 519–20.

37. Keynoush, *Saudi Arabia and Iran*, pp. 131–2; Reza Ekhtiari Amiri and Fakhreddin Soltani, 'Iraqi invasion of Kuwait as turning point in Iran–Saudi relationship', *Journal of Politics and Law* 4, 1 (2011): 188–94.

38. Wehrey *et al.*, *Saudi–Iranian Relations*, p. 20.

39. Terrill, 'The Saudi–Iranian Rivalry', p. 520.

40. Ibid. p. 520.

41. Ibid. p. 520.

42. Keynoush, *Saudi Arabia and Iran*, p. 11.

43. Wehrey *et al.*, *Saudi–Iranian Relations*, pp. 17–18.

44. Ibid. pp. 17–18.

45. Ibid. pp. 17–18.

46. Ibid. pp. 20–1

47. Ibid. p. 2.

48. Ibid. pp. 2–3.

49. Ibid. pp. 2–3.

50. Mabon, *Saudi Arabia and Iran*, p. 5.

51. Wehrey *et al.*, *Saudi–Iranian Relations*, p. 16.

52. Mabon, *Saudi Arabia and Iran*, p. 5.

53 Wehrey *et al.*, *Saudi–Iranian Relations*, pp. 2–3.

54. Ibid. p. 3.

55. Mabon, *Saudi Arabia and Iran*, p. xvi.
56. Ibid. p. xvi.
57. Ibid. p. xvi.
58. Ibid. p. xvi.
59. Wehrey *et al.*, *Saudi–Iranian Relations*, p. 3.
60. Ibid. p. 22.
61. Ibid. p. 25.
62. Vali Nasr, 'If the Arab Spring turns ugly', *The New York Times*, 27 August 2011, https://www.nytimes.com/2011/08/28/opinion/sunday/the-dangers-lurking-in-the-arab-spring.html.
63. Ibid.
64. Frederic Wehrey, 'Uprisings jolt the Saudi–Iranian rivalry', *Current History* 110, 740 (December 2011): 352.
65. Ibid. p. 352.
66. Ibrahim Fraihat, 'Iran and Saudi Arabia tensions', *CNN* interview, 7 January 2016, https://www.youtube.com/watch?v=pw9eqNruAto (last accessed 18 June 2019).
67. Ibrahim Fraihat, 'Nimr al Nimr: anatomy of a man', *Newsweek*, 13 January 2016, http://newsweekme.com/nimr-al-nimr-anatomy-of-a-man/ (last accessed 27 January 2018).
68. Daniel Serwer, quoted in Zack Beauchamp, 'Iran and Saudi Arabia's cold war is making the Middle East even more dangerous', *Vox*, 30 March 2015, http://www.vox.com/2015/3/30/8314513/saudi-arabia-iran.
69. Wehrey *et al.*, *Saudi–Iranian Relations*, p. 43.
70. Ibid. p. 21.
71. Ibid. p. 22.
72. Ibid. p. 22.
73. Ibid. pp. 22–3.
74. Ibid. p. 27.
75. Adel Altoraifi, 'The rise and demise of Saudi–Iranian rapprochement (1997–2009)', PhD Dissertation, London School of Economics, 2012, p. 251.
76. Ibid. p. 251.
77. Ibid. p. 251.
78. Ibid. p. 251.
79. Ibid. p. 38.
80. Ibid. p. 38.
81. Ibid. p. 38.

82. Prasanta Kumar Pradhan, 'The GCC–Iran conflict and its strategic implications for the Gulf region', *Strategic Analysis* 35, 2 (March 2011): 272.

83. Altoraifi, 'The rise and demise', p. 240.

84. Wehrey *et al.*, *Saudi–Iranian Relations*, p. 38.

85. Pradhan, 'The GCC–Iran conflict', p. 268.

86. Ibid. p. 269.

87. Ibid. p. 269.

88. Ibid. p. 269.

89. Ibid. p. 274.

90. Ibid. p. 268.

91. Altoraifi, 'The rise and demise', p. 252.

92. Ibid. p. 252.

93. Angus McDowall, 'Saudi King sits next to Iran's Ahmadinejad in goodwill gesture', *Reuters*, 14 August 2012, http://www.reuters.com/article/2012/08/14/us-saudi-iran-syria-summit-idUSBRE87D14H20120814.

94. Ibid.

95. Ibid.

96. Beauchamp, 'Iran and Saudi Arabia's cold war'.

97. Andrew Hammond, 'Saudi Arabia: cultivating sectarian spaces', in ECFR Gulf Analysis, *The Gulf and Sectarianism*, November 2013, pp. 7–9, http://www.ecfr.eu/page/-/ECFR91_GULF_ANALYSIS_AW.pdf.

98. Ibid. p. 7.

99. *Al Jazeera*, https://bit.ly/2Kkd6aT (last accessed 15 June 2019).

100. *The National*, https://bit.ly/2wXgy2E (last accessed 15 June 2019).

101. Saeed Kamali Dehghan, 'Iran's Supreme Leader accuses Saudis of "genocide" in Yemen', *The Guardian*, 9 April 2015, http://www.theguardian.com/world/2015/apr/09/iranian-president-rouhani-yemen-ceasefire.

102. Ibid.

103. Ibid.

104. 'Iran summons Saudi diplomat over plane interception', *Tehran Times*, 26 April 2015, http://www.tehrantimes.com/index_View.asp?code=246338.

105. Ibid.

106. 'Thousands of Iraq's Shia protest against Decisive Storm operation in Yemen', *Middle East Monitor*, 1 April 2015, https://www.middleeastmonitor.com/news/middle-east/17837-thousands-of-iraqs-shia-protest-decisive-storm-operation-in-yemen.

107. Ibid.

108. Michael R. Gordon and Eric Schmitt, 'Tensions flare between Iraq and Saudi Arabia in U.S. coalition', *The New York Times*, 15 April 2015, http://www.nytimes.com/2015/04/16/world/middleeast/iraqi-prime-minister-criticizes-saudi-intervention-in-yemen.html?_r=1.

109. Fatima Ayub, 'Introduction', in ECFR Gulf Analysis, *The Gulf and Sectarianism*, November 2013, p. 2, http://www.ecfr.eu/page/-/ECFR91_GULF_ANALYSIS_AW.pdf.

110. Mohammad Ali Shabani, 'Iran: strategist or sectarian', in ECFR Gulf Analysis, *The Gulf and Sectarianism*, p. 18.

111. Ibid. p. 18.

112. Ibid. p. 20.

113. Ibid. pp. 18–19.

114. Wehrey *et al.*, *Saudi–Iranian Relations*, p. 29.

115. Ibid. p. 29.

116. Ibid. p. 29.

117. Ibid. p. 29.

118. Ibid. p. 96.

119. Hammond, 'Saudi Arabia: cultivating sectarian spaces', p. 7.

120. Ibid. p. 7.

121. Ibid. p. 7.

122. Shabani, 'Iran: strategist or sectarian', p. 19.

123. Wehrey *et al.*, *Saudi–Iranian Relations*, p. 30.

124. Ibid. p. 30.

125. Ibid. p. 30.

126. Ibid. p. 30.

127. Hammond, 'Saudi Arabia: cultivating sectarian spaces', p. 7.

128. Wehrey *et al.*, *Saudi–Iranian Relations*, p. 43.

129. Ibid. p. 96.

2

Conflict Issues

Security

Security is at the core of the conflict between Iran and Saudi Arabia. Each party believes its actions towards the other are necessary to guarantee its own security needs. Security in this context is realised as a zero-sum outcome, where the advancement of the security of one party is perceived to be at the expense of the other. A clear clash of security interests has resulted in the Iranian–Saudi conflict entering a vicious cycle of escalatory actions and reactions in an example of what international relations scholars have dubbed a security dilemma. A security dilemma can be conceptualised as

> one side, fearing attack, ramps up defense spending or supports a regional proxy in order to guard against a perceived threat. The other side sees that as threatening – what if they're planning to attack? – and feels compelled to respond in kind. This creates a self-sustaining cycle in which both countries take actions that are designed to make their country more secure, but end up scaring the other side and thus raising both the chances and the potential severity of conflict.[1]

Historical examples of security dilemmas include Europe prior to World War I, the US–Soviet Cold War, and now what many scholars refer to as the 'new Middle East cold war'[2] or a 'new Arab cold war'.[3] However, Curtis Ryan adds another dimension to understanding security in Middle East politics by making the argument that 'regime security remains the key driver of alliance politics in the Middle East',[4] unlike what some traditional international relations theory tries to explain in terms of system-structure, anarchy and external threats.[5]

The Saudi perspective

Saudi Arabia has many reasons to believe that Iran's foreign policy towards the Gulf region represents a serious security threat. Indeed, Iranian policies, as seen by Riyadh, target not only the Gulf region and its regimes but also the entire Arab world. Saudi Arabia firmly believes that Iran's approach toward the region is hegemonic, expansionist and aggressive, and that the only way to stop it is by confronting, not accommodating, Iran's actions. Saudi Arabia's perception of Iranian aggression is not entirely baseless, as a number of indicators over the last few decades have clearly shown that Iran is deliberately trying to expand its influence in, and control of, the region.

Shortly after the 1979 revolution toppled the Shah's regime in Tehran, the Islamic Republic of Iran's first Supreme Leader, Ayatollah Ruhollah Khomeini, declared, 'We shall export our revolution to the whole world.' As for Gulf rulers who refused to submit to the revolution, they would be 'put to the sword and dispatched to hell'.[6] This revolution 'invigorated the shattered spirit of the Shias in Saudi Arabia as well as the Shias elsewhere in the Muslim world'[7] and, with the combination of other factors, Shia Muslims started to pose a 'serious challenge for Riyadh'.[8] Almost four decades later, the fear of Iran 'exporting the revolution' still influences the foreign policies of Saudi Arabia and its Gulf neighbours, especially in how they read and respond to Iran. It significantly underlines Saudi Arabia's perception of being under threat from Tehran. At this point, it does not matter whether Iran is genuinely seeking to export its revolution – as long as there is no Iranian statement that is equivalent in weight to counter it, that stated ambition will always remain a hindrance to rapprochement between the two countries. For Saudi Arabia, 'exporting the revolution' is a point of reference when trying to make sense of its relationship with Iran, which always leads to viewing it as a significant security threat.

Iranian actions on the ground have proved that the notion of 'exporting the revolution' is not just rhetorical. In the years following its revolution, Iran backed a coup attempt in Bahrain in 1981, bombings in Kuwait in 1983 (including an attempted assassination of the country's emir in 1985), anti-Saudi demonstrations during the hajj, and other actions targeting Gulf regimes.[9] Furthermore, Iran has long been implicated in the 1996 Khobar Towers bombing in Saudi Arabia and was ultimately found liable by a US court.[10] The attack represented a blunt violation of Saudi territory and security and is always cited by Saudis as evidence of the threat Iran poses to the Gulf region. More recently, Iran has been accused of spying in Kuwait and possibly other Gulf states, making the threat Iran continues to pose to the region's security that much more credible and urgent.[11]

In recent years, especially after the outbreak of the Arab Spring, Iran has increased the intensity and frequency of its threats against Saudi Arabia. The most dangerous escalation, as seen by Saudi Arabia, has concerned the issue of 'encirclement'. That is, Saudi Arabia views Iran as using both its political and military influence to nearly complete a circle around it, raising Riyadh's security threat alert to probably its highest level in recent history. Figure 2.1 shows where Iran has an established influence in countries around Saudi Arabia supported by armed militias.

To the Kingdom's east, Iran controls the entire eastern region of the Gulf and the Strait of Hormuz. To the north, there is an Iran-friendly Iraqi government and even Iranian Revolutionary Guard Corps (IRGC) units roaming different parts of the country. Qassem Suleimani, the head of the IRGC's elite Quds Force, served as a military advisor to the Iraqi government. To the northwest, Syria and Lebanon have the strongest Iranian political and military presence outside the Islamic Republic's borders. As previously noted, the Iran-backed Houthi militia lurks on Saudi Arabia's southern border, from where it has launched a number of ballistic missiles toward Saudi cities, airports, and vital targets like oil facilities. Just before the Saudi-led coalition's war in Yemen started in March 2015, the Houthis were performing military exercises along the border. Lastly, to the Kingdom's west, there is an Egyptian regime under Abdel-Fattah el-Sisi, who has occasionally flirted with Iran to blackmail Saudi Arabia for more money. Egypt has even welcomed the top-ranking security official of the Assad regime – Iran's primary ally – to Cairo, purportedly to coordinate

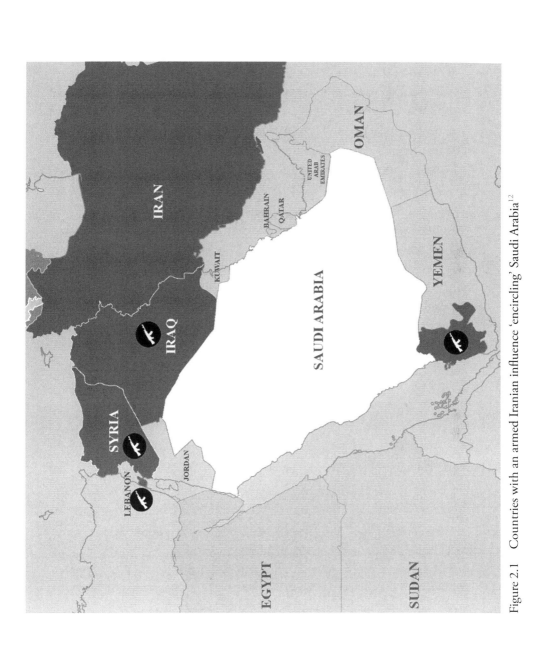

Figure 2.1 Countries with an armed Iranian influence 'encircling' Saudi Arabia[12]

counterterrorism efforts.[13] With the presence of regimes and militias that are loyal to Iran all around it, including on its borders, Saudi Arabia feels that it has no choice but to treat the situation as a planned and aggressive Iranian policy targeting not only Saudi Arabia, but the whole Gulf region – if not the entire Sunni Arab world.

In addition to 'actual influence' exerted by Iran, there are also areas with a 'perceived influence' of Iranian threat around Saudi Arabia's borders. The combination of actual and perceived influence seriously raises Saudi concerns about its own security and the source of the threat, Iran. Figure 2.2 shows the perceived threat of Iranian influence to Saudi borders.

In the two countries' attempt to balance their geopolitical relations, both Oman and Qatar have been historically viewed by Saudi Arabia as enjoying 'close ties' with Iran. Riyadh mentions this reason for the 2017 Qatari crisis with Saudi Arabia, the UAE, Bahrain and Egypt. Such a perceived influence would always be an area of concern for Saudi Arabia in any possible future confrontation with Iran. Though Bahrain has historically showed firm support for Saudi Arabia's foreign policy, the fact that the country has a significant Shia presence among its citizens causes concern for Saudi Arabia with regard to their relationship with Iran. In addition, Iran has made statements in the past claiming ownership of the Bahrain Islands.[15] Lastly, a Shia presence in the eastern part of Saudi Arabia (particularly in the Qatif area)[16] also contributes to Riyadh's perception of Iranian influence. It should be noted that the execution in 2016 of a Shia cleric, Nimr al-Nimr – who comes from this area – subsequently led to the severance of diplomatic relations between Iran and Saudi Arabia, as crowds attacked and burned the Saudi embassy in Tehran.

However, the most alarming threat to Saudi Arabia's security is the Iranian model of spreading armed militias loyal to Tehran throughout the region. Most notably, Iran was successful in building Hezbollah, the powerful Shia militia in Lebanon, and has attempted to replicate that model in a number of Arab countries, especially those surrounding Saudi Arabia. These militias are seen by Saudi Arabia as threatening, destabilising forces that, through their activities from Lebanon to Syria, to Iraq and to Yemen, threaten regional (and Saudi) security. In fact, these militias cannot be underestimated as with time they have grown in power and numbers, with

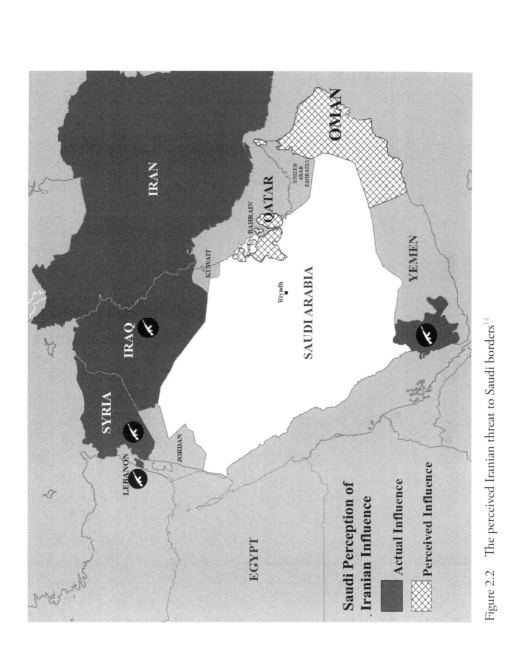

Figure 2.2 The perceived Iranian threat to Saudi borders[14]

more than fifty Shia militias now in Iraq alone.[17] In September 2016, Hadi Al-Ameri,[18] the leader of the powerful Shia Badr organisation, stated that the umbrella group of militias known as the Popular Mobilization Force (or Hashid al-Shaabi) is the most powerful force in Iraq, implying that it is even stronger than the country's army.[19]

The threat posed by Iran goes beyond its ability to destabilise neighbouring countries through militias to directly targeting regimes, particularly those of Gulf states, including Saudi Arabia. Khomeini made statements explicitly aimed at delegitimising the rule of Gulf regimes, which were seen as a call to topple them. As William Quandt explains, the 1979 Islamic revolution 'brought to power a man who had explicitly argued that Islam and hereditary kingship were incompatible, a threatening message, to say the least, in Riyadh'.[20] In response, Saudi Arabia and the other Gulf monarchies in 1981 formed the Gulf Cooperation Council (GCC), an organisation initially designed to counter and contain Iranian influence.[21]

Khomeini's successor, Ali Khamenei, has also launched rhetorical attacks against the Saudi regime, most recently to delegitimise its role in managing Islam's holiest sites. In 2016, he accused Saudi Arabia of being a 'small and puny Satan', adding that 'the world of Islam, including Muslim governments and peoples, must familiarize themselves with the Saudi rulers and correctly understand their blasphemous, faithless, dependent and materialistic nature'. He added, 'Because of these rulers' oppressive behavior towards God's guests, the world of Islam must fundamentally reconsider the management of the two holy places and the issue of hajj.'[22] The content of this attack, as well as the fact that it was delivered by Iran's Supreme Leader, makes it clear that Iran wants to delegitimise the Saudi regime, and perhaps eventually change it. In fact, as Khamenei's comments were directed to the Islamic world, his attack could also be seen as calling for all Muslims to revolt against the Saudi regime's custodianship of Mecca and Medina. No matter what such statements really mean, it is significant in itself that they are perceived to present serious threats to the survival of the Saudi regime, threats that Saudi Arabia of course vows to resist. In this particular case, Saudi Arabia's Grand Mufti Sheikh Abdulaziz Al-Sheikh responded to Khamenei's attack with a statement declaring that Iranians are 'not Muslims'.[23]

In this context, a Saudi official explained that the only way for Saudi Arabia to stop treating Iran as a serious security threat, is for

Iran to change its behaviour towards the Gulf, which has always been aggressive. Saudi Arabia wants Iran to stop its intervention in the Gulf region, and particularly to refrain from creating armed Shia militias as in Yemen and Iraq. In addition, Iran should end its recruitment of students as spies in the Gulf and its funding of attacks similar to Khobar in 1996. Finally, stop talking on behalf of Shias in the Gulf who are citizens of their own countries, not Iranian citizens. That is when Iran will cease to be a security threat to the Gulf region.[24]

The Iranian perspective

Security is also the major driver of Iran's foreign policy. Hassan Ahmadian, an adjunct professor at the University of Tehran and a senior research fellow at the Center for Strategic Research, explains that Iran bases its foreign policy on four major threats to its national security: the United States, Israel, the global system, and instability in neighbouring countries.[25]

There seems to be agreement among scholars of Iran and the Gulf that Iran treats the United States as a major threat to its national security. Regardless of American intentions, Iran believes that US foreign policy can cause serious damage to Iran's security. Accordingly, Iran has chosen to form its foreign policy to respond to this threat, including by destabilising the Gulf, as it is home to the United States' primary allies in the Middle East.

Interestingly, much like Saudi Arabia, Iran fears encirclement. As Ali Vaez, Senior Iran Analyst at the International Crisis Group, describes,

Since the 1979 revolution, Iran has viewed itself as encircled by the United States, inferior in conventional military capability to most of its neighbours and excluded from the region's security architecture. To defend itself, it has relied on its so called forward defence policy, which is based on deterring its enemies from attacking it through employing proxies on their borders. As long as the above-mentioned conditions remain unaltered, so will Iran's regional policies.[26]

Figure 2.3 shows the 'encirclement' of Iran by American military bases. These are air force, naval and army bases, aircraft carriers and radar facilities spread

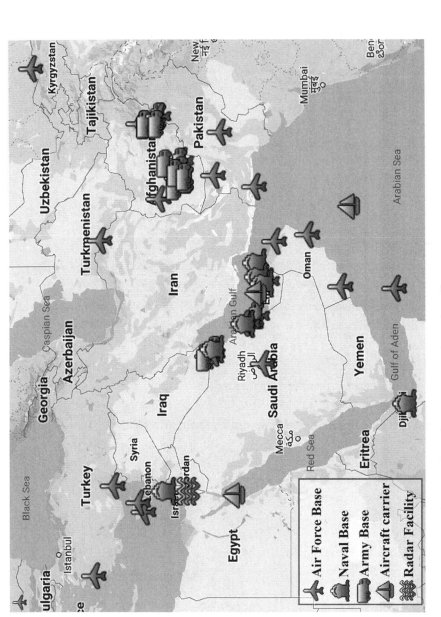

Figure 2.3 'Encirclement' of Iran by American military bases[27]

in neighbouring countries like Iraq, Bahrain, Qatar and Afghanistan. Being surrounded by all these military installations leaves Iran feeling nervous, vulnerable and exposed to American attacks at any time.

Steven Wright, a Gulf scholar at Hamad Bin Khalifa University in Doha, agrees that the American threat serves as a major mechanism driving Iran's foreign policy in the region. In particular, he points out that there are American bases in almost every country adjacent to Iran, such as Afghanistan, Iraq, Bahrain, Qatar, and others.[28] Indeed, the full list of nations within or near the Middle East where the United States maintains a military presence also includes Saudi Arabia itself, the United Arab Emirates, Qatar, Oman, Kuwait, Turkey, Pakistan, Jordan, Israel and Djibouti.[29] Referring to the American presence in the Gulf, an Iranian scholar noted, 'Our neighbours always bring outsiders to the region and they present a serious security threat to our country.'[30] A scholar from the Arab Gulf responded by invoking Iran's seizure in 1971 of Abu Musa, Greater Tunb and Lesser Tunb, islands over which the UAE claims sovereignty. He said,

> I don't want to bring foreign powers to the region. The Brits colonised this region and I don't want them back. But when the Iranian Shah took three islands by force he did not consult anyone. Today, Iran refuses to solve it by arbitration or other forms of intervention or even talk about it.[31]

However, Iran sees Saudi Arabia taking an active role in advancing the threat to Iran's security through its alliance with the United States. Seyed Hossein Mousavian, Head of the Foreign Relations Committee of Iran's National Security Council (1997–2005), argues that Saudi Arabia has always posed a security threat to Iran, first by supporting Saddam Hussein in his war against Iran (1980–8), and later by encouraging the United States 'to cut off the head of the snake', referring to Iran, as per the Wikileaks documents.[32]

More broadly, the United States being a threat to Iran means that the international order itself is biased against Iran and its values, given that this system is controlled by the United States. On this level, Iran is concerned about its own values and the need to maintain them in an age of globalisation. In other words, Iran aims not just to protect itself against a possible attack by the United States, but also proactively engages in building regional and international coalitions – including by expanding its influence in Arab countries even if it clashes with Saudi interests – to counter external influence on the region.

The threat from Israel also reinforces security as a core driver of Iran's foreign policy in the region. Mehran Kamrava, Director of the Center for Regional and International Studies at Georgetown University School of Foreign Service in Qatar, argues that Iran's security concerns and fear of an Israeli attack has a major role in influencing Iran's foreign behaviour. Ehud Barak's statement that Israel had come very close to attacking Iran three times in the past made Iranians even more convinced that security must be a priority.[33] On the other hand, Steven Wright places less importance on Israel as a source of threat to Iran's security because Iran knows that Israel cannot attack without full American backing, lessening the need for concern.[34]

Since Iran considers itself to be under threat from the United States, Israel, and even the international system, it believes the best way to defend itself is by building coalitions in the region and expanding its influence. According to Professor Ahmadian, 'Iran works with international players like Russia and China to counter America and weaken the basis of the international order that America leads.'[35]

The challenge for the Middle East in this context comes when Iran's building of coalitions and establishment of allied militias clash with Saudi Arabia's perceived security needs. While Iran tries to establish and support militias in a number of Arab countries, purportedly to counter American influence and deter the Israeli threat, it simultaneously encroaches on the security of Saudi Arabia and other Gulf countries, especially when Iran's allies happen to encircle Saudi Arabia. In fact, the situation can be seen as an example of a challenge to the basic human needs theory in conflict resolution, where both conflict parties have basic needs at stake, making compromise difficult.

However, Saudis question whether Iran is genuinely facing serious threats to its security, arguing that no other country has helped improve Iranian security the way the United States has. Specifically, the United States gave Iran what it could not achieve in eight brutal years of war – the removal of its arch rival and gravest threat, Saddam Hussein – without Iran having to fire one bullet. The Americans also removed a hostile regime in Afghanistan, and Iran actually cooperated in both cases. More recently, Iran and the United States have found themselves on the same side of the campaign against the Islamic State. Indeed, in May 2015, Qassem Suleimani was fighting ISIS on the ground alongside the Iraqi army outside Fallujah while US fighter jets were attacking the extremists from the air.

The fight against Sunni extremists like ISIS, Al-Qaida and other groups represents another major clash between Iranian and Saudi security agendas. Mahjoob Zweiri, an Iran scholar at Qatar University, explains that Iran builds its security strategy to fight outside its borders so that they do not have to fight inside: 'they learned the lessons of the Iraq–Iran war in 1980 when Saddam took about 105 kilometres of their land'.[36] Iran considers the spread of Sunni extremist groups, not unreasonably, to be a direct threat to its own security. In attempting to counter that threat, Iran undermines the political objectives of Iraq Sunni communities that do not necessarily support extremist groups, but very clearly oppose the Iran-backed government in Baghdad. These Sunni communities are close allies of Saudi Arabia, which attempts to counter Iranian influence through them. What makes this aspect of the security situation even more complicated is that Iran considers Saudi Arabia to be a supporter of Sunni extremist groups, if not directly then at least through its ideology of Wahhabism that provides guidance for violent extremism like Al-Qaida[37] in the region and against Iran – something that Saudi Arabia denies.

The nuclear deal

Since the American invasion of Iraq in 2003, no factor has exacerbated the security crisis between Iran and Saudi Arabia more than the signing of the Joint Comprehensive Plan of Action (JCPOA), or nuclear deal between Iran and the P5+1 (United States, Russia, China, France, United Kingdom, plus Germany) in 2015.[38] The deal pushed the Iranian–Saudi conflict across a new threshold, moving it from a stage of proxies battling in Syria and Iraq to direct – though not armed – confrontation between Riyadh and Tehran. The signing of the nuclear deal by the Obama administration in particular signalled to the Saudis that they had been betrayed by their traditional security guarantor the United States, and that they then had to take matters into their own hands when it came to standing up against 'Iran's intervention' in the region.

There have been a number of statements by Saudi officials and opinion leaders asserting that they are not concerned by the nature of the deal itself but instead are worried about Iran's foreign policy behaviour after the deal, especially towards the Arab region. The first reaction to the announcement of the deal between Iran and the P5+1 came from Saudi Foreign Minister Adel al-Jubeir, who is known for his hawkish positions on Iran. Jubeir said, 'Iran should use this agreement to improve the situation inside Iran and should not try to use it for "adventurism" in the region.'[39] Furthermore, influential Saudi opinion leader, Jamal Khashoggi explained, 'We are not against a deal that addresses Iran's nuclear activities; we are concerned about the fact that this will allow Iran to increase its meddling in its neighbours' internal affairs.'[40]

However, a number of factors explain Saudi anger about the deal with Iran. First, the West managed the entire negotiation process without involving Saudi Arabia, a neighbouring and primary rival of Iran, whose national security is at stake regardless of the negotiations' results; to make matters worse, neighbouring Oman, not traditionally aligned with the rest of the GCC, was involved in the process. Second, the negotiations and the deal itself completely ignored Iran's foreign policy behaviour, including its history of meddling in the internal affairs of Gulf states. In other words, Saudi Arabia saw the deal as giving Iran free reign to continue intervening in the region, including within Gulf states, America's traditional security allies. Third, given Saudi reliance on the United States as its primary security guarantor and provider of military equipment, Washington's signing of the deal was seen as a blunt betrayal, which left Saudi Arabia feeling abandoned and vulnerable. Fourth, this was not the first time that the West had made a deal with Iran and its allies, as a similar deal had been made with the Assad regime – Iran's ally – after its alleged use of chemical weapons against Syrian civilians. That agreement led the regime to surrender its chemical weapons programme in return for a free hand to crush the Syrian opposition, including Saudi-linked militias. Indeed, Saudi Arabia's primary concern with the nuclear deal stemmed from its assumption that if Iran was funding proxies in three civil wars – in Syria, Iraq and Yemen – while under sanctions, then one could only imagine what it would do once sanctions were lifted and billions of dollars in frozen assets released. Ultimately, for Saudi Arabia, Iran was given both a free hand to meddle and the resources to do so on a greater scale, which would only result in the region being destabilised even further.

Experts on the Gulf and Iran agree in general that the nuclear deal added significant tension to the complex Iranian–Saudi relations and exacerbated the security crisis in the Middle East. Vali Nasr argues,

> The nuclear deal only added fuel to the fire. Saudi Arabia interpreted the agreement as an American tilt toward Iran – one that would not only bring gains to Tehran, but also to the Shia side of the ledger in the Middle East. Hence Sunnis have had to redouble their efforts to block Shia gains. Saudi Arabia's foreign policy has become more confrontational since the Iran nuclear deal, emphasizing the sectarian divide.[41]

Marc Lynch notes that the nuclear deal produced added instability in the region and argues specifically that sectarian tension would worsen. He suggests,

> Saudi Arabia views Iran's reintegration into the international order and its evolving relationship with Washington as a profound threat to its own regional position. Mobilizing anti-Shia sectarianism is a familiar move in its effort to sustain Iranian containment and isolation.[42]

Alex Vatanka, an Iran expert at the Middle East Institute in Washington, DC, holds that the increased tensions could have been avoided if the Obama administration had taken a different approach to the nuclear deal. Asked about the Gulf states' frustration over the Obama administration not including their interests in the nuclear negotiations, he said the United States could have linked Iran's foreign policy in the region to the nuclear issue, but chose not to do so.[43] Steven Wright agrees that the Obama administration has played a destructive role in the Iranian–Saudi conflict by putting containment on the shelf and instead starting to reconcile with Iran while not involving Saudi Arabia in this process, raising Saudi suspicions about the deal and possible changes to overall security arrangements in the Gulf. Wright thus views the United States' decision to keep Saudi Arabia out of the negotiations as a major mistake.[44]

The increased tensions resulting from the nuclear deal immediately translated into action as Saudi Arabia took a number of escalatory measures the year after it was signed. Feeling betrayed by the United States, its traditional security ally, Saudi Arabia in turn adopted a strategy of confrontation with Iran to counter its 'meddling'. In his first year in power, King Salman put together three coalitions, all independent of the United States. First came a coalition of ten Arab countries in March 2015 to undertake Operation Decisive Storm in Yemen against the Houthis and forces loyal to Ali Abdullah Saleh.[45] Next, in mid-December 2015, Saudi Arabia established a military alliance, made up of thirty-four predominantly Muslim countries, to fight terrorism.[46] This group notably excluded Iran, Iraq, Syria and Lebanon, leading some analysts to call it a 'Sunni Coalition' as it seemed to reflect the sectarian division within the Muslim world. Third came the announcement, on 29 December 2015, that Saudi Arabia and Turkey were planning 'to create a "strategic cooperation council" to strengthen military, economic and investment cooperation between the two states'.[47]

This third announcement came only days before the Saudis took a different sort of escalatory step: the execution of Sheikh Nimr al-Nimr, the activist Shia cleric who was known for his harsh criticism of the Saudi regime. The Saudi government executed Sheikh al-Nimr both to spite Iran, which had taken up his cause, and to signal to the Obama administration, which had pressured Riyadh not to execute al-Nimr, that it was willing and able to act independently. Hussein Ibish, a Gulf expert at the Arab Gulf States Institute in Washington, DC, suggests that Saudi Arabia was actually sending three messages: first, it was demonstrating to the Iranians that it did not fear their threats and was willing to do whatever was necessary to counter them. Second, Riyadh was informing the Obama administration that it did not trust them and thus would act independently. Third, the execution was intended to smother any domestic discussion about the line of succession and was a warning to any Al-Qaida elements.[48]

With the arrival of the Trump administration and its aggressive criticism of the nuclear deal, the relationship between Washington and Riyadh returned to its traditional status of a strong alliance. The trust between the two parties was regained at the Riyadh summit in May 2017, Trump's first state visit of his presidency, and since that time they have essentially had one voice of escalation against Tehran. It is important to note here that this coalition has significantly deepened the security crisis between Iran and Saudi Arabia, as Tehran has become more convinced than ever of the security danger the Saudi regime – through its alliance with the United States – presents to its national security. If there had been a chance for the security crisis between Iran and Saudi Arabia to be resolved during the Obama administration – despite Saudi frustration – the Trump administration has now made that virtually impossible, especially after Trump's official withdrawal from the nuclear deal agreement in May 2018.

Sectarianism

Lawrence G. Potter defines sectarianism in a neutral way, explaining that 'it goes back to the idea of a sect, a group with distinctive religious, political, or philosophical beliefs'.[49] Sectarianism often has a 'negative connotation, denoting that a group sets itself off from society and thereby raises tensions'.[50] Notably, Fanar Haddad contends that the negativity most often associated with the term sectarianism is 'neither helpful nor is it accurate'.[51] He therefore aptly divides sectarianism into three broad categories: assertive, passive and banal. First, assertive sectarianism occurs when members of the other sect are largely absent, as opposed to what is the case for aggressive sectarianism, a subtype of this; the difference between these two types of sectarianism lies in whether displays of sectarian identity are pejorative (aggressive) or not (passive). Second, passive sectarianism involves members of a sect not shying away from asserting their sectarian identity if the occasion requires it, yet they must be induced to do so through provocation or through religious obligations. A contrasting subtype is apologetic sectarianism, when a person feels uncomfortable displaying sectarian symbols at any time. Third, banal sectarianism is devoid of any active dynamics and restricts itself to the background of one's conception of self.

Other complex definitions of the term sectarianism take into account the political realities which give rise to sectarian tendencies. Sectarianism, depending on political context, can be described as 'a neologism born in the age of nationalism to signify the antithesis of nation; its meaning is predicated on and constructed against a territorially-bounded liberal nation-state'.[52] Such a concept is particularly useful in the Middle East, where sectarian differences predated the establishment of nation-states. The cases of Iraq and Lebanon are particularly instructive in this description. Azmi Bishara takes the argument a step further to introduce what he calls the 'imagined sects'. Accordingly, it is

> the perception of dependence on religion or doctrine in association with millions of people, who do not know each other, have never formed a group or felt a belonging to a major social and religious group based on a common past of narratives, stories and legends, and consequent practices and limited understanding of legitimacy'.[53]

Darwich and Fakhoury explain the debate between two approaches to the understanding of the relationship between sectarianism and conflict, primordial versus instrumental. Accordingly,

> primordial approaches presume that sectarian identities, assumed to be natural, are the main driver of conflict. They consider primordial loyalties – such as sect and ethnicity – to be endemic, and the ensuing conflicts inevitable. On the other hand, the instrumental approach emphasizes the role of power politics, alliances and material structures. It explains conflicts as being driven by regional rivalries and the exigencies of balance-of-power dynamics, viewing sectarian identities as tools open to manipulation and exploitation by political elites.[54]

The question, therefore, becomes whether sectarianism is inevitable or is a product of its institutional environment.

In any region, state weakness or state failure tends to promote 'recourse to identities that do not align with the nation-state, such as sect, ethnicity, or tribe, to prove community'.[55] In such environments, sectarian conflict can be considered a symptom of political conflict rather than its cause.[56] As Aaron Reese explains,

> Left alone, however, it could become a cause of violence as groups strike pre-emptively against perceived threats to their communities or pursue revenge. Further violence then creates a vicious cycle of state weakness and perceived illegitimacy, which continues to lead citizens to feel less secure and to identify more with sub- and trans-national groups.[57]

The creation of an 'us versus them' rhetoric often emerges in such situations, further threatening the unity of nation-states and promoting the rise of sectarian identities.[58]

Because sectarianism often emerges in spaces where national identities are weaker than religious affiliations, the Middle East, as a region traditionally known for weak or ineffective governance, is rife with such conflict. Though most often associated with the Sunni–Shia division, it is important to note, however, that sectarianism does not solely concern religious differences. Fanar Haddad, for example, views sectarian groups in Iraq as 'competing subnational mass-group identities. As such, the dynamics are in essence very similar to other such competing groups, be they racial, national, ethnic, or even ideological.' Sectarian identities, like ethnic ones, are constantly changing and being renegotiated.[59]

Nonetheless, the primary sectarian clash in the Arab and Muslim context remains between Shia and Sunni sects of Islam. Notably, '[t]he doctrinal split between the Sunni and Shi'a is not itself an a priori determinant of conflict or tension'.[60] The Shia and Sunni are not in themselves monolithic or homogeneous groups in the slightest and may be divided into a variety of social, economic and political categories.[61]

Despite this complexity, Shia–Sunni sectarianism has taken on political importance at different times in the Arab and Muslim context. As Frederic Wehrey points out, 'At various points in history . . . sectarian identity has assumed greater prominence. Political elites have instrumentalized it, and ordinary citizens have defined themselves by it to the exclusion of other affinities.'[62]

In the Arab and Muslim context, Fanar Haddad contends that sectarianism has been driven by four primary factors: external influence, economic competition, competing myth-symbol complexes and contested cultural ownership of the nation.[63] Notably, then, states, either foreign or local, appear to influence the degree to which sectarian divisions matter in a given political context, yet these divisions must be in place initially to be re-activated. Haddad explains: 'State policy and officially sanctioned discrimination undoubtedly exacerbate sectarian tensions; however, more often than not, the state can only amplify extant fissures and tendencies and is unlikely to be able to create new ones overnight.'[64] Certainly, regimes in the Middle East have used sectarian claims to bolster their own positions among domestic and regional populations, while in the cases of Syria and Iraq, rulers have used associations with particular sects to ensure they have a reliable band of supporters.[65] Nonetheless, these rulers did not by any means *create* sectarian divisions but certainly have helped to reproduce and instrumentalise them.

Despite the state's ability to manipulate sectarian divisions at times, state weakness has also been cited as a primary driver of sectarianism in the Arab and Middle East context. Sectarianism, like other sub-national tribal or regional ascriptive identities, tends to increase as the power of the state decreases.[66] Certainly, '[w]hen the state is unable to provide basic security and services for its citizens, they have to look to those communities that will protect them and in which they feel safe'.[67] The cases of Lebanon, Libya and Yemen in particular prove the validity of this claim.

Sectarianism in the conflict between Iran and Saudi Arabia

The scholarly community remains polarised over the degree to which sectarianism motivates various conflicts in the Middle East. In particular, there is an unresolved debate among scholars specialising in Middle Eastern studies over whether the Iranian–Saudi cold war has been caused by sectarianism (and thus is primordial) or if the rivalry goes beyond religious animosity (and is therefore merely instrumental). While some argue that sectarianism represents the driving mechanism of many Middle East conflicts today, including the Iranian–Saudi conflict, others see it simply as a tool that has been conveniently used by both parties to advance their political agendas.

This chapter argues that Sunni–Shia sectarianism has not recently played a causal role in today's Middle East conflicts, and in particular the one between Iran and Saudi Arabia. Rather, that rivalry is driven by factors like geopolitics, leadership and security needs. Nonetheless, the politicisation of sectarianism by both parties to mobilise support for their political agendas has served as a reinforcing mechanism for Iranian–Saudi animosity, thus causing further conflict escalation. In this case, sectarianism is a means rather than a cause of the rivalry. Indeed, the extensive and varied use of sectarianism by both governments, mainstream and social media, clergy, and even think tanks on both sides has turned sectarianism into a cause for further escalation of the conflict. Such escalation can be seen in Syria, Yemen, Iraq and Lebanon. It should also be mentioned that factors external to Iran and Saudi Arabia have contributed to the politicisation of sectarianism and its role in intensifying their conflict, including the American invasion of Iraq in 2003 and the Arab Spring in 2011, among others.

External players in this conflict, like Western policymakers, have contributed to the primordial versus instrumental debate when it comes to explaining causes of the Iran–Saudi conflict. They have generally viewed the nature of the tension between Iran and Saudi Arabia as a primordial conflict driven by ancient religious differences and rivalry between Sunni and Shia Muslims. This belief is widespread, especially within the policy and media communities. In addition to the fact that many policymakers and journalists believe it is a sectarian conflict, each group has reason to cling to that belief. Policymakers would like to attribute the causes of the tension to factors internal to the rival states themselves, so they can neither be blamed for contributing to its escalation nor be expected to do something to contain it. If 'they' are fighting among 'themselves', there is little 'we' can do about it. In this regard, Paul Dixon warns of the 'sectarian narrative'[68] becoming a mechanism to explain conflicts and blame the other. Sectarianism is a derogatory term used to describe the 'other' rather than 'us'.[69] It is 'associated with narratives that emphasize the role of religion and sectarianism, rather than say politics, in explaining current conflicts in the Middle East'.[70]

President Obama's assertion in his 2016 State of the Union address that the region's conflicts 'date back millennia' is perhaps the clearest example of the preference of Western policymakers to view Middle East tensions as being caused by an ancient and unavoidable sectarianism. For Western journalists and media organisations, presenting tensions as essentially sectarian is also tempting, as it helps them produce reports that are simple for average readers to understand and absorb. Delving into the complexities of the Middle East's conflicts is a much tougher task than simply explaining conflicts by stating that Sunnis are on one side and Shias on the other. However, this oversimplification in explaining conflicts as resulting from Sunni–Shia tensions never does justice to understanding the real causes of the conflicts and obscures the need to formulate suitable strategies to deal with them.

Sectarianism defining politics

The argument that sectarianism plays a causal role in the Iran–Saudi conflict and the politics of the Middle East is well presented by scholars like Vali Nasr. He sees sectarianism as 'an age-old source that has flared up from time to time to mold Islamic history, theology, law, and politics'.[71] He adds, 'it has been far more important in shaping the Middle East than many realize or acknowledge . . . The overall Sunni–Shia conflict will play a large role in defining the Middle East as a whole and shaping its relations with the outside world.'[72] By the same token, Toby Matthiesen argues that the main development of the modern era is 'the transformation of religious group-identities into politically salient ethno-sectarian identities'.[73] Accordingly, sectarian identities, in particular of minority Shia populations in the Gulf, 'have become almost like a marker of ethnicity', and so it follows, in his view, that sectarian conflicts resemble ethnic conflicts in many respects.[74] Thus such conflicts are 'not just about "religious" beliefs, although for example in Saudi Arabia religious hatred against non-Wahhabis is an important factor. It is rather religion in its social context that matters.'[75] Certainly, since the Iranian revolution, Shiism has become increasingly politicised, creating a challenge for Sunni political Islam and making politicised strands of Shiism threatening to Sunni Islamists.[76] Sectarianism and geopolitics have therefore become increasingly intertwined, in particular between Saudi Arabia and Iran, but also in places with mixed Sunni–Shia populations like Bahrain, Iraq and Syria.[77]

Adding to the political importance of sectarian politics is a general lack of effective institutions, in particular in the Gulf, outside of the religious sector. Certainly,

> the region's unique lack of political institutions or an economic basis for class-based politics (due to the rentier economy) makes ethnic and sectarian categories the most viable bases for political coordination. This means that political coalitions in the Gulf will naturally tend to form along these same group-based distinctions.[78]

In the Gulf environment, where civil society is severely restricted, religion provides the most likely venue for political discussion.

Sectarianism, then, provides a motive for conflict and escalation in the context of Iranian and Saudi relations. Shireen Hunter, Research Professor at the Center for Muslim-Christian Understanding at Georgetown University and a former Iranian diplomat (1966–78) argues,

> Ethnic and sectarian differences certainly create a background more conducive to conflict than friendship between Iran and Saudi Arabia. Because of its Wahhabi beliefs Saudi Arabia is more anti-Shia than the other Sunni schools such as Hanafi and even Shafei. Abdul Wahhab was viscerally anti-Shia.[79]

It is about politics

The opposite view to sectarianism playing a causal role suggests that this conflict is in essence about politics. Anoushiravan Ehteshami rejects the notion that the Iran–Saudi rivalry stems from theological and ideological differences, or from historical rivalry between Arabs, Persians and Ottoman.[80] Furthermore, Gregory Gause believes that pitting Sunni against Shia 'does not do justice to the complexities of the new Middle East cold war'.[81] He contends that sectarianism is in fact the *reflection* of political competition in the region, rather than its root cause:

Riyadh and Tehran are playing a balance of power game. They are using sectarianism in that game, yet their motivations are not centuries-long religious disputes but a simple contest for regional influence. Neither side publicly asserts that they are engaged in a sectarian fight – in fact, each blames the other for introducing sectarian divisiveness into regional politics. That neither will admit to sectarian motives, even while using sectarianism to build patron-client relations, gives some indication of what they think regional audiences do and do not want to hear.[82]

Engaging with sectarian identities has proven useful for Saudi Arabia and Iran in mobilising domestic political support, which bolsters their power in the region more broadly. The fact that Iran and Saudi Arabia have reached out to allies outside of their sectarian circle, however, may suggest the superficiality of sectarianism as a principal cause of conflict.[83]

Baqer Alnajjar, a sociology professor at the University of Bahrain, agrees that Riyadh and Tehran's alliances go beyond sectarian lines. Indeed, he notes that Saudi Arabia's primary allies in Lebanon are the liberal al-Mustaqbal party and the predominantly Christian March 14th alliance.[84] In Yemen, Saudi Arabia supported the Shia Imamate in the 1960s. On the other hand, Iran supported the Sunni Hamas in Palestine and Christian Armenia against the majority-Shia Azerbaijan. It is a political conflict, but religion helps to mobilise a support base, Alnajjar explains. Valbjorn and Bank concur that Iran attempts to gain influence in the Arab world 'by behaving "more Arab than the Arabs", especially when it came to presenting itself as the "real defender of the Palestinian cause", thereby insinuating that the "real enemies" of the Arab people are their own regimes'.[85]

Fatima al-Smadi, an Iran expert at Al Jazeera Center for Studies in Doha, attempts to remove this confusion between sectarianism and politics in Iran's foreign policy by emphasising Iran's use of 'political Shiaism'.[86] She says that Iran's primary concern is for loyalists who carry its political views regardless of whether they believe in Iran's 'Velayat-e Faqih' (Guardianship of the Jurist) system of religious governance or not. For example, there are Sunni Afghan MPs – whom Iran supports – voting in favour of Iran's view on the security agreement between Afghanistan and the United States in their parliament and Iran does not care too much whether those parliamentarians believe in Velayat-e Faqih. In its search for power and influence, Iran supports not only the Shia but Sunni as well who are willing to support its political views. Al-Smadi adds that Iran supports dozens of media institutions including Sunni outlets who are now celebrating the Day of Ashura.

Marc Lynch agrees that Middle East conflicts today cannot be explained by sectarianism as a driving force. He argues,

> The idea of an unending, primordial conflict between Sunnis and Shias explains little about the ebbs and flows of regional politics. This is not a resurgence of a 1,400-year-old conflict. Sectarianism today is intense, but that is because of politics. The continuing reverberations of the U.S. occupation of Iraq, the Syrian civil war and the Iranian nuclear deal have far more to do with the current spike in sectarianism than some timeless essence of religious difference.[87]

Frederic Wehrey *et al.* concede that, aside from sectarian sources of conflict between Sunni Saudi Arabia and Shia Iran, some purely political issues drive the conflict. Saudi Arabia's links to the United States have polarised the two, as Iran hopes to lead a rejectionist stand against Western involvement in the Middle East and thus become the primary power broker in the region.

> Tehran continues to regard Riyadh as America's principal local proxy and a buffer against Iran taking what it feels is its rightful place as the region's preeminent power. From its perspective, Saudi Arabia harbors a deep-seated distrust of Iran, stemming from the 1979 Revolution and its explicit call for overturning the Sunni monarchical order. Yet even before this ideological challenge, Riyadh long perceived a stark asymmetry between its own national power and that of Iran, in terms of demography, industrial capacity, and military strength.[88]

Rather than seeking to diffuse obvious tensions between the two major Gulf players, the United States has sought to use Saudi Arabia as 'an "Arab balancer" against Iran'.[89] This strategy has become particularly evident during the Trump administration, as Saudi Arabia is instrumental in his policy to deter Iran. Relations between Iran and Saudi Arabia thus often reflect regional changes or broader American interests, rather than strictly national concerns.

Politicising sectarianism, escalating conflict

While it seems to play a minimal role as a motivator of the Iranian–Saudi cold war, the use of sectarianism has undeniably motivated further escalation and made the conflict more resistant to resolution. The two parties are not motivated by religious belief or ideology, but rather are tapping into these religious resources to strengthen their own alliances against each other. Religious differences in Iraq, Yemen, Bahrain, Syria and Lebanon come in very handy for Tehran and Riyadh with powerful resources for building alliances and potentially prevailing in these places. Simon Mabon notes this difficulty of separating politics and sectarianism arguing that they actually feed into each other. He suggests, that there are 'two spheres in which Iran and Saudi Arabia compete, namely ideological and geopolitical'.[90] These two spheres played a central role in shaping the rivalry after the 1979 Islamic revolution and 'although they can be viewed as separate entities, feed into each other'.

The politicisation of sectarianism in the Iranian–Saudi context takes different forms. As a first example, Iran has appointed itself as the 'defender of the Shia cause' worldwide, and with that title comes the role of 'leader' of the world's Shias. Saudi Arabia, on the other hand, has mobilised Sunnis to curtail what it sees as Shia expansion in the Muslim world. It is not a coincidence that Iran has supported Shias in Yemen, specifically the Zaydi-Houthi rebellion. Houthi leaders have received religious, political, financial and, some believe, military support from Tehran to build a Shia militia on Saudi Arabia's southern borders. Saudi Arabia, for its part, is alleged to have supported a prominent Sunni Salafi academy in the town of Dammaj, in the heart of the Zaydi Shia-dominated province of Saad in northern Yemen, now a Houthi stronghold.[91]

While Saudi Arabia supported the Sunni minority government in Bahrain by sending the Peninsula Shield Force to crush its revolution in February 2011, Iran has voiced its strong support for its majority Shia population to convert Bahrain into a 'proxy arena of competition between Tehran and Riyadh'.[92] When the latter executed Sheikh Nimr al-Nimr, an outspoken Shia activist cleric who openly criticised the Saudi regime, in January 2016, Iran's Supreme Leader Ayatollah Ali Khamenei and President Hassan Rouhani condemned the move, and an Iranian mob attacked the Saudi embassy in Tehran, setting it on fire. The incident led to Saudi Arabia severing diplomatic relations with Iran. More recently, when Bahraini authorities stripped top Shia cleric Sheikh Isa Qassim of his citizenship in June 2016, General Qassem Suleimani, the commander of Iran's elite Quds Force, warned Bahrain's leaders that their aggression risked setting the country on fire.[93] Obviously, Iran would not have responded in the same manner in either Bahrain or Saudi Arabia if al-Nimr and Qassim were not influential Shia figures.

As a second example, Iran and Saudi Arabia have used sectarianism to reinforce their political positions internally and to gain regime legitimacy. Justin Gengler looks at the political economy of sectarianism in the Middle East, highlighting the strong 'incentives that rulers face to cultivate non-economic sources of legitimacy in order to maintain the necessary preponderance'.[94] This dynamic is especially important given the nature of the rentier social contract in Saudi Arabia which places pressure on Riyadh to deliver economically to its citizens, regardless of international economic circumstances. Gengler argues that,

> by feeding intercommunal distrust, sowing fear of external threats, and emphasizing their unique ability to guarantee security, ruling elites can reinforce backing among loyalists and dampen incentives for protest among reformists more cheaply than through the standard provision of material benefits.[95]

Toby Dodge concurs by attributing the rise of sectarianism in the Gulf primarily to the behaviour of the ruling elites – rather than to ideological difference or religious competition – and suggests that ultimately it will be the leaders changing positions that could resolve the crisis. In his words, 'Sectarian politics is primarily driven by ruling elites and secondarily by state weakness.'[96] To remedy sectarian conflict, then, he posits that ruling elites must 'move away from heralding their population in sectarian forms to a new politics based on citizenship'.[97] Frederic Wehrey similarly considers sectarianism in the Gulf context to be

> the result of a damaged ruling bargain: the legitimacy deficit of Gulf rulers, feeble or dysfunctional participatory institutions, and uneven access to political and economic capital bear much of the blame for the prominence of Sunni–Shia tensions in times of regional tumult.[98]

Marc Lynch, on the other hand, explains the use of sectarianism by rulers as a means to manage their religious minorities. He argues,

> The Saudi regime, most obviously, systematically uses sectarianism in order to intimidate and control its own Shia citizens at home and to combat Iranian influence regionally. Saudi leaders may or may not genuinely hate Shias, but they know that sectarian conflict is a useful strategy.[99]

By the same token, the Shia majority government in Iraq used similar tactics in the management of the relationship with their Sunni community. According to Lynch, 'a stronger state under the control of Nouri al-Maliki is too easily used to protect Shia privilege and repress Sunni opponents'.[100]

Iran also capitalises on sectarianism as a means of boosting regime legitimacy. Speaking out in defence of Shia communities in Bahrain, Yemen, Syria, Lebanon and Iraq sends a strong signal to Iran's majority Shia society that their regime is eager to back their fellow Shias in the region. Having General Suleimani appear alongside Shia Popular Mobilization Forces (Hashd al-Shaabi) as they fight the Sunni extremists of the Islamic State in Iraq, for instance, demonstrates clearly to Iranians just how invested their leadership is in protecting the larger global Shia community. In fact, defending the Shia cause in the region has historically defined the legitimacy of the regime inside Iran. When the Iranian regime disengages from championing the Shia cause in the region, it will have to earn its legitimacy through other means, particularly by delivering on promised (and severely needed) economic reforms. Particularly when Iran was under Western sanctions due to its nuclear project, the government had limited flexibility to address economic grievances, making the use of the Shia cause to bolster its legitimacy that much more vital.[101]

Finally, it is not only Iran and Saudi Arabia that have politicised sectarianism and allowed it to activate further conflict escalation in the Gulf; external third parties have engaged in this behaviour as well, particularly the United States. In fact, it could be said that the primary contribution of American foreign policy toward the Middle East is the awakening of political sectarianism as a catalyst of conflict.

In 2003, American forces invaded Iraq and toppled Saddam Hussein's Sunni-dominated regime, which had helped to maintain a balance within the regional order as Iran's chief rival. As many have noted, the United States basically did for Iran what it was not able to achieve in eight years of a brutal war with Iraq (1980–8), and Iran did not have to fire even one bullet. This vigorous American intervention undoubtedly changed the region's balance of power, positioning Iran to pursue what Saudi Arabia calls 'an expansionist policy' in the Arab world. Even more importantly, however, is that by replacing Saddam with a Shia-dominated government that aligned its agenda with Tehran, the United States helped to establish sectarianism as a dividing line and an impetus for conflict. This instrumentalisation was key to the failure of state building after the removal of the Saddam Hussein regime and to alienating the Sunni community from having a meaningful role in the rebuilding process.

The United States compounded this error by enabling Nouri al-Maliki to become prime minister in 2006. *The New Yorker* reported that a CIA officer suggested Maliki as a candidate to the US ambassador at the time, who then helped coordinate his rise to power.[102] According to Kenneth Pollack, the United States chose al-Maliki not because he was a suitable leader, but mainly because he was the person that the Shia political leadership agreed did not pose a threat to any of them. In his words, al-Maliki 'is not a leader, and he was not from the first leadership of the Da'wa party . . . The selection of Maliki was not the best decision of the American decision makers.'[103] After being appointed, al-Maliki emerged as one of the most controversial leaders in Iraq, and it became abundantly clear that he was pursuing sectarian policies that were driving Iraq deeper into chaos. By late 2011, al-Maliki was not remotely hiding his sectarian agenda, stating during an interview that 'I am Shia first and Iraqi second'. He also contended that, 'Those who killed al-Husein are not finished yet. They are here today. The supporters of Husein and supporters of Yazid are fighting in a vicious and stubborn confrontation.'[104] Nevertheless, al-Maliki enjoyed American support for eight years.

Outside of Iraq, the United States had also already removed a radical Sunni government, the Taliban, from power in Afghanistan, on Iran's eastern border. This move also strengthened Iran's position in the region.

Whether directly, by the primary parties themselves, or by a third party, like the United States, the politicisation of sectarianism has changed the Iranian–Saudi rivalry. Specifically, it has caused it to widen and deepen, making it more resilient to management, containment or resolution.

Conflict widening

Since the 2003 US invasion of Iraq, the conflict between Iran and Saudi Arabia has widened in terms of the parties involved, whether primary, secondary or merely invested. The conflict has pulled in several other regional and even European players, to the point where it will be difficult to resolve without seriously addressing their involvement. Involved parties include the Syrian regime, the Iraqi government and its Shia-dominated Popular

Mobilization Forces (Hashd al-Shaabi), Yemen's Houthis, Bahrain, and even the Gulf countries that participated in the Saudi-led coalition's war against the Houthi–Saleh alliance in Yemen. These new stakeholders bring new sets of interests and needs, and resolving the conflict without addressing them, at least to some degree, will not be feasible. With time, furthermore, the conflict has spread in a top-down fashion, moving from the leadership level of the two countries to their own populations, thus making it even more intractable. With this wide involvement from neighbouring stakeholders and the parties' own populations, the conflict has definitely become more complex, making it more resilient to resolution. Therefore, any effective solution to this conflict will have to address the grassroots level on both sides, not just the political leaderships.

Conflict deepening

Conflicts have a tendency to develop layers of complexity by generating new issues that differ – to varying degrees – from the original causes of the outbreak of the conflict. This is exactly the case with the Iranian–Saudi conflict with regards to the issue of sectarianism. While sectarianism probably did not cause the original conflict (as many scholars argue), it cannot be denied that it has today been converted into a cause of the conflict's escalation and thus will need to be accounted for in any sustainable resolution. Sectarianism was hardly noticed in politics or at a social level in Yemen before its conflict became part of the Iranian–Saudi cold war. The Zaydi Shia minority and Shafei Sunni majority lived side by side in peace and harmony with no obvious tension. The Houthi movement, which is Zaydi Shia, was probably the only exception since it emerged as a result of a mixture of ideological, economic, political and social grievances against central government. But the Houthi movement could be seen as the exception that proves the rule. That is, despite the fact that the Houthis fought six wars against the central government between 2004 and 2010, the conflict never triggered an obvious sectarian division within Yemeni society. The six wars remained contained between the central government and the Houthis in the northern district, Saada. It was only after links between the Houthis and Iran started to develop, mainly in 2009, with the Saudis seeing it as an Iranian expansion on its southern border, that sectarianism began to emerge. Only then did wider Yemeni society start to link the Houthis to a sectarian agenda supported by Iran for its own reasons. Unfortunately, sectarianism in Yemen today has become intense; divisions have started to appear, with the South seen as Shafei Sunni and the north as Zaydi Shia.

Sectarianism, as a new issue emerging from the Iranian–Saudi cold war, has also played a destructive role in other parts of the region, most notably Iraq, Syria, Lebanon and Bahrain. In fact, it has played a role in disrupting harmony and worsening relations between Sunni and Shia Muslims in countries that seemed stable and not deeply affected by the polarisation that is emerging from the Iranian–Saudi cold war. In Kuwait, for example, the Shia minority has come to be viewed by some as agents of Iran in the country, despite the fact that Shia figures stand strongly against external loyalties and see themselves as an integral part of Kuwaiti society. 'We became labelled by some Kuwaitis as the "tails of Majous". Thank you, Iran, for this,'[105] one Kuwaiti Shia participant in a workshop held in Doha in 2016 explained to the Iranian participants.

Even in countries like Jordan and Palestine, I have noticed high tension on a public level against Shia Muslims, though there are only very small Shia populations in these countries and many residents have never met a Shia person in his or her life. When I researched the reasons behind this dynamic, it became obvious that it is driven by Iran's involvement in wars, especially in Syria. Over time, the public have started to see a sectarian dimension to these conflicts, as it is not by accident that Iran is heavily supporting the Shias involved in them. Even worse, they are seeing Shia Afghanis and Iraqis being recruited by Iranian security units to fight in Syria against the Sunni opposition to Assad.

Iran is in fact aware of this widespread level of anti-Shia attitude in the Arab world, which is very concerning for Tehran; it constantly tries to present its foreign policy as being 'aggressively non-sectarian', to appeal to Arab populations beyond Shias.[106] In defence of Iran's non-sectarian foreign policy, one official in Hezbollah's research wing cited two issues at its centre: the Palestinian cause and facing down the Western presence in the Middle East.[107] This might appeal to a minority among the Arab population, but the majority still continues to view the foreign policy of both Iran and Saudi Arabia through sectarian lenses. As Shahram Akbarzadeh puts it, while Iran purports to represent the interests of the Muslim *Umma*, its close relationships with the government in Baghdad as well as with Shia militia groups tend to substantiate accusations that Iran is the lynchpin of the Shia Crescent. The matter is made worse when Iranian authorities habitually refer to the Shia community in Iraq as brothers and Iran's natural partners.[108]

Geopolitics, Leadership and Influence

Geopolitical factors are unlikely to have produced this conflict on their own, but have instead been activated by other complementary factors, like the sectarianism discussed above, the pursuit of global leadership, and the level of worldwide and regional influence.

Geopolitics

According to Andrew Cooper, '[t]his [Iran–Saudi rivalry] is probably the big geopolitical story of the next decade'.[109] Leadership and influence are only the 'software' of the Iran–Saudi rivalry, yet both parties seek to secure the 'hardware' to carry it, which is geographical influence. The importance of geopolitics in this conflict is that both countries realise it is only the control of the geography of the region that will make leadership, power and even hegemony possible.

Iran and Saudi Arabia's rivalry manifests itself in a proactive pursuit of the maximisation of power, influence and geopolitical gains. As explained by Henner Furttig, the geography of the Gulf represents a major lifeline for both Iran and Saudi Arabia, given that both countries remain largely reliant on oil.[110] As such, 'secure transit routes through the Gulf and Strait of Hormuz are essential'.[111] However, the mere existence of these geopolitical factors does not necessarily lead to direct competition and conflict among the relevant parties. That is, conflict is not a default outcome for the existence of geopolitical factors in the region and instead depends on what the parties themselves make of these factors. Geopolitical factors do not exist in a vacuum; other factors are sustaining and manipulating them. The fact that there is geopolitical conflict between the two parties is because Riyadh and Tehran, for a variety of reasons, chose this path.

As well argued by Sharifi-Yazdi, the conflict between Iran and Saudi Arabia is not all about the resources, but a combination of factors: 'territorial disputes are commonly driven by issues extraneous to the historic, legal or functional details of the territory and disputes themselves'.[112] These factors include, but are not limited to, a 'state's innate quest for power and hegemony, the associated economic and strategic value of some territory and shifts in interstate and regional power balance'.[113]

The radical change in the region's geopolitical map is driving Saudi nervousness about the conflict with Iran. Before the 2003 American invasion of Iraq, Iran was sandwiched between two Sunni governments – Saddam Hussein in Iraq and the Taliban in Afghanistan – that kept Iran geographically contained within its own boundaries. However, after 2003, two pro-Iran governments were installed in Baghdad and Afghanistan, definitively ending the containment of Iran while contributing to what Saudi Arabia sees as a geopolitical encirclement of Iranian influence.

Saudi Arabia's concerns about Iran's prospective geopolitical gains are not entirely groundless. The history of the relationship between the two has many examples of when Iran's appetite for expansion translated into serious plans and actions. For example, in 1973, Iran's shah convinced President Richard Nixon and Secretary of State Henry Kissinger to approve a military contingency plan, which entailed the United States and Iran invading Kuwait and Saudi Arabia and seizing their oil fields in the event of a regional threat coming either from Iraq or Gaddafi-like radicals. As Cooper put it, '[t]his would be the US approving an Iranian invasion of Saudi Arabia and you wonder why Saudi Arabia is nervous about this American–Iranian collaboration.'[114] Additionally, Iran seized control of three disputed islands from the United Arab Emirates in 1971 without consulting that country, and has not accepted mediation or arbitration to resolve the matter.

Luciano Zaccara, an Iran expert at Qatar University's Gulf Studies Program, argues that the geopolitical situation has not changed since the Islamic revolution, but rather the way that Iran has sought to achieve its geopolitical aims has shifted. He claims that the Shah was able to achieve Iran's geopolitical objectives using both hard and soft power, while the Islamic Republic has relied more on hard power. The Shah allied with the United States against Nasserism, Communism and Baathism, in addition to helping Oman's sultan crush the Dhofar revolution. The Islamic Republic introduced a new ideology, but the geopolitical objectives before and after the Islamic revolution remained the same.[115]

Recently, Iran and Saudi Arabia have been fighting a geopolitical battle in which a decisive victory by one of the parties may change the nature of the Middle East's regional order. The Saudi fight for Iraq and Syria since 2003 is to prevent the formation of the 'Shia Crescent',[116] which in theory starts in Iran, goes through Iraq and Syria, and ends in Lebanon, thereby encompassing the entire northern part of Saudi Arabia's borders. Iran's expansion in Yemen also allows it to threaten Saudi Arabia's 1,800 kilometre (1,100 mile) southern border through their ally (or proxy, as Saudi sees it), the Houthis. Furthermore, Iran's influence in Yemen will privilege its talks, primarily with the West, as it gives Iran proximity to the Mandeb Strait, the path for trade between Europe and much of Asia. Nearly 4 million barrels of oil pass through the Mandeb Strait daily.[117]

Saudi Arabia sees the Iranian geopolitical project as an existential threat and thus considers defeating this project as necessary to building its own regional order. This is not a battle that Saudi Arabia and its allies are going to abandon easily. As Bruce Riedel puts it, 'Yemen to Saudi Arabia is like Cuba to the United States.'[118] This comparison also explains why Saudi Arabia has not given up on Iraq since 2003 and Syria since 2011. Saudi Arabia sees no choice other than to have its say in shaping the geopolitics of the region in order to maintain its national security, particularly along its borders. Unfortunately, both Iran and Saudi Arabia see this as a zero-sum game, where the geopolitical gains of one party will necessarily be at the expense of the other. Until this perception of the geopolitical game changes, both neighbours will likely continue the battle through any means available to them.

Leadership

According to Hussein Ibish of the Arab Gulf States Institute in Washington, the root cause of the Iran–Saudi rivalry is geopolitical competition for power, influence and leadership.[119] While it can be difficult to distinguish between sectarian, security-focused and geopolitical motivations, the desire of both Iran and Saudi Arabia to lead and influence the Muslim world can be clearly seen in the statements, policies and actions of their governments, he adds.

Competition between Tehran and Riyadh for leadership of the Muslim world, as well as to serve essentially as the boss – or the policeman – of the Gulf region, is not totally new. Its recent history dates back to 1979, the Islamic revolution in Tehran. Chubin, Shahram and Tripp explain that the establishment of the Islamic Republic of Iran 'considerably worsened Iran–Saudi relations, not least by expanding their rivalry to Islamic leadership',[120] and, according to Simon Mabon, 'the nature of geopolitical competition'.[121] Both states began competing, particularly over Islamic leadership. Indeed, '[t]he importance of Islam, serving as a legitimizing tool for regimes in both Riyadh and Tehran',[122] makes it vital for both regimes to fight for leadership of the Muslim world as legitimacy comes embedded in leadership.

Kim Ghattas makes a similar argument, stating that

> this is not a theological debate or even a purely Sunni–Shia struggle. This is a war about power, a struggle for the leadership of the Muslim world that really kicked off in 1979, with the return of Ayatollah Ruhollah Khomeini to Iran . . . For Riyadh, the rise of a theocratic power next door, which had ambitions as a transnational leader of all Muslims, was a direct threat to its role as the custodian of the two holy mosques, so it embarked on an unrelenting mission to maintain its religious bona fides.[123]

Perceptions of the Iranian threat within Saudi Arabia were fuelled by facts on the ground related to Iran's foreign policy behaviour in the region. For example, the creation of Hezbollah al-Hijaz in 1987 (al-Hijaz is the Saudi district where the two holy mosques are) was seen as an Iranian attack to the heart of Saudi Arabia, especially with this newly created group calling for 'the establishment of an Islamic Republic in the Arabian Peninsula after the Iranian model'.[124] Furthermore, especially during the early days of the Islamic revolution, Khomeini was frequently 'sending his propagandists on pilgrimage to Mecca since 1979 to challenge the legitimacy of Saudi control over the Holy Places'.[125]

Though Iran's 1979 revolution is often considered to mark the outbreak of the current Iran–Saudi rivalry, the power struggle between the two neighbours can be traced back to decades earlier. Iran's interest in policing the Gulf region and leading the Middle East and Muslim world precedes Khomeini's rise to power. His desire to 'export the revolution' was only a change of the means by which Iran wanted to lead. The nature of Iran's regime changed from secular to Islamist, but the objective of leading and policing the region remained unchanged.

Senior Iran analyst at the International Crisis Group, Ali Vaes, agrees that the competition between Iran and Saudi Arabia emanates from a balance of power rivalry and that it began prior to 1979. He argues that the key to understanding it is the triangular relationship between Iran, Saudi Arabia and Iraq over the past five decades. As he describes it, in the 1960s and 1970s, Iran and Saudi Arabia, both monarchies aligned with the United States and wary of the Baathist republican regime in Baghdad, sided together against Iraq. Then, in 1979, the equation shifted and the Saudis and Iraqis united against the revolutionary regime in Tehran. The balance shifted once again after the 2003 invasion of Iraq, and this time Iran and Iraq sided together against Saudi Arabia. For Vaes, these realignments demonstrate that sectarian considerations are not the primary factor in these countries' strategic calculus. Instead, whenever the triangle's balance vacillates, the country that is isolated resorts to sectarianism as an 'instrument to compensate for its strategic solitude'.[126]

Limiting Iran's expansion in the Arab world helps Saudi Arabia sustain its leadership role in the Muslim world. Saudi Arabia does not hide its claim to leadership of the Muslim world. It is home to Islam's two most religiously significant mosques, found in Mecca and Medina, and accordingly the king carries the title of 'Custodian of the Two Holy Places'. The management of the hajj, during which approximately two million pilgrims visit from all over the Muslim world each year, gives Saudi Arabia a renewable soft power source that cannot be matched by any other state. In fact, that is why Iran has called many times for removing from Saudi Arabia its management role and giving it to a committee of representatives from several Muslim countries. In the words of Ali Khamenei in September 2016, 'because of these (Saudi) rulers' oppressive behaviour towards God's guests (pilgrims), the world of Islam must fundamentally reconsider the management of the two holy places and the issue of haj'.[127] Granting Iran some role in the management of the pilgrimage would boost Iran's influence and undermine Saudi Arabia's soft power and leadership role in the Muslim world.

Saudi Arabia's leadership role in relation to Iran is also sustained by the fact that the headquarters of the Organization for Islamic Cooperation (OIC) is located in Jeddah. The OIC is in theory the 'United Nations of the Muslim world', and its presence in Jeddah allows Saudi Arabia to set the agenda of debates within the Muslim member states. Historically, Iran has also challenged Saudi Arabia in this venue, and the organisation has on many occasions turned into the battleground for Iranian–Saudi rivalry.

In addition, Saudi Arabia has relied heavily on a strategy of building alliances to reinforce its leadership role within the Muslim countries and slowly limit Iran's potential for leadership. March Lynch claims that

> Saudi diplomacy has focused intently on efforts to consolidate its leadership of a reconstituted 'Sunni' regional order. Riyadh recently announced with much fanfare an 'Islamic Coalition'[128] against terrorism and has presented its Yemen war coalition as a model for Arab collective action.[129]

Whether it is the Islamic Coalition against terrorism or Arab Coalition in Yemen, Saudi Arabia's leadership role has been reinforced and Iran has been further excluded through these arrangements. However, these coalitions have not been easily sustained over time, leading Saudi Arabia to search for other alliances that could serve to enhance its leadership role.

The conflict with Iran also gives the Saudi regime an opportunity to boost its power domestically, especially since 'royal political and economic power has caused a substantial amount of jealousy and political friction within Saudi society'.[130] The Saudi regime has capitalised on the Saudi public's rejection of Iran's expansionist policies in the Arab region, benefiting internally by spearheading efforts to counter Iran's influence. Generally, fighting a war leads to the consolidation of internal unity against the external threat. The Saudi regime's decisive and confrontational policy – also called King Salman's doctrine[131] – against Iran's perceived sectarian war has had a similar impact of strengthening the popular backing of Saudi Arabia's leadership. In other words, the conflict with Iran has aided the internal legitimacy and power of the Saudi regime.

The Iranian regime has also benefited domestically from the conflict with Saudi Arabia. Alex Vatanka, Iran expert at the Middle East Institute in Washington, DC, explains that the legitimacy of the Iranian regime is partially built upon its leadership role in the region. Specifically, Iran's Revolutionary Guards emphasise their opposition to what they call the 'Great Satan',[132] – a code name that Iran's Supreme Leader Khomeini first, and Khamenei now, used for the United States – and if that stance were to change, the regime would likely face opposition from the Iranian people.[133]

Internationally, while the Saudi monarch has historically served as the Custodian of the Two Holy Places, Iran's Supreme Leader has taken on the informal role of Custodian of the Shia Faith. Iran's assumption of a leadership role in the Shia community in the Muslim world, including within Arab countries, has been a key factor in escalating the tension between Riyadh and Tehran. This became clear when an Iranian crowd responded to Saudi Arabia's execution of Shia cleric Nimr Al-Nimr by attacking and burning the Saudi embassy in Tehran. One of Saudi Arabia's primary conditions for resolving the conflict with Iran is that the latter stops acting like the leader of the Shia communities in Arab countries and instead treats fellow Shias as citizens of their own countries. It is not a coincidence that Tehran's primary allies in the Arab countries are the Shias in Lebanon, Iraq and Yemen, among others.

It should be mentioned, however, that the relationship between Iran and the Shia communities of the Arab world is quite complex. There is no distinct division between Iran defending the cause of Shia minorities in Arab countries and using this cause to advance its drive for regional leadership. Abbas Kadhim, senior fellow and director of the Atlantic Council's Iraq initiative, explains that Iran wants to be a hegemon like it was during the Shah's time. While it does not want to occupy neighbouring countries, it certainly wants to be respected as a regional power and seen as the 'policeman of the Gulf'. As for leading the Shia, Iran wants to use them as its 'sandbag defence' in advancing its ambitions for regional leadership.[134] Thomas Juneau concedes that Iran invests in arming its regional allies to advance its leadership position in the region. He says that Iran

seeks to boost its deterrence, by arming its partners so that they could retaliate against U.S. interests or partners in the event of a war. More broadly, Iran uses these ties to build influence in weak polities, aiming to position itself as an indispensable regional power.[135]

Iran may be pursuing security and sectarian agendas in the Arab region, but they cannot be separated from the underlying driver of its foreign policy – its hope of achieving regional leadership and geopolitical gains. In fact, all three components complement each other for Iran. It could be argued that the best way for Iran to satisfy its security needs – or to successfully advance toward its 'sectarian agenda' – would be to prevail in the region in terms of leadership and policing of the regional order. In fact, 'Iran sees itself as uniquely qualified to determine, at the very least, the destiny of the Gulf sub region'.[136] This dynamic complicates the conflict between the two countries as Iran perceives itself as a 'natural state', with a history and geography, surrounded by 'artificial states' created or supported by the West in recent history.[137]

Iran's foreign policy behaviour is heavily influenced by its history as an ancient civilisation, and, to a large extent, Tehran believes that this history should translate to a leadership position in the region. Iranian narratives frequently cite the age of countries as a factor that should determine their position in the regional order. Especially with some quite young Arab countries on the other side of the Gulf (e.g. the UAE and Qatar) playing an active role in international politics thanks largely to the discovery of oil fields in the Arabian Peninsula, Iran has developed a sense of being entitled to lead the region and rebuild its ancient Persian empire. Haider Said, an Iraqi expert on Iran and the Gulf, claims, 'Iran has emperor ambitions and expansionism is accordingly the guiding principle of Iranian foreign policy in the region.'[138] By the same token, Jamal Khashoggi explains,

[t]here is a belief within Saudi that religion drives Iran's policies and that Iranians believe that their ultimate role in history is to support the Shia everywhere. The Iranian government represents the fundamentalist version of Shia Islam and wants to create a Shia empire. This imperial vision, the Saudis believe, includes Mecca and Medina.[139]

Naser Hadian, a political science professor at the University of Tehran, does not completely refute what Khashoggi argues about Iran's leadership role in the region, yet the two differ over how Iran endeavours to achieve its leadership ambitions. While Khashoggi sees religion and public support for the Shia cause as a means that Iran uses to achieve its leadership role,

Hadian points to an international dimension, in particular to Iran standing up to American and Israeli hegemony in the region and thus countering Saudi Arabia. As Hadian describes it, Iran views the world through the prism of the United States and Israel being its primary enemies. As a result, Iran is involved where it is in the region because of its desire to deter the United States and Israel, not to compete with Saudi Arabia. Iran does not view Saudi Arabia as a major threat, but Tehran recognises that Riyadh views Iran as its number one threat.[140]

The External Factor

The conflict between Iran and Saudi Arabia does not exist in a vacuum. Indeed, the future direction of the conflict is not solely determined by the issues explained earlier, such as security, sectarianism and leadership or solely by domestic factors of regime legitimacy and survival; the regional and international context definitely have a role. Historically, the conflict has interacted with regional and international factors that have significantly contributed to de-escalation on some occasions and exacerbation on others. Today, unfortunately, international factors have significantly contributed to escalation, and it is thus difficult to imagine a mutually acceptable resolution unless this situation changes. The two prominent international actors that are involved in the current conflict escalation are the United States and Israel. As Keith Smith emphasises, the Gulf regional security complex is of strategic importance for the US, perhaps more than any other,[141] and for that reason, Washington cannot afford to stay neutral in conflicts there. Indeed, the interaction of a number of factors, notably political economy, political stability and energy security, have placed the Gulf prominently within critical US national security calculations.[142]

Previously, in the global context of the Cold War between the United States and the Soviet Union, Richard Nixon's administration in 1969 considered the best way to protect American interests in the Gulf region against the Communist threat to 'rely heavily on the two key states of Iran and Saudi Arabia, a strategy that quickly became known as the Twin Pillar policy'.[143] This strategy was part of a major policy review by Nixon that sought to redefine security interests 'at a time of competing demands on US military forces and a growing reluctance by the American public to support what were seen as potentially costly foreign commitments'.[144] The result of the Twin Pillar policy was that the Shah of Iran collaborated closely with Saudi Arabia and other Gulf monarchies without concerns about sectarianism and Arab–Persian nationalism to disrupt such an American security interest. The Shah of Iran even sent his armed forces to help the Sultan of Oman in 1973 to crush the Dhofar rebellion without this provoking any objections from Saudi Arabia about an Iranian military presence in the Arabian Peninsula.

By the same token, Jimmy Carter in 1977 declared the Gulf region to be of vital interest to the United States,[145] which resulted in further consolidation of the pre-existing security collaboration between Riyadh and Tehran. However, this dynamic changed with the Iranian revolution in 1979 and removal of the Shah's regime. This change in leadership led to what became known as America's 'dual containment' policies. That is, the United States 'pursued a policy of balancing Iran and Iraq against each other as a means of maintaining a degree of regional stability and to protect the smaller oil-rich Arab states on the southern side of the Gulf'.[146]

However, with the removal of Saddam Hussein's Baathist regime in Iraq in 2003, the American policy towards the Gulf shifted to a 'protracted stalemate', neither removing the Iranian threat to Arab Gulf states nor allowing Tehran to dominate the region. The mere existence of the Iranian threat in the Gulf perfectly served American interests during this period, as it continued to justify US military presence in the region, provide security guarantees to the Arab Gulf states, and retain control of oil resources. Once again, the US played up the Iranian threat when Trump made his first foreign visit to Saudi Arabia. In particular, during the May 2017 Riyadh summit, Trump and King Salman

> signed documents which included an arms deal which the White House described as worth $350 billion over the next decade. A day earlier Pentagon officials had told The Associated Press that 'the immediate sale' was worth $110 billion and included 'Abrams tanks, combat ships, missile defense systems, radar, and communications and cyber security technology'.[147]

Donald Trump did not hide his agenda in the Gulf, as the conflict for him is about providing security to Gulf rulers to contain the Iranian threat. He even made undiplomatic remarks about the role of the US military in the Gulf and how the US is financially benefiting, publicly stating that he had warned Saudi Arabia's King Salman he would not last in power 'for two weeks' without the backing of the US military.[148] On another occasion, Trump publicly stated that getting cash from the Saudi King was easier than collecting rent 'from a tenant in a bad location in New York city',[149] and 'it is safer too'. Saudi Foreign Minister Adel al Jubeir rejected Trump's comments, telling CNN that the Saudi Kingdom 'carries its own weight' as an ally.[150] Trump used the same financial logic to justify his withdrawal from the Iran nuclear deal, stating the deal was 'not [for] long enough' and asserted that he would 'never have given $150 billion back to Tehran'.[151]

The conflict between Iran and Saudi Arabia has entered a phase of 'protracted stalemate' that benefited not only the US, but Israel as well. Israel has invested heavily in this stalemate taking the conflict to a new level, benefiting in three major ways. First, because of the so-called 'Iranian threat', the US is expected to provide financial aid and military technology to ensure Israel's military superiority in the Middle East, a long-standing American commitment that had shaped US–Israeli relations. After the US signed the Joint Comprehensive Plan of Action (JCPOA) with Iran in 2015, the Obama administration signed a military aid package with Israel in September 2016, requiring the US to give Israel $38 billion over the next ten years, the largest aid package in US history.[152] The Israeli government strongly fought against American approval of the nuclear deal with Iran, arguing that such an agreement would increase the Iranian threat against Tel Aviv. As a result, Washington rushed to provide the most generous military aid package in its history to Israel to defuse the impact of the 'Iranian threat' and again ensure Israel's military superiority in the region.

As a second benefit of the policy, Israel was able to convince Saudi Arabia that the 'Iranian threat' was a concern for countries, and thus they had to cooperate to counter it. In this dynamic, Israel was granted a historic achievement of starting a normalisation process with one of the key countries in the Arab–Israeli conflict, also a leading country in the Muslim world. The official Arab boycott of Israel is considered one of the pressures on Israel to accept the Saudi-led Arab Peace Initiative[153] – also called the Saudi initiative – of the 2002 Arab summit in Beirut. The initiative called for full normalisation of the entire Arab region with Israel, in exchange for Israeli withdrawal from the Arab land it occupied in 1967 and a 'just settlement' of the Palestinian refugee problem, as recommended by the UN Security Council. With this development, Saudi Arabia undermined its own peace initiative to settle one of the longest conflicts in the world, that of Israel–Palestine, and started to lose one of its major power cards, full normalisation for full withdrawal.

Israeli–Saudi collaboration to counter the 'Iranian threat' started before the proposal of the peace plan, but 'reports about meetings between Israel and Saudi Arabia began circulating shortly after the 2006 war between Israel and Hizballah'.[154] After the 2006 war with Israel, Hezbollah gained unprecedented popularity with 'the Arab on the street', which meant an increased Iranian influence in the region and increasing anxiety for both Israel and Saudi Arabia, mainly about the hegemonic Saudi role in the region[155] and Israeli control of the conflict with the Palestinians.

Another major factor that fostered Israeli–Saudi collaboration against Iran was the Obama administration's handling of the Iranian nuclear project and the signing of the deal in 2015. Indeed, '[p]olicymakers in Israel expressed deep unease at what they viewed as U.S. "retrenchment" in the Middle East under the Obama administration, which they saw as undercutting the United States' supporters and emboldening its enemies in the region.'[156] It should be mentioned that Saudi Arabia also became very frustrated with the Obama administration, and particularly by the exclusion of Riyadh from the nuclear negotiation with Iran. Saudi Arabia felt betrayed by the Obama government, a dynamic which encouraged Israel to engage further with Riyadh and make additional political inroads through normalisation with Saudi Arabia.

As the third benefit of the 'protracted stalemate', Israel capitalised on the arrival of Donald Trump to power in 2016 by convincing him to link the confrontation with Iran to the Israel–Palestine conflict. Trump escalated the situation by withdrawing from the nuclear deal with Iran and imposing the harshest ever sanctions on Tehran, while simultaneously moving the US embassy from Tel Aviv to Jerusalem, recognising Jerusalem as the capital of Israel and pronouncing the Syrian Golan Heights to be part of Israel.[157] These calculations all formed part of what became known as Trump's 'deal of the century' in which 'the US administration is simply ticking off most of the Israeli right's wishlist'[158] while offering economic benefits rather than a state to the Palestinians.

By linking Gulf politics with Israel–Palestine, the Trump administration abandoned a longstanding American principle of 'compartmentalization of regional security', which treats the issue of the security of oil reserves (Gulf security) and that of the Israel/Palestine issue and Israel's security as separate concerns'.[159] Theoretically, this 'deal' should bring the 'protracted stalemate' phase of the Iran–Saudi conflict to an end, as it aims to end Iranian influence in the region, including its support to groups like Hezbollah in Lebanon and the Houthis in Yemen. Hence, Abdelkader Faeez, director of the Al Jazeera media network in Tehran, argues that the Trump administration and Israel will succeed in limiting Iranian regional influence if they can successfully implement the 'deal of the century', but if they fail, they will prove Iran to have a more important regional influence than they currently envision.[160]

Finally, it is obvious that, with the incorporation of external factors and especially under the Trump administration, the conflict between Iran and Saudi Arabia has moved from being bilateral to multilateral or regional. This dynamic adds complexity and new challenges to resolution. Usually, when other parties join a conflict, each one comes with its own set of interests, demands and needs that it expects to be satisfied in any future negotiation. Even more complicated is the fact that interests do not always match. They can clash or at least move into a state of protracted stalemate, as is the case with this conflict between Iran, Saudi Arabia, the United States and Israel. As Simon Mabon argues,

> the role of the United States both in the Persian Gulf and Middle East has been an area of antagonism. The United States maintains a strong visible presence within the Persian Gulf and Middle East, which challenges Iran's desire for regional security, to be engendered solely by regional actors. Given the strategic importance of the Middle East for the United States, a reconsidered role would have to come from Washington, meaning that a key aspect of the rivalry remains beyond the control of Saudi Arabia or Iran.[161]

Notes

1. Beauchamp, 'Iran and Saudi Arabia's cold war'. For academic definitions and the theoretical underpinnings of the concept of the security dilemma, see Herbert Butterfield, *History and Human Relations* (London: Collins, 1951); John Herz,

Political Realism and Political Idealism: A Study in Theories and Realities (Chicago: University of Chicago Press, 1951); Robert Jervis, *Perception and Misperception in International Politics* (Princeton: Princeton University Press, 1976), chap. 3; and Jervis, 'Cooperation under the security dilemma', *World Politics* 30, 2 (January 1978): 167–214.

2. F. Gregory Gause III, *Beyond Sectarianism: The New Middle East Cold War*, Analysis paper no. 11 (Doha: Brookings Doha Center, 2014). The term 'Arab cold war' was first used to describe inter-Arab rivalry in the tense times of the 1950s and 1960s by Malcolm Kerr in his study of ideology in international politics. Malcolm Kerr, *The Arab Cold War, 1958–1964: A Study of the Ideology in Politics* (Oxford: Oxford University Press, 1965).

3. Morten Valbjorn and Andre Bank, 'The new Arab cold war: rediscovering the Arab dimension of Middle East regional politics', *Review of International Studies* 38, 1 (2012): 3–24. Curtis R. Ryan, 'The new Arab cold war and the struggle for Syria', *Middle East Report* 262 (2012): 28–31.

4. Curtis R. Ryan, 'Regime security and shifting alliances in the Middle East', *Project on Middle East Political Science (POMEPS)*, briefings 31, October 2017, https://pomeps.org/2015/08/20/regime-security-and-shifting-alliances-in-the-middle-east/.

5. Stephen M. Walt, *The Origins of Alliances* (Ithaca: Cornell University Press, 1987).

6. As quoted in Robin Wright, *Sacred Rage: The Wrath of Militant Islam* (New York: Simon & Schuster, 2001), p. 27.

7. Fouad N. Ibrahim, *The Shi'is of Saudi Arabia* (London: Saqi, 2006), p. 117.

8. Simon Mabon, 'Kingdom in crisis? The Arab Spring and instability in Saudi Arabia', *Contemporary Security Policy* 33, 3 (2012): 530–3.

9. Suzanne Maloney, *Iran's Long Reach: Iran as a Pivotal State in the Muslim World* (Washington: US Institute of Peace Press, 2008), p. 27.

10. Carol D. Leonnig, 'Iran held liable in Khobar attack', *Washington Post*, 23 December 2006, http://www.washingtonpost.com/wp-dyn/content/article/2006/12/22/AR2006122200455.html.

11. Rory Jones, 'Kuwait charges 26 suspects with plotting attacks against it', *Wall Street Journal*, 1 September 2015, http://www.wsj.com/articles/kuwait-charges-26-suspects-with-plotting-attacks-against-it-1441132841.

12. Source: created by the author. Original map adapted from Julien Barnes-Dacey, Ellie Geranmayeh and Hugh Lovatt, 'The Middle East's new battle lines', *European Council on Foreign Relations*, https://www.ecfr.eu/mena/battle_lines/ (last accessed 14 June 2019).

13. Ahmed Aboulenein, 'Syrian security chief makes public Cairo visit – SANA', *Reuters*, 17 October 2016, http://uk.reuters.com/article/uk-mideast-crisis-syria-egypt-idUKKBN12H2AM.

14. Source: created by the author. Original map adapted from Julien Barnes-Dacey, Ellie Geranmayeh and Hugh Lovatt, 'The Middle East's new battle lines', *European Council on Foreign Relations*, https://www.ecfr.eu/mena/battle_lines/ (last accessed 14 June 2019).

15. Majid Khadduri, 'Iran's claim to the sovereignty of Bahrayn', *American Journal of International Law* 45, 4 (October 1951): 631–47.

16. Source of map of Shia presence in east of Saudi Arabia: *The Economist*, https://econ.st/2Rg6if1 (last accessed 14 June 2019).

17. 'Fears in Iraqi government army over Shiite militias' power', *Associated Press*, 21 March 2016, https://www.yahoo.com/news/fears-iraqi-government-army-over-060458082.html?ref=gs.

18. Hadi al-Ameri is considered one of Iran's most loyal Iraqi figures – he fought with Iran against his own country in the 1980–8 war. Some call him 'Iran's General in Iraq'. For more see 'Hadi al-Ameri . . . Iran's "General" in Iraq', *Al Jazeera*, 28 February 2016, https://goo.gl/ZgyrEE.

19. 'Al-Amiri: Hashid al-Shaabi is the strongest in Iraq', *Al Jazeera*, 1 September 2016, https://goo.gl/YVpoJr.

20. William Quandt, *Saudi Arabia in the 1980s: Foreign Policy, Security, and Oil* (Washington: Brookings Institution Press, 1981), p. 39.

21. Beauchamp, 'Iran and Saudi Arabia's cold war'.

22. 'Iran calls for "puny Satan" Saudi Arabia to be stripped of Hajj duties', *Middle East Eye*, 5 September 2016, http://www.middleeasteye.net/news/iran-calls-small-and-puny-satan-saudi-arabia-be-stripped-hajj-management-1644348841.

23. Dahlia Nehme, 'Top Saudi cleric says Iran leaders not Muslims as haj row mounts', *Reuters*, 7 September 2016, http://www.reuters.com/article/us-saudi-iran-mufti-idUSKCN11D0HV.

24. Saudi official, interview and discussion with the author, Riyadh, Saudi Arabia, May 2016.

25. Email exchange with the author, May 2016.

26. Email exchange with the author, February 2016.

27. Source: Google maps – American military bases around Iran, https://bit.ly/2KR5ufA (last accessed 14 June 2019).

28. Interview and discussion with the author, Doha, Qatar, May 2015.

29. David Vine, 'America still has hundreds of military bases worldwide. Have they made us any safer?', *Mother Jones*, 14 November 2014, http://www.motherjones.

com/politics/2014/11/america-still-has-hundreds-military-bases-worldwide-have-they-made-us-any-safer.

30. Iranian participant at a Qatar University workshop in March 2016. Identity withheld under the Chatham House rule.

31. Gulf participant at a Qatar University workshop in March 2016. Identity withheld under the Chatham House rule.

32. Interview and discussion with the author, Doha, Qatar, May 2016; *Wikileaks*, https://wikileaks.org/plusd/cables/08RIYADH649_a.html.

33. Interview and discussion with the author, Doha, Qatar, September 2015.

34. Interview and discussion with the author, Doha, Qatar, May 2015.

35. Email exchange with the author, May 2016.

36. Interview and discussion with the author, Doha, Qatar, May 2015.

37. John Bradley, 'Al Qaeda and the House of Saud: eternal enemies or secret bedfellows?', *The Washington Quarterly* 28, 4 (2005): pp. 139–52.

38. Ibrahim Fraihat, 'Room for containment: the Iran deal and the neighboring Arab states', in Payam Mohseni (ed.), *Iran and the Arab World After the Nuclear Deal* (Cambridge, MA: Harvard Kennedy School, 2015), pp. 44–6, http://belfercenter.ksg.harvard.edu/files/Impact%20on%20Arab%20World%20-%20Web.pdf.

39. Saeid Jafari, 'How Iran should approach the GCC', *Al-Monitor*, 3 August 2015, http://www.al-monitor.com/pulse/originals/2015/08/iran-gcc-relations.html.

40. Interview and discussion with the author, Doha, Qatar, April 2016.

41. Vali Nasr, 'The war for Islam', *Foreign Policy*, 22 January 2016, http://foreignpolicy.com/2016/01/22/the-war-for-islam-sunni-shiite-iraq-syria/.

42. Marc Lynch, 'Why Saudi Arabia escalated the Middle East's sectarian conflict', *Washington Post*, 4 January 2016, https://www.washingtonpost.com/news/monkey-cage/wp/2016/01/04/why-saudi-arabia-escalated-the-middle-easts-sectarian-conflict/.

43. *Al Jazeera* TV channel interview with Alex Vatanka on 17 January 2016.

44. Author's interview and discussion, Doha, October 2016.

45. Nick Thompson and Inez Torre, 'Yemen: who's joining Saudi Arabia's fight against the Houthis?', *CNN*, 30 March 2015, http://edition.cnn.com/2015/03/27/world/yemen-saudi-coalition-map/.

46. Noah Browning and John Irish, 'Saudi Arabia announces 34-state Islamic military alliance against terrorism', *Reuters*, 15 December 2015, http://www.reuters.com/article/us-saudi-security-idUSKBN0TX2PG20151215.

47. 'Saudi Arabia, Turkey to set up "strategic cooperation council"', *Russia Today*, 29 December 2015, https://www.rt.com/news/327391-turkey-saudi-arabia-erdogan-syria/.

48. Interview by Carol Castiel, 'Encounter', *Voice of America*, 15 January 2016, http://www.voanews.com/audio/3126883.html.

49. Lawrence G. Potter, 'Introduction', in Lawrence G. Potter (ed.), *Sectarian Politics in the Persian Gulf* (London: C. Hurst & Co., 2013), p. 2.

50. Ibid. p. 2.

51. Fanar Haddad, *Sectarianism in Iraq: Antagonistic Visions of Unity* (New York: Columbia University Press, 2011), p. 25.

52. Ussama Makdisi, 'Reconstructing the nation-state: the modernity of sectarianism in Lebanon', *Middle East Report* 200 (July–September 1996): 24.

53. Azmi Bishara, *Sect, Sectarianism, and Imagined Sect* (Doha: Arab Center for Research and Policy Studies, 2018), p. 64.

54. May Darwich and Tamirace Fakhoury, 'Casting the Other as an existential threat: the securitisation of sectarianism in the international relations of the Syria crisis', *Global Discourse* 6, 4 (2017): 712–32.

55. Aaron Reese, 'Sectarian and regional conflict in the Middle East', *Middle East Security Report* 13 (July 2013): 7.

56. Ibid. p. 7.

57. Ibid. p. 7.

58. Ibid. p. 9.

59. Potter, 'Introduction', p. 2.

60. Frederic M. Wehrey, *Sectarian Politics in the Gulf: From the Iraq War to the Arab Uprisings* (New York: Columbia University Press, 2014), p. xiii.

61. Haddad, *Sectarianism in Iraq*, p. 8.

62. Wehrey, *Sectarian Politics in the Gulf*, p. xiii.

63. Haddad, *Sectarianism in Iraq*, p. 10.

64. Ibid. p. 7.

65. Ibid. p. 7.

66. F. Gregory Gause III, 'Sectarianism and the politics of the new Middle East', Brookings Institution, *Up Front* blog, 8 June 2013, http://www.brookings.edu/blogs/up-front/posts/2013/06/08-sectarianism-politics-new-middle-east-gause.

67. Ibid.

68. Paul Dixon, 'Beyond sectarianism in the Middle East? Comparative perspectives on group conflicts', in Frederic Wehrey (ed.), *Beyond Sunni and Shia: The Roots of Sectarianism in a Changing Middle East* (London: C. Hurst & Co., 2017), p. 11.

69. Ibid. p. 16.

70. Ibid. p. 16.

71. Vali Nasr, *The Shia Revival: How Conflicts within Islam Will Shape the Future* (New York: W. W. Norton & Company, 2007), p. 22.

72. Ibid. p. 24.

73. Toby Matthiesen, 'Sectarianism in the Middle East', *Boston University Institute on Culture, Religion & World Affairs*, 20 March 2014, p. 3, https://www.bu.edu/cura/files/2013/10/Matthiesen.pdf.

74. Ibid. p. 4.

75. Ibid. p. 4.

76. Ibid. p. 3.

77. Ibid. p. 3.

78. Potter, 'Introduction', p. 7.

79. Shireen Hunter, former Iranian diplomat (1966–78) and Research Professor at the Center for Muslim-Christian Understanding at Georgetown University, email exchange with the author, February 2016.

80. Anoushiravan Ehteshami, 'Iran and its immediate neighborhood', in Anoushira-van Ehteshami and Mahjoub Zweiri (eds), *Iran's Foreign Policy from Khatami to Ahmadinejad* (Reading: Ithaca Press, 2008), pp. 129–30.

81. Gause, *Beyond Sectarianism*.

82. Ibid.

83. Ibid.

84. Interview and discussion with the author, Doha, Qatar, May 2015.

85. Valbjorn and Bank, 'The new Arab cold war', p. 19.

86. Interview and discussion with the author, Doha, Qatar, June 2015.

87. Lynch, 'Why Saudi Arabia escalated'.

88. Wehrey *et al.*, *Saudi–Iranian Relations*, p. 2.

89. Ibid. p. 5.

90. Mabon, *Saudi Arabia and Iran*, p. 42.

91. In late 2011, the Houthis besieged Dammaj before agreeing to a ceasefire. The conflict resumed in late 2013, and in early 2014 the Salafis were forced to evacuate the school and town entirely. See Peter Theo Curtis, 'A militia, a madrassa, and the story behind a siege in Yemen', *New Republic*, 30 January 2012, https://newrepublic.com/article/100214/yemen-shia-militia-sunni-madrassa?page=0%2C1; Nasser al-Sakkaf, 'Salafis forced to flee Dammaj, government forces unable to protect them, they say', *Yemen Times*, 16 January 2014, http://www.yementimes.com/en/1747/

news/3365/Salafis-forced-to-flee-Dammaj-government-forces-unable-to-protect-them-they-say.htm.

92. Simon Mabon, 'The battle for Bahrain: Iranian–Saudi rivalry', *Middle East Policy* XIX, 2 (Summer 2012): 84–97, p. 84.

93. 'Iran general warns Bahrain after Shia cleric stripped of citizenship', *BBC News*, 20 June 2016, http://www.bbc.com/news/world-middle-east-36578844.

94. Justin Gengler, 'The political economy of sectarianism: how Gulf regimes exploit identity politics as a survival strategy', in Frederic Wehrey (ed.), *Beyond Sunni and Shia: The Roots of Sectarianism in a Changing Middle East* (London: C. Hurst & Co., 2017), p. 183.

95. Justin Gengler, *The Political Economy of Sectarianism in the Gulf* (Washington: Carnegie Endowment for International Peace, 2016), p. 6.

96. Toby Dodge, 'Seeking to understand the rise of sectarianism in the Middle East: the case study of Iraq', *Project on Middle East Political Science*, 19 March 2014, http://pomeps.org/2014/03/19/seeking-to-explain-the-rise-of-sectarianism-in-the-middle-east-the-case-study-of-iraq/.

97. Ibid.

98. Wehrey, *Sectarian Politics in the Gulf*, p. xii.

99. Marc Lynch, 'The entrepreneurs of cynical sectarianism', in Marc Lynch (ed.), *The Politics of Sectarianism* (Washington: Project on Middle East Political Science, 2013), http://pomeps.org/wp-content/uploads/2014/06/POMEPS_Studies4_Sectarianism.pdf.

100. Ibid.

101. For more on how sectarian foreign policy sustains domestic regimes, see 'POMEPS Conversations 28 with Toby Matthiesen', interview by Marc Lynch, *Project on Middle East Political Science*, 1 November 2013, http://pomeps.org/2013/11/01/pomeps-conversation-28-with-toby-matthiesen-1112013/; and Wehrey, 'The roots and future of sectarianism'.

102. Dexter Filkins, 'What we left behind', *New Yorker*, 28 April 2014, http://www.newyorker.com/magazine/2014/04/28/what-we-left-behind.

103. 'The black box: Nouri al-Maliki . . . the whole story', *Al Jazeera* video, 18 October 2015, https://goo.gl/e6UQeA.

104. Ibid. Al-Husein bin Ali is the grandson of Prophet Mohammed who became the Imam of Shia in AD 670. Yazid was appointed the Ummayad Caliph by his father Muawiyah. Al-Husein refused to pledge allegiance to Yazid. When the people of Kufah pledged allegiance to al-Husein, who was based in Mecca,

he travelled to Kufah but the army of Yazid intercepted him near Karbala and killed him. His death became a rallying cry that further defined the Shia sect and their cause; it became the chosen trauma of the Shias and a part of their identity today. In this context, Maliki considers that the battle of Karbala – that ended with the killing of al-Husein – is not over yet and the fight with the Sunni extremists, who he called the supporters of Yazid, still continues today. To frame the conflict as a continuation of the battle of Karbala is a clear example of the use of sectarianism to advance his political agenda and ensure the Shia's loyalty to his reign.

105. The author, observing the interaction in a Gulf–Iran workshop organised by the Gulf Research Center at Qatar University in 2016. The workshop was held under the Chatham House rule where discussion can be cited without revealing the identities of speakers.

106. Wehrey *et al.*, *Saudi–Iranian Relations*, p. 21.

107. Ibid. p. 22.

108. Akbarzadeh, 'Iran and Daesh', p. 49.

109. Andrew Cooper, speaking at an event hosted by the American–Iranian Council, 8 February 2016, https://www.youtube.com/watch?v=PHcfTvHqcpc.

110. Henner Fürtig, *Iran's Rivalry with Saudi Arabia between the Gulf Wars* (Reading: Ithaca Press, 2006).

111. Mabon, *Saudi Arabia and Iran*, p. 55.

112. Sharifi-Yazdi, *Arab–Iranian Rivalry in the Persian Gulf*, p. 268.

113. Ibid. p. 268.

114. Cooper, event hosted by the American–Iranian Council.

115. Interview and discussion with the author, Doha, September 2015.

116. Morten Valbjorn and Andre Bank, 'Signs of a new Arab cold war: the 2006 Lebanon war and the Sunni-Shi'i divide', *Middle East Report* 242 (Spring 2007), p. 11.

117. Robin Mills, 'Risky routes: energy transit in the Middle East', Brookings Doha Center, Analysis Paper no. 17, April 2016, https://www.brookings.edu/research/risky-routes-energy-transit-in-the-middle-east/.

118. Interview and discussion with the author, Washington, DC, April 2016.

119. Interview and discussion with the author, Washington, DC, September 2015.

120. Chubin and Tripp, *Iran–Saudi Arabia Relations and Regional Order*, p. 53.

121. Mabon, *Saudi Arabia and Iran*, p. 42.

122. Ibid. p. 51.

123. Kim Ghattas, 'The Saudi cold war with Iran heats up', *Foreign Policy*, 15 July 2015, https://foreignpolicy.com/2015/07/15/the-saudi-cold-war-with-iran-heats-up/.

124. Toby Matthiesen, 'Hizballah al-Hijaz: a history of the most radical Saudi Shi'a opposition group', *Middle East Journal* 64, 2 (2010): 179–97, p. 194.

125. Lewis B. Ware *et al.*, *Low Intensity Conflict in the Third World* (Alabama: Air University Press, 1988), p. 8.

126. Email exchange with the author, February 2016.

127. 'Iran suggests Saudi should not run Muslim pilgrimage', *Reuters*, 5 September 2016, https://www.reuters.com/article/saudi-haj-iran/iran-suggests-saudi-should-not-run-muslim-pilgrimage-idUSL8N1BH1DS.

128. Ahmed Al Omran and Asa Fitch, 'Saudi Arabia forms Muslim anti-terror coalition', *Wall Street Journal*, 15 December 2015, http://www.wsj.com/articles/saudi-arabia-forms-muslim-anti-terror-coalition-1450191561.

129. Lynch, 'Why Saudi Arabia escalated'.

130. Anthony H. Cordesman, *Saudi Arabia: Guarding the Desert Kingdom* (Oxford: Oxford University Press, 1997), p. 26.

131. Nawaf Obaid, 'The Salman doctrine: the Saudi reply to Obama's weakness', Harvard Kennedy School, *Belfer Center for Science and International Affairs*, 30 March 2016, https://www.belfercenter.org/publication/salman-doctrine-saudi-reply-obamas-weakness.

132. Hamid Dabashi, 'Who is the "Great Satan"?', *Al Jazeera*, 20 September 2015, http://www.aljazeera.com/indepth/opinion/2015/09/great-satan-150920072643884.html.

133. Discussion with the author, Doha, January 2016.

134. Interview and discussion with the author, Washington, DC, September 2015.

135. Thomas Juneau, 'No, Yemen's Houthis actually aren't Iranian puppets', *Monkey Cage* blog, *Washington Post*, 16 May 2016, https://www.washingtonpost.com/news/monkey-cage/wp/2016/05/16/contrary-to-popular-belief-houthis-arent-iranian-proxies/.

136. Anoushiravan Ehteshami, 'The foreign policy of Iran', in Raymond Hinnebusch and Anoushiravan Ehteshami (eds), *The Middle East in the International System* (London: Lynne Reiner Publishers, 2002), p. 286.

137. Mabon, *Saudi Arabia and Iran*, p. 60.

138. Interview and discussion with the author, Doha, November 2015.

139. Interview and discussion with the author, Doha, November 2015.

140. Interview and discussion with the author, Doha, April 2016.

141. Keith Smith, 'Realist foreign policy analysis with a twist: the Persian Gulf security complex and the rise and fall of dual containment', *Foreign Policy Analysis* 12, 3 (2016): 315–33.

142. Simon Mabon, 'Muting the trumpets of sabotage: Saudi Arabia, the US and the quest to securitize Iran', *British Journal of Middle Eastern Studies* 45, 5 (2017): 1–18.

143. Gary Sick, 'The United States in the Persian Gulf, from twin pillars to dual containment', in David Lesch and Mark Haas (eds), *The Middle East and the United States, History, Politics, and Ideologies* (Boulder: Westview Press, 2005), p. 328.

144. Ibid. p. 328.

145. Henner Fürtig, 'Conflict and cooperation in the Persian Gulf: the interregional order and US policy', *The Middle East Journal* 61, 4 (2007), p. 631.

146. Sick, 'The United States in the Persian Gulf', p. 335.

147. Dilip Hiro, *Cold War in the Islamic World: Saudi Arabia, Iran and the Struggle for Supremacy* (Oxford: Oxford University Press, 2019), p. 317.

148. 'Trump: I told Saudi king he wouldn't last without US support', *Reuters*, https://www.reuters.com/article/us-usa-trump-saudi/trump-i-told-saudi-king-he-wouldnt-last-without-u-s-support-idUSKCN1MD066 (last accessed 4 June 2019).

149. 'President Trump compares a phone call with the King to collecting rent', *C-Span*, https://www.c-span.org/video/?c4794551/collecting-nyc-tenant (last accessed 4 June 2019).

150. Hiro, *Cold War in the Islamic World*, p. 315.

151. Ibid. p. 315.

152. 'US, Israel sign $38 billion military aid package', *Reuters*, https://www.reuters.com/article/us-usa-israel-statement/u-s-israel-sign-38-billion-military-aid-package-idUSKCN11K2CI (last accessed 4 June 2019).

153. 'Arab Peace Initiative, full text', *The Guardian*, https://www.theguardian.com/world/2002/mar/28/israel7 (last accessed 6 June 2019).

154. Jacob Abadi, 'Saudi Arabia's rapprochement with Israel: the national security imperatives', *Middle Eastern Studies* 55, 3 (2019), p. 11.

155. Ibid. p. 11.

156. Kristian Ulrichsen, 'Palestinians sidelined in Saudi–Emirati rapprochement with Israel', *Journal of Palestine Studies* 47, 4 (2018), p. 83.

157. 'Trump recognizes Golan Heights as Israeli', *Reuters*, https://reut.rs/2Ws97v9 (last accessed 6 June 2019).

158. David Gardner, 'Trump's "deal of the century" offers nothing good to the Palestinians', *Financial Times*, https://www.ft.com/content/40d77344-b04a-11e8-8d14-6f049d06439c (last accessed 6 June 2019).

159. Pinar Bilgin, *Regional Security in the Middle East: A Critical Perspective* (New York: Routledge Curzon, 2005), p. 151.

160. Abdalkader Faeez, director of *Al Jazeera* office in Tehran, interview and discussion with the author, June 2019.

161. Mabon, *Saudi Arabia and Iran*, pp. 219–21.

3

Conflict Management

Conceptualising the management and resolution of this conflict is not as simple as it might sound. The challenges that an effective management system faces do not stem only from the difficult issues of the conflict – explained in the previous chapter – but also from the dynamics that this conflict experiences. Those dynamics play a dangerous role in actively pushing the conflict into further escalation and thus make management and solution increasingly elusive.

Active dynamics operating in the Iran–Saudi conflict environment have been largely responsible for the advancement of the conflict from one phase to another. Those dynamics operating outside the direct control of the parties themselves push the conflict to intractability and make it more difficult to contain and eventually resolve. In fact, current dynamics suggest some alarming scenarios about the extent to which those active dynamics could potentially push the conflict, including direct war between Iran and Saudi Arabia.

Mistrust is a major dynamic that has contributed to the worsening of the relationship between the two neighbouring countries. Because of the serious trust deficit, every single move on either side tends to be received and interpreted as escalatory. In 1973–5, Iran sent approximately 5,000 troops to Oman to help Sultan Qaboos defeat rebels, without any major objections from Saudi Arabia.[1] However, with mistrust now shaping the relationship between Iran and its Gulf neighbours, even a statement related to internal Gulf affairs would be seen as highly suspicious by Saudi Arabia and could be interpreted as a threat to its national security.

Another major escalation-accelerating dynamic in this conflict is the fact that the two parties view it as a zero-sum game, where one side's gains are necessarily seen as the other side's losses. Iran considers any progress made by the opposition against the Assad regime in Syria as both harming its role in the region and benefiting Saudi Arabia's position. Similarly, Saudi Arabia views an increase of power of the Houthi rebels as an extension of Iranian influence on its southern border.

A polarising narrative has also become instrumental in reinforcing the escalation of tensions, not only between Iran and Saudi Arabia but throughout the region, along such lines as Sunni–Shia, Arab–Persian and Iran–Arab Gulf states. For Iran, it is a battle between the 'axis of resistance' (to the West) against collaborators with or proxies of the West. However, for Saudi Arabia the narrative is a Shia, Safawi and Persian attack against a Sunni Arab region. The principle of being 'either with us or against us' correctly describes the current scenario.

Polarisation has reached unprecedented levels. During the Iraq–Iran war (1980–8), the polarisation was limited mostly to the two warring countries, and extended at a certain level to a few other Gulf countries. Today, however, it has reached almost every house in the Arab region, dividing communities and even families in countries like Syria, Iraq and Yemen. With such deep division, neutrality becomes difficult to maintain.

The atrocities committed in Syria in particular have forced everyone in the region to take a position. Because of Iran's staunch support for the Assad regime, the general Arab public has developed a high level of antagonism against any Iranian, Shia or Persian influence. On the other hand, individuals belonging to the Iranian camp have developed similar feelings towards Saudi Arabia, Turkey and Qatar, who are seen as the supporters of the revolution against the Assad regime. It should be noted that media on both sides, much of which is government-linked, have played a key role in reinforcing the polarisation and thus have contributed to the escalation of tensions.

A lack of communication between the countries has contributed to this environment, which is rife with misperceptions, stereotypes and mistrust since diplomatic relations were severed in 2016. With no verification mechanism or official diplomatic contract, both parties develop their own perceptions and understandings as fact, exacerbating the polarisation.

In conclusion, designing a conflict management and resolution system to address both the issues and dynamics of this conflict will require a two-step process: first, focusing on management of the crisis and, second, addressing a lasting resolution between Iran and Saudi Arabia. This process should not be understood as being strictly linear: both processes should proceed simultaneously; advances in the 'management process' can help achieve advances in the 'resolution process', and vice versa. This chapter will address a containment strategy for the Iran–Saudi rivalry, to serve as a way to stop the escalation of the conflict and take the first step towards achieving a lasting resolution. Chapter 4 will then address finding a comprehensive resolution strategy, aided by having this conflict management strategy in place.

An effective conflict containment strategy should at least include: crisis management tools, confidence-building measures, dialogue, and building zones of peace.

Crisis Management System

Halting the escalation of this conflict is necessary and should be treated as a high priority. Leaving the conflict with no restraining mechanism will cause deeper damage through their proxies in the region, which could evolve into direct war between Riyadh and Tehran in the future. Deep damage will be harder to repair in the future and generally leads to the perpetuation of the conflict. Effective crisis management tools will certainly help to contain the conflict and prevent the outbreak of new cycles of escalation. Crisis management tools should respond to conflict issues as they develop, rather than waiting for the pace of official government protocol.

Riyadh–Tehran hotline

One of the major crisis management tools used should be the establishment of a hotline[2] between the governments of Iran and Saudi Arabia. A focal point should be designated from each side, so that one person has direct access to communication with the highest decision maker on both sides. For example, on the Iranian side, the focal point should be linked with either the Supreme Leader or the President and on the Saudi side the link should be with either the King or the Crown Prince. Having direct access to the highest level of the decision-making process is useful, as it overcomes bureaucratic barriers, especially in emergency situations.

This development could certainly help prevent escalation on the ground. Wars do not always begin as deliberate political decisions. Instead, it is common for wars to start when events on the ground drive the political leadership to respond by attacking.

For example, in April 2015, when an Iranian plane attempted to break the Saudi-imposed blockade on Yemen by landing in Sanaa, Saudi fighter jets flew extremely close to it and ultimately destroyed the airport runways to prevent it from landing.[3] It was reported that two Saudi F-15s came so close to the Iranian plane that the pilots could see each other's faces.[4] If an accident had occurred, it would have been reported that the Iranian plane was downed by a Saudi fighter jet. No doubt the street pressure in Tehran would have been tremendous, and Iran's leadership would have had little choice but to respond – perhaps even militarily – thereby sparking a direct confrontation between the two countries. In this case, and in other similar situations, the existence of a hotline between Riyadh and Tehran would be of particular help to manage crises quickly and prevent a war.

The importance of direct communication became clear during the peak of the Cold War. After narrowly avoiding a serious direct confrontation during the Cuban Missile Crisis of 1961, Moscow and Washington signed a memorandum of understanding (MoU) establishing the Moscow–Washington hotline, which was designed to allow for 'rapid and reliable' communication between the two countries in times of crisis.[5] The MoU was signed on 20 June 1963 in Geneva.[6] Although known in popular culture as the 'red telephone', the hotline was never a telephone line; it first employed teletype equipment, followed in 1986 by fax technology, and finally, in 2008, by a secure computer link over which messages are exchanged via email.[7] The link has been used several times, including during the 1967 Arab–Israeli war when the United States used it to prevent possible misunderstanding of US fleet movement in the Mediterranean.[8]

This mechanism is also believed to have been utilised in 1971 during the Pakistan–India War, in 1973 during the Arab–Israeli War, in 1974 when Turkey invaded Cyprus, and again in 1979 when the Soviets invaded Afghanistan.[9] The Moscow–Washington hotline is not the only such example of a hotline between rival governments; other examples include Islamabad–New Delhi, London–Moscow, Paris–Moscow and Seoul–Pyongyang. When

North Korea decided to de-escalate the tension with South Korea in January 2018, it reopened the border hotline with Seoul, 'restoring a channel of direct dialogue and signaling a possible thaw in relations between the two Koreas after years of hair-trigger tensions'.[10] Instigation of most of these hotlines followed the near-outbreak of a direct war between countries with even more acrimonious relations than Saudi Arabia and Iran; there is therefore no compelling reason not to establish a similar Riyadh–Tehran hotline.

Exchange of senior governments' visits

While having top Iranian and Saudi officials – even the heads of state – exchange visits may sound unrealistic given the high level of tension between the two states, it is a proposal that both countries should consider. In conflict situations, where parties weigh options ranging from peace to war, direct state visits are not an unreasonable avenue to consider, especially when states agree to seek to manage the conflict, rather than leaving it to spin completely out of control. For example, high-level US and Soviet officials exchanged a number of visits even at peak times of the Cold War. In 1959, President Eisenhower invited and hosted the Soviet Premier, Nikita Khrushchev, for a two-week visit, and, in 1972, President Nixon visited Moscow.[11] Both Moscow and Washington were motivated by a desire to maintain effective management of the Cold War, despite being unable to resolve their differences.

Visits at the level of heads of state between Riyadh and Tehran have occurred in the past, even during the term of Iran's hard-line president, Mahmoud Ahmadinejad. The goal of these visits was to ease relations and explore ways to resolve differences. Ahmadinejad visited Riyadh in 2007 for a summit with King Abdullah, as his predecessor, Mohammad Khatami, had done in 1999 when Abdullah was still Crown Prince.[12] As Crown Prince, Abdullah visited Tehran in 1997 to attend the Organization of the Islamic Conference summit.[13] While these visits did not fully resolve the issues at hand, the conflict during the times of King Abdullah and Ahmadinejad was significantly better managed compared to the times of King Salman and Hassan Rouhani.

After the Arab Spring (2011), exchanges of visits to both capitals stopped completely at the level of heads of state and were significantly reduced at other government levels. Even when meetings did take place outside the two countries, such as on the side of international conferences, they became more of a protocol exercise with no tangible results ever produced. For example, Saud al-Faisal, during the First Arab Cooperation and Economic Forum with Central Asia and Azerbaijan in May 2014, had invited his Iranian counterpart to Riyadh in an effort to negotiate their differences.[14] The invitation was intended to 'control the conflict, not resolve it, because there are no signs of a Saudi–Iranian agreement on Syria, Iraq, Bahrain or Yemen'.[15] With little enthusiasm or belief in the necessity of managing the conflict on both sides, such invitations have thus far had little impact.

Technical committees

Technical coordination committees, or meetings of experts, could also contribute to a de-escalation of tension between Iran and Saudi Arabia. Unlike official dialogue between the two parties, technical committees can open lines of communication while at the same time addressing Saudi concerns over potentially legitimising Iranian intransigence. Technical can include experts, not government officials, and their communication can focus on finding approaches and formulas that address the interests of both parties. Such interest-based discussions should aim to reach a win-win arrangement to address the underlying causes and conditions that fuel the conflict.

Such a committee could discuss, for example, the issue of falling oil prices, which has been a serious point of tension between Iran and Saudi Arabia during the years of conflict. Many analysts have speculated that Riyadh has deliberately attempted to drive prices down to undermine Iran's national budget.[16] Saudi Arabia has firmly denied manipulating the oil price, maintaining that the reduction is purely a result of market forces.[17] A Saudi–Iranian technical committee on oil prices could easily investigate, discuss, and come to conclusions on the issue. Its findings would likely help reduce tensions and prevent actions based on one party's own perceptions. If the expert committee meetings prove successful in tackling some issues, their scope could be expanded to facilitate discussion of larger issues between the two parties, like regional security and spheres of influence.

In addition, Iranian and Saudi experts could discuss issues of mutual concern in the Gulf, especially those of an environmental and maritime nature, since this is an area largely divorced from sectarianism or the political agendas of both parties. Instead, such meetings would simply serve to address issues related to how the current nuclear activities of Iran, and possibly of Saudi Arabia in the future, could affect the environment of the region (e.g. water pollution in the Gulf) and what arrangements could be made to prevent it. Severe water pollution would be disastrous for both Iran and Saudi Arabia and both share a common interest of preventing this from happening.

Such cooperation to manage conflict is not without precedent: United States and former Soviet Union scientists worked together not only to devise verification methods for important bilateral treaties – which furthered mutual trust between the two states – but also to find solutions to problems important to both states. For example, in October 1986, Ronald Reagan and Mikhail Gorbachev met in Reykjavik, Iceland, where they tasked Soviet and US scientists with developing verification techniques to help ratify the 1974 Threshold Test Ban Treaty (TTBT). This meeting led to the Joint Verification Experiments, which brought scientists from the top Soviet nuclear weapons institutes to a top secret US nuclear test site in Nevada and top US nuclear specialists to the Soviet's test site in Semi-palatinsk in the same year, 1988.[18] According to Siegfried Hecker, who was the Director of the US Los Alamos National Laboratory from 1986–97, '[t]he Joint Verification Experiments exposed each side to the idea that we could work toward a common objective instead of as adversaries. We gained respect for one another, and the meetings cracked open the door to future scientific collaboration.'[19]

Confidence-Building Measures

Confidence-building measures (CBMs) involve 'a series of actions that are negotiated, agreed upon, and implemented by the conflict parties in order to build confidence, without specifically focusing on the root causes of the conflict'.[20] Another definition focuses on their ability to enhance actors' feelings of confidence or ability to trust negotiating parties; confidence-building measures thus 'may be defined as arrangements designed to enhance such assurance of mind and belief in the trustworthiness of states and the facts they create'.[21] Therefore, such measures do not touch on the heart of matters at hand in negotiations, but rather set the scene for productive conflict resolution.[22] Certainly, '[e]ven if the parties are ready and willing to engage, the negotiations can only be successful if the participants trust their negotiating partner(s)'.[23]

Confidence-building measures will prove particularly important in the case of Iran and Saudi Arabia because their policy positions remain diametrically opposed, making it unrealistic to deal with the root causes of the conflict in first encounters. The mistrust that engulfs the entire region likewise makes the arrangement of CBMs a necessary first step towards a resolution. The main goal of CBMs would be to set the scene for a conflict resolution process between Iran and Saudi Arabia; they are not in any way expected to resolve all the differences between Riyadh and Tehran.

As an example, Saudi concerns over Iranian expansionism and the Kingdom's encirclement are real, and many of Saudi Arabia's foreign policy decisions can be explained on those grounds. Iran could take the initiative – not just make statements – to address this concern, assuring the region that its role is that of a partner, not a hegemon, possibly leading to tangible results. Iranian Foreign Minister Javad Zarif has repeatedly emphasised the need for Iran and Saudi Arabia to work together to resolve the region's political crises and has stressed Iran's willingness to do so, but the Saudi leadership has yet to buy into this argument.[24]

Importantly, CBMs can include formal and informal measures, both inside and outside the security sector (where they were first applied).[25] Such flexibility is a hallmark of this tool for conflict resolution since CBMs are 'tailored to each actor as necessary'.[26] Indeed, CBMs taken on each side need not be symmetrical but must demonstrate that each party is 'committed to the [conflict resolution] process by requiring all involved to make different choices and implement different policies'.[27] Lacking such commitment, parties can become 'locked in a cycle of negotiation, defection, and investigation, and calls for more CBMs to get the process back on track'.[28]

One immediate step could be in reviving the 2001 security pact signed between the two countries when Hasan Rouhani was in the Iranian National Security Council in 1997 and Imir Nayef Ben Abdul-Aziz was the Saudi Minister of Interior.[29] The pact, which took two years to negotiate, was signed to combat terrorism, drug-trafficking and organised crime. In addition, it covered measures on border surveillance and co-operation between their police forces.[30] This document could provide an important starting point that addresses major security concerns for both countries, which are at the heart of the conflict.

CBMs can either entail legally binding commitments or simply be political declarations, depending on the type of measures used and their goals.[31] While a legal obligation is obviously more binding, making political commitments 'may be more conducive to a *process* of expanded practice as a result of challenge and the possible engines of mutual example'.[32] They can also simply involve '*declaratory* undertakings or obligations which involve specific *actions*'.[33] Declarations are important expressions of goals and reiterate commitment to the process of conflict resolution and often precede concrete actions.[34] Holst divides CBMs into four different functions: information, notification, observation and stabilisation (with some overlap among them).[35]

One missed opportunity for an influential 'declaratory' CBM was Iran not apologising for the attack on Saudi Arabia's embassy in Tehran in January 2016, as demanded by Riyadh.[36] Regardless of Iran's objections to the execution of Saudi cleric Nimr al-Nimr that spurred this attack, an apology was clearly needed, since international law was violated because Iran failed to provide adequate protection of a diplomatic mission. Many other countries took a stance on the execution – but they did not respond by allowing an attack on the Saudi missions in their capitals.

By the same token, Iranians were frustrated by Saudi Arabia not apologising for the death of 464 Iranian pilgrimages in the October 2015 hajj stampede.[37] Apologising would not have implicated the Saudi authorities in the incident but would have shown solidarity and sympathy with the tragedy; an apology could have been powerful in promoting de-escalation and laying the ground for the parties to collaborate. One of the participants in a workshop organised by Georgetown University on Iran–Saudi relations in Doha commented on this issue, saying that

> the death of Iranian pilgrimages made Iranians furious about the incident, especially because we know what the Saudi Wahhabi position on the Iranian Shia is – considering them as infidels – so a lack of apology from the authorities just confirmed our thinking of how they view us.[38]

Before CBM can be implemented, a period of pre-negotiation must have laid the groundwork for a commitment to resolution of the conflict at hand.[39] Certainly, rather than solving the conflict themselves, 'CBMs constitute building blocks which could provide operational substance to the notion of common security'.[40] They are ultimately meant as a 'political *demonstration* of good will and common interest'[41] and, as such, 'only affect the margins of international conflict'.[42] Obviously, the severing of diplomatic relationships between Iran and Saudi Arabia in January 2016 hinders the effectiveness of CBMs regardless of the source. However, with the help of a third party, CBMs could help provide the first step for restoring diplomatic relations, not necessarily preparing the scene for conflict resolution negotiations.

CBMs have three main objectives: to prevent escalation, initiate and deepen negotiations, and consolidate the process and its outcome.[43] As Mason and Siegfried explain,

> the aim of CBMs is not to make people like each other or to address the root causes of conflict. Rather, the idea is to help build a working trust by addressing easier issues, which will then allow parties to address the root causes of a conflict through substantive negotiations. CBMs are therefore not an end in themselves, but rather useful steps in the ladder to negotiating and implementing peace agreements that address the key strategic concerns of the parties.[44]

Even a 'working' relationship between Saudi Arabia and Iran is blurred by feelings, perceptions, and even historical events. Many Iranians and Saudis base their positions on stereotyping or superficial issues. For example, Iranians view themselves as coming from a civilisation thousands of years old, while states of only a few decades exist on the other side of the Gulf. The Arab Gulf states in turn see this attitude as evidence of Iranian arrogance and national chauvinism. Credible CBMs, again, are useful to try and shake these perceptions, replacing personal feelings with professional working relationships.

Simon Mason and Matthias Siegfried determine five types of CBMs: political, security sector, economic and environmental, social, and humanitarian and cultural. Political CBMs aim to lay the groundwork for political resolution of a conflict through the creation of trust among parties involved, focusing either on negotiations or on altering the political landscape to enhance the potential for successful negotiations.[45] Ali Vaez of the International Crisis Group explains the trust issue saying,

> given the level of miscomprehension and mistrust between the two sides, it is crucial to complete track one negotiations with track two discussions and people to people exchanges at all levels. Confidence building measures will be essential as many years of compiling distrust cannot be overturned overnight.[46]

Security sector CBMs, the first type implemented, 'focus on avoiding escalation triggered by a misunderstanding of signals'.[47] Security issues are thus used to lay the groundwork for a stronger relationship between the negotiating parties.[48] Economic and environmental CBMs meanwhile

> focus on joint economic endeavors or activities dealing with natural resource management and environmental challenges. Opening trade routes can help to ease tensions and benefit both actors. Co-operation over economic issues can often be a first step in collaborating across conflict lines.[49]

Finally, social, humanitarian and cultural CBMs, often implemented before negotiations, tend to signal a willingness to undertake a peace process. In addition, they 'help the affected population, but also provide conflict parties with the fresh start that is needed if they seek to try negotiations'.[50]

The five levels of CBMs (security, economics, environment, cultural and humanitarian) are relevant to varying degrees to the Iran–Saudi rivalry in the Gulf region. Each approach offers a set of measures that can be taken to build trust and prepare the path for negotiation and conflict resolution. In the cultural or religious sphere, better collaboration between the two countries on the annual hajj (pilgrimage) – an issue that has created serious tension over the past three decades – could prepare the two sides for negotiation on other levels, such as the political, at a later date. Saudi Arabia could allow a larger involvement of Iran in the coordination of Iranian pilgrimages, potentially laying the seeds for trust to grow among the two sides.

Indeed, cultural contributions to confidence-building measures were also raised during the Soviet–US Cold War. The two parties agreed: 'The two sides reaffirm their intention to deepen cultural ties with one another and to encourage fuller familiarization with each other's cultural values. They will promote improved conditions for cultural exchanges and tourism.'[51]

The same logic applies to economic and environmental measures, where Iran, for example, could take the initiative to address environmental concerns that Saudi Arabia and the rest of the Gulf countries have regarding its nuclear activities; doing so would also send a powerful message about their willingness to collaborate. Moreover, on the economic level, Saudi Arabia could use its influence in the international oil market to try and address low oil prices, something that Iran has traditionally accused Saudi Arabia of being behind. In this regard, Soviet–US counterparts in the Cold War were aware of the potential of economic CBMs, as they agreed,

> [t]he USA and the USSR regard commercial and economic ties as an important and necessary element in the strengthening of their bilateral relations and thus will actively promote the growth of such ties. They will facilitate cooperation between the relevant organizations and enterprises of the two countries and the conclusion of appropriate agreements and contracts, including long-term ones.[52]

Though initiatives in the areas of culture, the environment and economics can help, CBMs in the areas of security and politics remain the most promising for a tangible outcome that may de-escalate tension between the two sides. Iran should start by launching an initiative that proves its seriousness about de-escalation and cooperating with Saudi Arabia. For example, Iran could use its leverage with the Houthis to stabilise Yemen, as Saudi Arabia considers stability in Yemen a core national security priority.

Iran should realise that its ability to stabilise Yemen will help Tehran achieve the level of regional influence to which it aspires, winning what it has not been able to achieve through several years of war in Syria. Iran emerging as part of the solution will invite other countries, particularly Saudi Arabia, to deal with Tehran on that ground, which is the win-win situation that the region needs to defuse the prevailing tensions.

CBMs in this context should never be used as an alternative to a meaningful conflict resolution approach between Iran and Saudi Arabia that tackles the deep issues between the two parties. If a lack of trust is not at the root of issues, CBMs can stall real change or resolution of conflicts and can distract from negotiations.[53] CBMs are needed at *this* stage of *this* conflict, however, because the mistrust between the two sides is considerable, making even initial negotiations all but impossible. Dialogue, track two diplomacy, and even formal mediation can all help in expanding the achievements of CBMs. As is the case in many world conflicts, any successful resolution will require a multi-method approach that incorporates various strategies.

Dialogue

Dialogue is another means by which conflict resolution can be facilitated, as it builds trust and understanding among parties to a conflict. Most such meetings 'take the form of organized group encounters of a size that allow face-to-face communication. They are usually conducted with persons below the top-leadership level. They are therefore not so much official negotiations as a form of political preliminaries.'[54] Indeed, like CBMs, dialogue 'is meant to complement other forms of diplomatic or political processes, or lay the groundwork for future and more formal talks, not replace them'.[55] In other words, '[a]s one popular formula puts it: "As long as you're talking, you can't be shooting."'[56]

In the context of the Iran–Saudi conflict, dialogue is not expected to replace, contradict or duplicate the work of the CBMs discussed earlier, but rather to build on the progress made by CBMs to contribute to the larger containment strategy for the conflict. This section discusses the prospects for a dialogue process, the conditions under which it might occur, and what form it could take to contribute to a de-escalation or containment phase of the Iran–Saudi conflict.

Certain conditions must be present for a dialogue to begin, brokered through a third party. According to the UN Development Programme (UNDP),

> [w]hen violence, hate, and mistrust remain stronger than the will to forge a consensus, or if there is a significant imbalance of power or a lack of political will among the participants, then the situation might not be ripe for dialogue. Moreover, participants must feel free to speak their minds without fear of retribution, or rejection.[57]

Indeed, in the case of violent conflict or in states where major divisions remain, crafting a dialogue is particularly difficult, especially as it takes the form of an ongoing process rather than a single meeting.[58] Furthermore,

> [d]ialogue stresses a long-term perspective . . . To find sustainable solutions requires time and patience. The process can be painstakingly slow and incremental, lasting anywhere from ten minutes to ten years – one-off interventions very often do not work to address deeply-rooted causes of conflict or to fully deal with complex issues.[59]

Challenges to Iranian–Saudi dialogue

There is no doubt that the conflict environment between Iran and Saudi Arabia offers challenging conditions for the possibility of initiating a dialogue, which could explain why there has not been any structured or meaningful dialogue between the two sides since the Iranian revolution in 1979. There is deep mistrust as well as a lack of political will to build bridges, combined with barely concealed hatred and even violence (though still carried out via proxies in the region) on both sides. The mistrust between the two sides can clearly be seen in the position of Jamal Khashoggi, who opined that Iran–Saudi dialogue would not necessarily stop Iran from using time to build militias in the Arab countries, 'providing the Assad regime in Syria with barrel bombs and if they can, the Houthis in Yemen as well'.[60]

Mistrust can also mix with stereotypes to form an even stronger hindrance to dialogue. Many in the Arab Gulf see Iran as merely using negotiation as a tactic to bore their opponents, achieving gains once the other side loses interest. Proponents of this argument use an Iranian rug-making analogy: craftsmen can spend months and sometimes a year working to complete one piece, and so the Iranians could spend years patiently negotiating – without giving up – to achieve even small gains.

Retribution on those involved in the dialogue also cannot be ruled out. This is particularly likely, given that both Iran and Saudi Arabia maintain highly centralised political systems where notably different views of the government are not tolerated. Individuals can be punished and institutions can be shut down if they challenge the position of central government. This centralisation of the political position has affected previous efforts at dialogue, including those held by Qatar University and Georgetown University in Doha.

Some Iranian participants came to the Doha-based workshops ready with talking points reflecting the official Iranian position, and almost all of them – in some workshops there were ten participants – showed no real difference in position. Most issues raised in the workshops resulted in one position being held by the entire team and that position, to a large extent, matched the position of the Iranian government.[61] When asked about this, some observers in the workshop explained that Iranian participants worried that their positions would be communicated back to Tehran, which could lead to serious trouble for them. However, it should be mentioned that with time and trust developing within the workshop, some participants started to open up and be more engaging in their discussion on prospects of resolution.

By the same token, potential Saudi participants refused to attend the dialogue sessions in the first place. Some invited individuals refused because they did not believe in dialogue with the Iranians – those who 'build armed militias in Arab countries' – but others declined due to their (well-founded) fears of what they could face when they got back to Saudi Arabia. Talking to Iranians in a third country like Qatar before the GCC rift could lead Saudi participants to face interrogation and other forms of retribution back home. Furthermore, the position of the Saudi participants who did attend the workshop was not meaningfully different from the that of the government, reflecting the centralisation of the narrative on this conflict.

Other challenges to a successful Iranian–Saudi dialogue certainly exist. In Khashoggi's view, dialogue simply will not take place when each side thinks it can win, or as long as this conflict is seen as a zero-sum game by both parties. Furthermore, as they are not fighting directly, neither party is truly feeling the cost of the conflict. Saudis will refuse to talk to the Iranians as long as they are intervening in Syria; as Khashoggi put it, 'ask Hezbollah and Iran to get out of Syria; then Saudi will talk. How do you talk to someone who is so adamant about causing all this death and destruction?'[62]

Another major challenge to beginning a dialogue between the two countries is a lack of understanding and empathy for each other's positions, interests and needs. Certainly, Saudi Arabia's view of Iran's foreign policy is that it is mainly about aggression, intervention and meddling in domestic Arab affairs, with its one objective being the 'export of the revolution'. The mechanisms driving Iran's foreign policy are too opaque to change this opinion. However, since it came into existence in 1979, the Iranian regime has been sanctioned and threatened, mainly by the United States and Israel. These measures have provoked vital security concerns for its survival and have also led to a psychological nervousness, especially when dealing with foreign affairs.

The Iranian government's survival mode has therefore driven its foreign policy behaviour to a large extent, and this has not given Tehran room to build a collaborative strategy with its neighbour that could be beneficial (for example, economically) for both of them. While Saudi Arabia demands an immediate and complete halt to Iran's foreign policy involvement in the Arab region, it refuses to recognise the security concerns that are at least partially responsible for Iran's behaviour.

By the same token, Iran's lack of empathy and understanding of Saudi Arabia's position is clearly seen in its refusal to accept that its foreign policy is causing an 'encirclement' of Saudi Arabia, interpreted by that country as a major threat to its national security and the survival of its regime. Iran's influence in Iraq, Syria and Yemen covers three sides of Saudi Arabia's borders. Iranian support of the Houthis' coup in September 2014, in particular, significantly exacerbated Saudi security concerns, as Riyadh saw only a powerful Iranian-backed armed militia emerging in control of security on its southern borders. By and large, the two parties are caught up in a vicious cycle of reproducing their own security concerns, which is exactly why dialogue is needed – and why it is challenging to establish.

A major obstacle to dialogue between Iran and Saudi Arabia is both sides' understanding that talks lead to concessions, which is something neither party is willing to provide. In other words, dialogue has not happened because both parties fear it might succeed. Of course, Saudi Arabia is not at all willing to compromise in Yemen since Iran is seen as having no right to be there, as noted by Khashoggi.[63] 'Iran must stop intervening in these places in the first place so that dialogue can be successful,' he said.[64] Iran is not willing to give concessions either, which is why their calls for dialogue seem to be lacking credibility. Paul Salem argues,

> Zarif [Iran's foreign minister] should be aware that any regional agreement will require fundamental policy shifts from Iran. It would mean giving up Hezbollah as an independent proxy army in Lebanon and channeling any

military aid through the Lebanese government . . . In short, it would mean a fundamental reversal of decades of Iranian policy. Can Rouhani or Zarif deliver such a change? If so, they will find that the Arab states are eager to engage with such an Iran; if not, it is hard to see on what basis a regional dialogue could be launched.[65]

What dialogue looks like

Despite these serious challenges, there is still hope for dialogue between Riyadh and Tehran. Alireza Yousef, head of the Politics and International Relations Institute in Tehran, explains, 'we are neighbours and brothers. Let us have a constructive dialogue. How are we ready to talk to the Americans, Europeans, but not with our Iranian brothers to exchange views? Dr Zarif wrote four articles asking to talk face to face.'[66] Seyed Hossein Mousavian adds to this by explaining his views of dialogue arguing, 'we need diplomacy like what we did on Iranian nuclear crisis. The way for Iran and Saudi Arabia to have immediate direct negotiation on security issues, bilateral security issues, regional security issues, and try to have resolve the problem.'[67]

These Iranian statements are important because they express goodwill and an interest in dialogue and in reaching solutions via peaceful means. However, statements that are not supported by actions are never sufficient for parties to move from their positions. Only through actions can Iranians make their calls for dialogue credible. In his response to the prospect of open negotiations with Iran without preconditions, Khashoggi responds,

> No, we need the Iranians to act; Hussein [Mousavian] is talking peace and acting war. Iranians must get out, take their militias out of Syria as a goodwill. Then we can sit with them and talk peace, and try to bring peace to Syria.[68]

It is true that Iranian statements have generally lacked credibility, but nevertheless they offer a clue as to how a dialogue might look. In his *New York Times* editorial, Iranian foreign minister Javad Zarif outlines the principles of dialogue:

> regional dialogue should be based on generally recognized principles and shared objectives, notably respect for sovereignty, territorial integrity and political independence of all states; inviolability of international boundaries;

non-interference in internal affairs; peaceful settlement of disputes; impermissibility of threat or use of force; and promotion of peace, stability, progress and prosperity in the region.[69]

This vision sounds optimistic, and some might see it as unrealistic or even part of the government of Iran's media campaign. Paul Salem, for example, explains,

> yet Iran is violating most of these principles in a large number of Arab countries. It arms and finances Hezbollah in Lebanon, arms and finances militias in Iraq, has sent its own military commanders and proxy militias to aid Assad in the barbaric opposite of 'peaceful settlement of disputes' with his own population, and has sent money and arms to the Houthi militia in Yemen, Hamas in Gaza, and other groups elsewhere.[70]

On the other hand, Qasem Mohebali – a former director general of the Iranian Ministry of Foreign Affairs' Middle East section – offers a more realistic view of how best Iran should approach dialogue with Saudi Arabia:

> Iran should assume a three-pronged approach. First, Iran should act nobly and should not threaten or use force against these countries. It might be true that these countries did not behave properly when Iran was under sanctions, but at present, increasing tension is not in our best interest. Second, we should hold direct talks with each of these countries instead of using a mediator. Third, we should engage in dialogue with Saudi Arabia. Saudi Arabia plays an undeniable role in the regional equations. We might have disagreements with Riyadh, but the most pragmatic thing is to try and manage these conflicts. We should try to decrease the tension between Iran and Saudi Arabia and bring it to a controllable level.[71]

While some Iranian analysts and politicians take a somewhat idealistic approach to dialogue, Saudi Arabia and the other Arab Gulf states generally want to see concrete action before talks begin. Iranian statements frequently mention the benefits of dialogue and the need for collaboration between the 'brothers' and 'neighbours' of the Gulf region. Kuwait professor and political analyst Abdullah Al-Shayji argues, 'it is only the dialogue of power that works with Iran'.[72] Jamal Khashoggi, on the other hand, is sceptical about the chances of dialogue with Iran but he concedes that if dialogue is to happen, it has to be an 'assertive dialogue'.[73] 'We need intervention not to dictate but to provide assurances.'[74]

Gulf experts' scepticism regarding a potential dialogue with Iran stretches to include not only reservation about the process of dialogue – as raised by Al-Shayji and Khashoggi – but even to the outcome of such a dialogue. A Kuwaiti Shia intellectual said the following about the initiatives that were sometimes launched to bring Sunnism and Shiism closer to each other, 'there is nothing called bringing the sects closer. It does not exist in real life. What we need is co-existence.'[75] It might sound frustrating to lose faith in the two parties becoming closer, but at least the speaker acknowledges that the end goal of dialogue can be simply co-existence rather than resolving the conflict outright.

Zones of Peace, a Non-Aligned Movement for the Iran–Saudi Cold War

One way to battle a fire is to remove flammable objects from its path. While this practice does not directly put out the fire, it crucially prevents it from spreading, improving chances of eventually controlling or extinguishing the fire completely. The zones-of-peace concept follows a similar logic, preventing a conflict from expanding to new territories, countering polarisation, and subsequently presenting potential intervention and conflict resolution efforts. In the context of the Iran–Saudi conflict, zones of peace would encourage countries in the region to shield themselves from a spill-over of the conflict, disengage from polarisation, and build a culture of peace that could potentially contribute to conflict de-escalation and peacebuilding.[76]

Jawaharlal Nehru first raised the notion of an 'area of peace' in the early 1950s, when he began to deal with Asian, African and Middle Eastern countries emerging from colonial rule. As he explained to the Lok Sabha (the lower house of India's parliament) in 1953, he was not trying to create a 'third force' to compete with the Cold War powers blocs, but rather

an area where peace might, perhaps, subsist, even if war was declared. That would be good, of course, for the countries there, but would be good for the world too, because the area would exercise some influence, when a crisis came, on avoidance of war.[77]

In 1955, the Bandung conference in Indonesia brought together twenty-nine countries and represented the first large-scale Asia–Africa summit – in line with Nehru's vision to work independently from a Cold War context. Most of the participants were newly independent states, intent on promoting economic and cultural cooperation among themselves and opposing any form of colonialism by any country. In addition, in 1961, the non-aligned movement was formally established in Belgrade, a testimony to the success of Nehru's vision, along with his co-founders: Tito in the former Yugoslavia and Naser in Egypt.

The new Middle East cold war resembles the US–USSR Cold War (1945–90) in many ways, most importantly in the high level of polarisation of the surrounding environments. Polarisation puts tremendous pressure on regional actors to take a side, in this case either with Iran or Saudi Arabia. Divisive statements like 'you are either with us or against us', used by George Bush after the 9/11 attacks, can start to dominate diplomatic rhetoric. Pressure from Riyadh and Tehran on other regional powers to join their side will always mount with every development in the crisis; however, yielding to the pressure will help neither Iran nor Saudi Arabia. Regional actors should not surrender to such pressure because, if they do, these states will become the new battlegrounds of the cold war, the 'fuel' to the conflict 'fire'.

What the Middle East regional order needs today is a non-aligned movement – or a 'peace zone' – that resists polarisation and alliance formation, serves as an impartial territory for the conflict primary parties to meet in, and exerts pressure on Iran and Saudi Arabia to refrain from meddling in other countries' internal affairs. The emergence of a non-aligned movement would prevent a concentration of power within any one country at the expense of another. This would address one of the root causes of the current Iran–Saudi cold war – the imbalance of power in the regional order that was created after the American invasion of Iraq in 2003 and the significant influence that Iran gained as a result.

In response to the dangerous escalation in Iran–Saudi rivalry, the most urgent task facing other countries in the region will be to resist pressure to join one of the two main blocs. The example of Yemen highlights how being dragged into the polarisation can deeply damage not only the country itself but the centres of the conflict (Riyadh and Tehran) as well.

Up until 2014, the Yemeni conflict was confined largely to Yemeni political actors. However, with the Houthis launching a coup against the central government and publicly allying themselves with Iran, neighbouring Saudi Arabia was provoked to join the conflict – as it saw Iran's presence on its southern borders as a security threat – leading to one of the most destructive wars in Yemen's recent history. Yemen emerged as the biggest loser in this conflict, but Iran has also had to fund a brutal civil war – on the Houthi side – and Saudi Arabia, with some regional partners, has been funding an unnecessary war for years. Yemen's strategic interest would have been upheld by strictly distancing itself from both Iran and Saudi Arabia and in preserving its own sovereignty and independence, or what we call here having its own zone of peace or non-aligned status within the Iran–Saudi rivalry.

A more extreme case even than Yemen, Lebanon has been a battleground for the Iran–Saudi rivalry since the early 1980s. Lebanon has been structurally linked to the Iran–Saudi conflict, with major political parties like Hezbollah – originally formed by an Iranian decision – linking its policies to Tehran, and al-Mustaqbal linking its policies to Riyadh. There is an almost equal division between the political parties within Lebanon, with the March 14 alliance receiving support from Riyadh and the March 8 alliance strongly backed by Tehran. Iran's expansion of influence in the region has linked the political future of Lebanon to that of the Iran–Saudi cold war.

On many occasions in the past decades, Lebanon has lost its sovereign decision-making ability to one or both of the central powers of the Iran–Saudi rivalry. One example was the country's inability to elect a president for almost twenty-nine months (May 2014–October 2016). During this period, parliament met for over forty-five sessions until Tehran was finally able to impose its ally, Michael Aoun, scoring important points in its rivalry with Saudi Arabia.[78] In order for Lebanon to become a zone of peace for this regional conflict, the Lebanese themselves first and foremost will have to decide how to disengage from this conflict. They need to reach a point where they are no longer forced to incur the cost of running a proxy conflict. Their political understanding will have to develop first, which will then allow them to proceed towards disengagement. A zone of peace 'exists as a state of mind before its physical dimensions take shape',[79] as Wallace Warfield argues.

Given its strong link to both primary conflict parties, Lebanon is unlikely to disengage from the regional rivalry in the foreseeable future, as the past three decades have shown. Lebanon's only means of disengaging from the conflict is either by structurally changing its political institutions or if the centres of conflict – Riyadh and Tehran – abandon Beirut (something similar to when the collapse of the Soviet Union released a number of developing countries from their link to the Cold War). Therefore, Lebanon is not a candidate to become a zone of peace in the near future.

To a certain extent, Iraq has followed in the steps of Lebanon by forging a strong alliance with Tehran, especially at the governmental level, and thus is becoming another key battleground for the rivalry in question. This is a fatal mistake for all involved – Iraq, Iran and Saudi Arabia. On the one hand, Iraq has linked the stability of its political future to that of the Iran–Saudi cold war, which does not seem likely to end anytime soon. On the other hand, however, Iraq joining Iran's bloc has only whetted Iran's appetite for further expansion in the region and further provoked Saudi Arabia, as the issue becomes a serious national security threat to Riyadh. All parties sink deeper in the conflict, wasting their resources and causing further misery, underdevelopment and chaos throughout the entire region.

No other factor could calm the Iran–Saudi conflict more than Iraq disengaging from the conflict and becoming a zone of peace. This would entail complete independence from the influence of Tehran and Riyadh and a truly impartial role of Baghdad, providing a space for the two rival neighbours to meet and bridge the gap between them. This would also, notably, be in the interest of Iraq itself. In this scenario, Iran's appetite for further expansion would be curbed because the geographical continuity with its other allies, Syria and Lebanon – or what Jordan's King called 'the Shia Crescent' back in 2004 – would be broken, and Saudi Arabia's security fears would be lessened.[80] As a result, both Iran and Saudi Arabia's objectives would be more rationalised and become closer to dialogue and reaching solutions. Whether Iraq can become a zone of peace depends on whether its political leadership decides to take this path – it is time for Iraq to try other avenues, and this is definitely one worth taking. Nevertheless, Iraqi protesters' burning of Iran's consulate in Basra in 2018 and attack on the consulate in Karbala in 2019 should send a strong message to both the Iranian and Iraqi leadership that the people will not accept being used in this rivalry forever.

Unlike Yemen, Lebanon and Iraq, Oman has maintained its own 'peace zone' in relation to the Iran–Saudi conflict. Historically, Oman has insisted on remaining neutral in this conflict and keeping good relations with both parties. Oman was and remains a founding member of the Gulf Cooperation Council (GCC) – established in 1981 to counter 'Iran's threat' to the region – yet also facilitated conflict resolution efforts with Iran. One of Oman's major mediation successes was paving the way for the signing of the nuclear agreement between Iran and the West – finally signed on 14 July 2015 – that contributed to distancing the Gulf region from what could have been an enormously destructive war.[81]

To a lesser degree when compared to Oman, Kuwait and Qatar have also tried to maintain a relatively balanced position towards Iran – their own 'peace zone' – while slightly tilting towards Saudi Arabia. Kuwait has not encountered serious challenges to its relationship with Iran 'partly due to its sizable Shia community, which acts as an influential pro-Iran lobby'.[82] Qatar, on the other hand, publicly supported the nuclear deal between Iran and the P5+1, as evidenced by foreign minister Khaled al-Attiyah praising the deal, stating that he was 'confident that what they undertook makes this region safer and more stable'.[83]

After the Iranian attack on Saudi Arabia's embassy in Tehran in protest of its execution of Saudi Shia cleric Nimr al-Nimr, Riyadh immediately cut diplomatic relations with Tehran.[84] While countries like Bahrain and Sudan immediately followed Saudi Arabia's lead, Kuwait and Qatar responded by only recalling their ambassadors to Iran.[85] It was not a coincidence that in February 2017 Iranian president Hasan Rouhani paid presidential visits to Oman and Kuwait, 'to consult with Oman to look at ways that Iran can remove the hostility that exists with other Arab regional countries' according to an Iranian diplomat in Muscat.[86]

Unfortunately, countries of the region are increasingly joining the conflict rather than disengaging from it. For example, Yemen joined in 2014 and Iraq in 2003, while attempts to disengage Syria from the Iranian bloc after the Arab Spring did not make any progress. This increased regional polarisation makes the need for a non-aligned movement more urgent than ever before, particularly as a means of countering this dangerous trend of escalation or 'conflict enlargement'.[87] If this trend continues, the region will experience more violence as seen in Syria, Yemen and Iraq. While completely reversing it may not be easy to achieve, the mere disruption of this trend of escalation will lead to conflict containment and assist in its resolution in the long run.

Of course, it is not easy to maintain peace zones in highly polarised conflicts. The pressure on countries in this region will be enormous as the race between the primary parties – Iran and Saudi Arabia – becomes more intense. Indeed, '[t]he most significant current source of division among the GCC states relates to Iran's role in the Middle East's evolving geopolitical order'.[88] As an example, Saudi Arabia, the UAE, Bahrain and Egypt imposed a sea, land and airspace blockade on Doha in May 2017 to try to change its policies, particularly in relation to Iran. One of the major demands of the Saudi-led group blockading Qatar was for the latter to end its relationship with Iran.[89] However, Doha responded by restoring full diplomatic relations with Tehran and returned its ambassador, previously withdrawn in sympathy with Saudi Arabia in the aftermath of the embassy attack. Economic cooperation between Qatar and Iran has improved as a result of the blockade. Qatar's strategy has been to improve relations with Iran since it now needs to use Iranian airspace and import food products, but this relationship has not evolved into an Iranian–Qatari alliance against Saudi Arabia. Qatar knows that Saudi Arabia is a permanent neighbour and will always be key to its national security strategy and so the closeness with Iran will have to be balanced as well.

The level of involvement of other countries in the rivalry varies. Beyond those who have taken clear sides, countries like Oman, Kuwait, Qatar and Jordan take a more cautious approach. Jordan's foreign minister Nasser Judeh called for a dialogue with Iran when he visited Tehran in 2015.[90] Such statements give hope for potential moderation of the conflict through peace zones and non-alignment, brought about in part by the independent actions of other countries in the region.

As discussed earlier, the idea of a non-aligned movement is not intended to be a passive approach to the conflict. Instead, it is expected to take an impartial approach to dealing with the conflicts of the region rather than disengaging entirely. Saudi Arabia, understandably, will expect a solid alliance from its Gulf neighbours to fight Iran and stop its 'aggression' towards

Arab countries. In fact, that is exactly the kind of impartial role these countries might take if they are convinced that is in fact what Iran is doing. Countries acting in this capacity would be better able to help Saudi Arabia contain Iran's expansion than playing the role of closely allied countries. Similarly, Iran's goal of building good relations with other countries in the region can also be facilitated by the peace zone. If such a non-aligned group builds high levels of credibility by being truly impartial, it will be able to help facilitate, build bridges, and even help Iran achieve the good relations that it claims to seek.

Notes

1. Marc Valeri, *Oman: Politics and Society in the Qaboos State* (London: C. Hurst & Co., 2009), p. 63.
2. Ibrahim Fraihat, 'Keeping Iran and Saudi Arabia from war', *Foreign Affairs*, 30 May 2016, https://www.foreignaffairs.com/articles/iran/2016-05-30/keeping-iran-and-saudi-arabia-war (last accessed 29 January 2017).
3. Mohammed Ghobari and Mohammed Mukhashaf, 'Saudi-led planes bomb Sanaa airport to stop Iranian plane landing', *Reuters*, 28 April 2015, http://www.reuters.com/article/us-yemen-security-airport-idUSKBN0NJ24120150428.
4. 'Video: Iranian "hero pilot" defies Saudi orders to leave Yemen', *France 24*, 1 May 2015, http://observers.france24.com/en/20150501-video-iranian-pilot-saudi-yemen.
5. 'Memorandum of understanding between the United States of America and the Union of Soviet Socialist Republics regarding the establishment of a direct communications link', US Department of State, 20 June 1963, http://www.state.gov/t/isn/4785.htm.
6. Thomas Graham Jr and Damien J. LaVera, 'The hotline agreements', in Thomas Graham Jr and Damien J. LaVera (eds), *Cornerstones of Security: Arms Control Treaties in the Nuclear Era* (Seattle: University of Washington Press, 2003), p. 20.
7. Ibid. p. 21.
8. Ibid. p. 20; Stanford Arms Control Group, 'Agreements and treaties other than SALT and the NPT', in Coit D. Blacker and Gloria Duffy (eds), *International Arms Control* (Palo Alto: Stanford University Press, 1984), p. 118.
9. Colonel Stephen L. Thacher, 'Crisis communications between super powers', Study Project, US Army War College, 12 February 1990, file:///C:/Users/dinterns/Downloads/ADA222248.pdf.

10. Choe Sang-Hun, 'North Korea reopens border hotline with South', *New York Times*, 3 January 2018, https://www.nytimes.com/2018/01/03/world/asia/north-korea-hotline-south.html.

11. Craig Daigle, 'The era of détente', in Artemy M. Kalinovsky and Craig Daigle (eds), *The Routledge Handbook of the Cold War* (New York: Routledge, 2014), pp. 195–208.

12. Hassan M. Fattah, 'Saudi–Iran meeting yields little substance', *New York Times*, 5 March 2007, http://www.nytimes.com/2007/03/05/world/middleeast/05saudi.html; Douglas Jehl, 'On trip to mend ties, Iran's President meets Saudi Prince', *New York Times*, 17 May 1999, http://www.nytimes.com/1999/05/17/world/on-trip-to-mend-ties-iran-s-president-meets-saudi-prince.html.

13. 'Iran welcomes old foes to Islamic summit', *CNN*, 8 December 1997, http://edition.cnn.com/WORLD/9712/08/islamic.conference/.

14. Abdulmajeed al-Buluwi, 'Saudi invitation a first step with Iran', *Al-Monitor*, 16 May 2014, http://www.al-monitor.com/pulse/originals/2014/05/saudi-arabia-iran-region-deescalation.html#ixzz3f1jZ7Vc5.

15. Ibid.

16. Dmitry Zhdannikov and Alex Lawler, 'Saudi oil policy uncertainty unleashes the conspiracy theorists', *Reuters*, 18 November 2014, http://www.reuters.com/article/opec-idUSL6N0T73VG20141118.

17. Matt Egan, 'Saudi Arabia: we're not crashing oil prices to hurt Iran', *CNN Money*, 19 January 2016, http://money.cnn.com/2016/01/19/investing/saudi-arabia-oil-prices-iran/.

18. Siegfried S. Hecker, 'Adventures in scientific nuclear diplomacy', *Physics Today* 64, 7 (July 2011): 31–7, https://fsi.stanford.edu/sites/default/files/Hecker_sciencediplomacy_physicstoday.pdf.

19. Ibid. p. 32.

20. Simon J. A. Mason and Matthias Siegfried, 'Confidence building measures (CBMs) in peace processes', in Luc Chounet-Cambas (ed.), *Managing Peace Processes: Process Related Questions. A Handbook for AU Practitioners*, vol. 1 (Addis Ababa: African Union and the Centre for Humanitarian Dialogue, 2013), pp. 57–78, p. 58.

21. Johan Jorgen Holst, 'Confidence-building measures: a conceptual framework', *Survival* 24, 1 (1983): 2–15, p. 2.

22. Rachel Bzostek and Allison Rogers, 'Oslo +20: reassessing the role of confidence building measures', *The Social Science Journal* 51, 2 (2014): 250–9, p. 252.

23. Ibid. p. 252.
24. Robin Emmott and Noah Barkin, 'Iran says ready to put rivalries aside with Saudi Arabia', *Reuters*, 12 February 2016, http://www.reuters.com/article/us-mideast-crisis-iran-saudi-idUSKCN0VL236.
25. Bzostek and Rogers, 'Oslo +20', p. 253.
26. Ibid. p. 256.
27. Ibid. p. 256.
28. Ibid. p. 256.
29. Seyyed Hossein Mousavian, former member of the Iranian Supreme National Security Council. Author's interview and discussion, March 2016.
30. 'Landmark Iran–Saudi security deal', *BBC*, April 2001, http://news.bbc.co.uk/2/hi/middle_east/1283010.stm.
31. Holst, 'Confidence-building measures', p. 5.
32. Ibid. p. 5.
33. Ibid. p. 4.
34. Ibid. p. 4.
35. Ibid. p. 4.
36. 'UN condemns attack on Saudi embassy in Iran', *BBC*, 5 January 2016, http://www.bbc.com/news/world-middle-east-35229385.
37. 'Hajj stampede: Iran death toll rises to 464', *BBC*, 1 October 2015, http://www.bbc.com/news/world-middle-east-34410484.
38. Author participation, workshop organised by the CIRS, Center for International and Regional Studies, at Georgetown University in Doha, September 2016. Identities withheld under the Chatham House rule.
39. Bzostek and Rogers, 'Oslo +20', p. 257.
40. Holst, 'Confidence-building measures', p. 2.
41. Ibid. p. 3.
42. Ibid. p. 5.
43. Mason and Siegfried, 'Confidence building measures', pp. 59–61.
44. Ibid. pp. 57–58.
45. Ibid. p. 64.
46. Author's interview and discussion, email correspondence, February 2016.
47. Mason and Siegfried, 'Confidence building measures', p. 64.
48. Ibid. p. 64.
49. Ibid. p. 66.
50. Ibid. p. 67.

51. 'Text of the basic principles of relations between the United States of America and the Union of Soviet Socialist Republics', *The American Presidency Project*, 29 May 1972, http://www.presidency.ucsb.edu/ws/?pid=3438.

52. Ibid.

53. Mason and Siegfried, 'Confidence building measures', pp. 72–5.

54. Norbert Ropers, 'From resolution to transformation: the role of dialogue projects', Berghof Research Center for Constructive Conflict Management, 2004, p. 4, http://edoc.vifapol.de/opus/volltexte/2011/2580/pdf/ropers_handbook.pdf.

55. United Nations Development Program (UNDP), 'Why dialogue matters for conflict prevention and peacebuilding', February 2009, p. 3, http://www.undp.org/content/dam/undp/library/crisis%20prevention/dialogue_conflict.pdf.

56. Ropers, 'From resolution to transformation', p. 2.

57. UNDP, 'Why dialogue matters', p. 3.

58. Ropers, 'From resolution to transformation', p. 4.

59. UNDP, 'Why dialogue matters', p. 3.

60. Author interview, Doha, November 2015.

61. Author participation in dialogue encounters, 2015–18.

62. Author interview, Doha, November 2015.

63. Ibid.

64. Ibid.

65. Paul Salem, 'A response to Iranian foreign minister Zarif', *The Middle East Institute*, 30 April 2015, http://www.mei.edu/content/article/irans-arab-policy-change-dialogue.

66. Comments made at 'Conference: The Arabs and Iran – Problems in the relationship', Al Jazeera Center for Studies, Doha, 16 February 2016, https://www.youtube.com/watch?v=UoUYA3wysLk (last accessed 10 February 2017).

67. 'Saudi Arabia vs Iran: is the cold war heating up?', *UpFront, Al Jazeera*, 16 January 2016, http://www.aljazeera.com/programmes/upfront/2016/01/saudi-arabia-iran-cold-war-heating-160115075435374.html.

68. 'Saudi Arabia vs Iran', *UpFront*.

69. Mohammad Javad Zarif, 'A message from Iran', *New York Times*, 20 April 2015, http://www.nytimes.com/2015/04/20/opinion/mohammad-javad-zarif-a-message-from-iran.html?_r=1.

70. Salem, 'A response to Iranian foreign minister Zarif'.

71. Jafari, 'How Iran should approach the GCC'.

72. Abdullah Al Shayji, panel discussion, Doha Forum, 22 May 2016.

73. Jamal Khashoggi, panel discussion, Doha Forum, 22 May 2016.

74. Ibid.

75. Arab–Iranian dialogue workshop, Georgetown University in Qatar, 13 January 2016.

76. Ibrahim Fraihat, 'Managing the Saudi–Iranian regional rivalry', a lecture delivered at Georgetown University on 8 November 2015, https://www.youtube.com/watch?v=snqUvvBEhzE (last accessed 18 June 2019).

77. Steven Hoffmann, *India and the China Crisis* (Berkeley: University of California Press, 1990), p. 50. Quoted in M. N. Das, *The Political Philosophy of Jawaharlal Nehru* (New York: John Day, 1961), p. 234.

78. 'Lebanon's parliament elects ex-general Michel Aoun president', *Deutsche Welle*, 31 October 2016, http://www.dw.com/en/lebanons-parliament-elects-ex-general-michel-aoun-president/a-36211650.

79. Wallace Warfield, 'Moving from civil war to civil society', *Peace Review* 9, 2 (1997): 249–54, p. 250.

80. Ian Black, 'Fear of a Shia full moon', *The Guardian*, 26 January 2007, https://www.theguardian.com/world/2007/jan/26/worlddispatch.ianblack.

81. 'Joint statement by EU High Representative Federica Mogherini and Iranian Foreign Minister Javad Zarif', *European Union*, 14 July 2015, http://eeas.europa.eu/statements-eeas/2015/150714_01_en.htm.

82. Jafari, 'How Iran should approach the GCC'.

83. 'Qatar says Gulf Arabs confident region safer with Iran deal', *Reuters*, 3 August 2015, http://www.reuters.com/article/us-iran-nuclear-gcc-qatar-idUSKCN0Q81Q320150803.

84. Fraihat, 'Nimr al Nimr'; Martin Chulov, 'Saudi Arabia cuts diplomatic ties with Iran after execution of cleric', *The Guardian*, 4 January 2016, https://www.theguardian.com/world/2016/jan/03/saudi-arabia-cuts-diplomatic-ties-with-iran-after-nimr-execution.

85. 'More countries back Saudi Arabia in Iran dispute', *Al Jazeera*, 6 January 2016, http://www.aljazeera.com/news/2016/01/nations-saudi-arabia-row-iran-160106125405507.html.

86. Saleh al-Shaibany, 'Rouhani meets rulers of Oman and Kuwait to reduce Iran–GCC tensions', *The National*, 15 February 2017, https://www.thenational.ae/world/rouhani-meets-rulers-of-oman-and-kuwait-to-reduce-iran-gcc-tensions-1.52558.

87. Mitchell, *The Structure of International Conflict*.

88. Giorgio Cafiero and Daniel Wagner, 'Iran exposes the myth of GCC unity', *The National Interest*, 7 September 2015, http://nationalinterest.org/feature/iran-exposes-the-myth-gcc-unity-13787.

89. Patrick Wintour, 'Qatar given 10 days to meet 13 sweeping demands by Saudi Arabia', *The Guardian*, 23 June 2017, https://www.theguardian.com/world/2017/jun/23/close-al-jazeera-saudi-arabia-issues-qatar-with-13-demands-to-end-blockade.

90. Maen al-Bayari, 'Jordanian opening with Tehran a sign of regional mood', *The New Arab*, 10 March 2015, https://www.alaraby.co.uk/english/comment/2015/3/10/jordanian-opening-with-tehran-a-sign-of-regional-mood.

4

Conflict Resolution

The previous chapter discussed approaches to managing, containing and preventing a further escalation of the conflict between Riyadh and Tehran. In this chapter, several approaches are proposed to find potential solutions to the conflict. While some approaches are proposed to address matters of the Iran–Saudi rivalry in the short term, others focus on long-term solutions that deal primarily with the underlying causes and conditions of the conflict. Only by adequately responding to the root causes of the rivalry can lasting stability, collaboration and rapprochement between Iran and Saudi Arabia be achieved.

Restoring the Regional Order's Balance of Power

It is generally argued that the American invasion of Iraq in 2003 created an imbalance of power between Iran and its Gulf neighbours, since the invasion led Baghdad to shift its regional allegiance to Tehran. Thus, in order to resolve the conflict between Iran and Saudi Arabia, the balance of power between the two must be restored.

Balance of power theory in international relations presumes that the more equal states are in terms of global power, the less likely they are to come into conflict. In essence, the theory 'rests on two critical variables: (1) the distribution of power among the states of the system and (2) the alliance configuration'.[1] The notion of no predominance, then, forms a critical part of the balance of power theory.[2] As Morton Kaplan explains,

> [t]he system tends to be maintained by the fact that even should any nation desire to become predominant itself, it must, to protect its own interests, act to prevent any other nation from accomplishing such an objective.

Like Adam Smith's 'unseen hand' of competition, the international system is policed informally by self-interest, without the necessity of a political subsystem.[3]

Critical to such a balance is 'a relatively equal balance of military power'.[4] Certainly, if one state is obviously stronger than others in terms of military capabilities, it is able to prey on the weaker states to gain greater power in the global system. If states have somewhat equal military abilities, however, they are less likely to enter into confrontations. The same can be said for other types of resources:

> The power balance model of conflict ... gives a rationale for the often made assumptions and observations that the probability of manifest conflict between two parties tends to increase as the parties become more equal in power resources. It does also lead to the not so obvious prediction that the risk for manifest conflict is greatest not when the parties are equal in power resources but rather when one of them has some edge in power resources over the other.[5]

Such a balance of global power is said to lead to peace due to the fact that rational choice logic dictates that actors, before beginning a conflict, will take into account the fact that neighbouring states have equal capabilities.[6] This balance becomes undone, however, with the entry of a state actor that 'does not play according to the rules of the game, such as one whose essential rules are oriented toward the establishment of some form of supranational political organization'.[7] Incorrect or incomplete information about other states' capabilities and posturing can also lead a national actor to act outside of the arranged order.[8] Also, due to the dynamic nature of state-to-state relations, if one state increases its capabilities vis-à-vis its neighbours, the balance falls apart.[9] In such a situation, logistics of this balancing process can also prove difficult and lead to its unravelling.[10] Ultimately, this model represents an ideal type that rarely exists in reality, due to the vast inequalities in the global system and difficulty in ascertaining states' military might from the outside. Furthermore, if such a balance did exist, it would likely be only short-lived, considering the dynamism of the global system; it is not as static in nature as this model would lead us to believe.

In 1988, Iran's Supreme Leader, Khomeini, made his famous statement on ending the war with Iraq: 'Taking this decision was more deadly than taking poison. I submitted myself to God's will and drank this drink for his satisfaction.'[11] With this, Iran accepted not only the end of its 'exporting the revolution' policy (at least temporarily) but, most importantly, the altered characteristics of a balanced regional order between Tehran and its Arab neighbours; as a result, the relationship between Iran and Saudi Arabia improved considerably in the following decade. However, it is generally believed that the current waves of tension between Iran and its Arab neighbours, especially in the Gulf region, began with the shift of the regional order to Iran's advantage after the American invasion of Iraq in 2003 and the removal of the Saddam Hussein regime. The replacement of an antagonistic government in Baghdad with one friendly to Tehran certainly gave Iran a stronger position within the regional order, with a continuity of influence starting in Iran through Iraq, Syria and Lebanon via Hezbollah. This rebalancing led Jordan's King Abdullah II to warn against a dominant Shia influence, calling this continuity the 'Shia Crescent'.[12] It should be noted that this 'Crescent' arcs above the entire northern border area of Saudi Arabia, which Riyadh sees as a threat to its national security. Thus, in order to bring the current Iran–Saudi rivalry – or battle for influence – to an end, the regional order will need to be rebalanced again.

How to restore the balance is certainly not an easy question. Scholars of Gulf and Middle East politics provide varying views on how this could be done. Fatima al-Smadi, an Iran scholar at Al Jazeera Center for Studies, argues that Saudi Arabia will not be able to restore the balance of power in the region without taking Iraq back to the Arab side: 'No rapprochement is possible without Iraq. The Arabs must retake Iraq and that is when rapprochement becomes possible.'[13] However, Iran considers maintaining influence in Iraq part of its national security strategy, whether against Saudi Arabia or others. In this regard, Keynoush argues,

> The safety of Iran's borders was best guaranteed if power in Iraq was shared among multiple political groups, and ideally if Baghdad was run by Shi'i factions with varying political orientations, to allow Iran to influence them more easily to secure their compliance in facing any potentially hostile trends against Tehran.[14]

Exacerbating the concerns of Saudi Arabia about Iranian expansion in Iraq, senior Iranian politicians do not hide their ambitions to control Iraq. In the words of Ali Younesi, a top advisor to Iran's President Hassan Rouhani, 'Iran is once again an empire whose influence extends to Iraq and beyond.' He added that, '[a]t the moment, Iraq is the bastion of our civilization. It is also our identity, culture and capital and this is true now as it was in the past.'[15]

This line of thinking indicates the extent to which Iraq is critical in rebalancing the regional order. In fact, one way to rebalance the regional power is to accept that Iraq must be independent from the influence of both Iran and Saudi Arabia – as well as from the United States. Until Iraq regains its uncompromised sovereignty, it will continue to be a battleground for both regional and international powers. Iraqi independence is critically important not only to rebalancing power between Iran and Saudi Arabia but even more so for its own national interest. By allying with one party over the other, Iraq is working against its own national interest no matter how much support it is receiving from any outside actor. Its reliance on outside actors is probably one reason that Iraq continued to struggle for years with a civil war and various types of instability: none of the interested parties (Iran, Saudi Arabia, the United States) is ready to give Iraq up. Iraqi independence is therefore more important than ever, as its ability to rid itself of external influence would position the country strongly to provide a bridge between Tehran and Riyadh and thus become a unifier of the two rivals rather than a divider. An independent Iraq has huge potential to take a regional role in impacting the centre of the Iran–Saudi cold war, and reflecting onto other areas of instability in the region. Iraq has large Shia and Sunni communities; a harmonious relationship between the two groups would send out a strong message and perhaps calm sectarian tension in the region. Furthermore, Iraq has the resources to play a regional role: it has a rich history that links the two parts of the Muslim world and even geographically bridges Iran, Saudi Arabia and the rest of the Arab region.

Unfortunately, Iraq has not demonstrated credible signs of independence from Iran or the United States. With Iran, there is an ideological factor at play. Iraqi groups like the Islamic Dawa Party, led by Nouri Al-Maliki, which are Shia-based, have been historically allied with Iran; since the removal of

Saddam Hussein from power in 2003, the relationship between Dawa and Tehran has only become stronger. By the same token, Iraqi independence from American control, especially on the security side, has not been realised, and Iraq's foreign policy remains affected by the security agenda of the United States in the Gulf region. In other words, since Iraq's independence in security and foreign policy seems unlikely in the foreseeable future, Saudi Arabia will need to look for other ways to balance the regional order with Iran.

Saudi Arabia understands that Iraq will not return to playing the same role it had during the days of Saddam Hussein. The alternative, according to Jamal Khashoggi, is a Syria more closely aligned with Saudi Arabia. He argues that Iran won Iraq after the American invasion in 2003, and Saudi Arabia therefore cannot afford to waste this opportunity – the Syrian revolution – to claim Syria, which is a natural ally given its Sunni majority.[16] He adds,

> the Iranians saw the US invasion as an opportunity to fulfil their expansionary agenda and they did not hesitate in taking it. Saudi now sees the civil war in Syria as a similar opportunity to tip the balance of power in its favour. Syria is an Arab country that lies very close to Saudi's northern border. A large portion of Saudi's trade goes through Syria. It has a Sunni majority. In addition, Saudis also have tribal and family links with the Syrians. If the Iranians were to stay, they would have to consistently use force to subjugate the population. This is something Saudi cannot allow.[17]

Theoretically, Syria can replace Iraq in rebalancing the regional order should it move from the Iranian camp to that of Saudi Arabia. Not only would such a move cut off Iran logistically from its powerful ally Hezbollah, in Lebanon, but would also disrupt the 'Shia Crescent' that Iran has aimed to build since 2003. In practical terms, however, Syria after the 2011 revolution has changed substantially. Syria has been weakened to the extent that it has lost control over its own territories. Instead of playing a regional role in balancing the regional order, it has become a battleground not only for an Iran–Saudi rivalry, but for many other regional and international forces that took part in controlling Syria, including Russia, the United States, Turkey, ISIS, Kurdish factions, and several other forces with boots on the ground. Obviously, Iran lost portions of its influence in Syria after the revolution, as it was forced to share control with other regional and international players, while in the past it had Syria fully on its side. In other words, relying on Syria to rebalance the regional order is not a very realistic option; even if the regime collapses and the revolutionaries win, post-war recovery is a process that takes years or even decades, and at every stage there is the threat of sliding back into violence. Syria will be a burden to whichever regional power claims control after the civil war, as it will require hundreds of billions of dollars for reconstruction. So, countries other than Syria are likelier to rebalance the regional order.

Professor Arshin Adib-Moghaddam, Chair of the Centre for Iranian Studies at the School of Oriental and African Studies (SOAS) in London, suggests almost a different approach to rebalancing the regional order and to ending the Iran–Saudi rivalry. He argues for building a security system in the Gulf that involves not only Iran and Saudi Arabia but also the United States:

> in the future, the order in the Persian Gulf may resemble what former President Nixon termed the 'dual pillar' policy in the 1970s which relied upon Saudi Arabia and the Shah's Iran to safeguard regional security. Of course, times have changed, and both Iran and Saudi Arabia are unlikely to create any unnecessary dependencies on Washington DC. But in the end this diplomatic crisis has to be addressed within a wider diplomatic context which requires the presence of the European Union and the United States. Iran and Saudi Arabia have an interest in regional security and if there is a concerted move in that direction both countries would follow suit. This may be the time to call for an Organization for Peace and Cooperation in West Asia along the lines of the OSCE which helped to pacify Europe after two world wars. I am in no doubt that such an initiative is viable and timely. To that end, the diplomatic presence of the EU and the United States is required.[18]

The 'twin pillars' policy worked in the 1970s mainly because all three parties – the United States, Iran and Saudi Arabia – had one common enemy during the Cold War– the USSR – whose defeat was a national security interest for all. No similar common enemy exists in the present day. Indeed, today, each country defines its national security interest in a very different way to each other, and in fact from the way it was defined in the 1970s. Iran is a close ally of Moscow today, while Saudi Arabia sees the biggest threat to its national security as the 'exporting of the revolution' from Tehran.

In theory, an American presence in the Gulf region should be able to balance all parties involved in the Gulf security system; it can deter Iranian expansion in the region and at the same time protect the Gulf monarchies. Even practically, the American security umbrella has contributed to the relative stability of the Gulf region and contained what could have been a more acute security confrontation. However, this arrangement has been in place since the end of the Cold War in 1990, while the region has recently become increasingly unstable, raising questions about the efficiency of a security system that is reliant on the United States. The major problem in rebalancing through a US security role in the Gulf region is that the US presence is a problem in itself, and so too is its absence. Both American presence and absence shift security dynamics significantly in a way that yields conflict and instability. The United States can be too powerful – where its presence undermines security assurances of some parties like Iran – yet a US absence triggers Iran's appetite for expansion, control and hegemony. Rebalancing the Middle East regional order through American involvement has three major problems, for the United States, Iran and Saudi Arabia.

First, the United States. American presence is already strong in the region, yet it has not made the Iran–Saudi cold war any less vicious. More importantly, it is not certain that Washington itself under the Trump administration is interested in taking an active security role in the Gulf region. There is already an intense debate within the scholarly community about whether American foreign policy is in retreat in the Middle East or whether a commitment still exists to engineering the security architecture of the region. Former Secretary of State Hillary Clinton's Pivot-to-Asia argument is testimony to American foreign policy's hesitation to long-term commitment in the Middle East. In her words, '[t]he future of politics will be decided in Asia, not Afghanistan or Iraq, and the United States will be right at the center of the action'.[19]

Without going into too much detail about this debate, it can be safely stated that there is no consensus across different American administrations about the country's role in mediating between Iran and Saudi Arabia. The Obama administration, for example, signed the nuclear deal with Iran independently from Saudi Arabia; President Obama later stated that Saudi Arabia needs to share the region with Iran. He told *The Atlantic*:

The competition between the Saudis and the Iranians, which has helped to feed proxy wars and chaos in Syria and Iraq and Yemen, requires the U.S. to say to our friends, as well as to the Iranians, that they need to find an effective way to share the neighborhood and institute some sort of cold peace.[20]

However, this scenario changed substantially under the Trump administration, which forged an open alliance with Saudi Arabia during the Riyadh summit in May 2017 that emphasised huge arms sales to Saudi Arabia as well as, perhaps even more importantly, uniting to confront Iranian power in the region. President Trump went even further by withdrawing from the nuclear deal with Iran and imposing the harshest sanctions ever against Tehran – a policy that likely resulted from Saudi Arabia being a pillar of this new American policy towards Iran.

Second, Iran. American involvement exacerbates the root causes of the Iran–Saudi regional rivalry through a heavy American military presence in the Gulf that contributes to the tension in the first place, at least from an Iranian perspective. For Iran, American bases in the Gulf present a direct threat to its national interest and necessitate the pursuit of an independent security strategy to protect itself from the 'American–Saudi alliance' against Tehran. An American presence in the Gulf can never reassure Iran – at least under the current leadership – for many reasons, including the fact that this presence prevents Tehran from pursuing its objective of being a decision-making regional power. Iran will therefore continue to pursue a strategy of neutralising the American deterrence in order to prevail or at least share with the other regional powers in guarding the regional security order.

Third, Saudi Arabia. American military presence in the Gulf is equally problematic for Saudi Arabia. Over the past decades, this presence has created a high level of 'security dependency' from Saudi Arabia towards Washington. Saudi Arabia has not been able to build an independent security strategy to protect itself from the 'Iranian expansion' without mainly relying on American help. This dependency has left Riyadh vulnerable to political changes, lobbying, and other political development in Washington, DC. Saudi Arabia must establish its own security strategy so that it may stand on its own, rather than remaining dependent on a controversial American presence in the region, which is subject to change with each presidential election.

This discussion takes us to our proposed solution to rebalancing with Iran through developing Saudi Arabia's own power – possibly with neighbouring Gulf states – rather than relying on others like the United States, Iraq or Syria to do so. The Gulf Cooperation Council in 1981 was built on the premise that Gulf countries must unite to counter the power of Iran and its attempts to 'export its revolution'. Despite the progress the GCC has made in a number of areas, the Council has not yet been able to fully build its own security strategy without relying on external vendors. In this regard, Professor Abdullah Al Shayji, a Gulf studies expert at Kuwait University, suggests that it is what he calls 'the balance of terror' that will resolve the conflict with Iran.[21] Accordingly, 'Iran should be deterred in order to engage in meaningful solutions'. He adds that, as with the US–USSR Cold War, where it was only the 'balance of terror' that deterred parties on both sides and ultimately forced them to engage in peacemaking, in his view, the Arab–Iranian cold war will be resolved in a similar way.[22]

No matter how strong the alliances are that Saudi Arabia can build, whether with the US or other players, there will never be a sustainable alternative to building its own security strategy that relies mostly on its own power if the goal is countering Iranian power. Developing its own self-sufficient powerbase will allow for a balance of power between Riyadh and Tehran, which is a situation likely conducive to reaching conflict settlement. In situations of power imbalance, as described above, the powerful party loses incentive to make concessions to reach solutions. The moment that Saudi Arabia is able to face Iran without the help of the United States, a solution to the rivalry and other forms of proxy wars becomes possible. Saudi Arabia has made significant progress in this area with regards its air force, which is said to balance or exceed that of Iran. Nevertheless, there is much more to be done.

One last approach to rebalancing the regional order and ending the rivalry is through the expansion of the order itself to include new influential players, especially from neighbouring countries. That is, instead of looking at a regional order that contains only Iran and neighbouring Arab states, countries like Turkey and Pakistan could also be part of a political system that covers West Asia and North Africa (WANA). In this regard, Jane Kinninmont explains, 'the increasing interest of rising Asian powers . . . could represent an opportunity to reconceptualize Gulf security not as the burden or asset of a superpower, but as a "global public good" that should be governed multilaterally'.[23]

WANA is of critical importance as Turkey and Pakistan are essential parts of the larger political and security architecture of West Asia. Both parties are involved to a large extent in the Iran–Saudi rivalry. Several dimensions of their foreign policy intersect with key aspects of Iranian and Arab conflicts; they are by no means separated from developments in Syria, Iraq and Yemen. Terrorism and sectarianism are also at the core of Pakistan and Turkey's national security matters. Equally importantly, if direct war between Iran and Saudi Arabia broke out, both Turkey and Pakistan would have to take sides, since such a development would present a direct threat to their national interest. Turkey was the first country to be directly affected by the civil war in Syria through the inflow of refugees and incidences of terrorism, making its direct involvement inevitable. Pakistan has historically relied on generous financial support from Saudi Arabia but at the same time does not want to engage in a conflict with Iran – with which Pakistan shares 909 kilometres of borders. Sectarianism, an issue at the core of Iran–Saudi rivalry, has been a source of instability and there has been a history of violent attacks between Sunni and Shia groups.

The incorporation of Turkey and Pakistan into a larger regional order like WANA would fundamentally shift the equation from Iran–Arab rivalry to a totally new arrangement where Pakistan's primary interest would be the balance of this new system, meaning that it would not have to choose between Iran and Saudi Arabia. Their incorporation into the new system would create a new venue for building political alliances and potentially ending the state of polarisation between Arabs and Iranians or Sunnis and Shias. Countries of the size and power of Turkey and Pakistan are unlikely to be absorbed by the current polarisation and thus can more easily maintain independent foreign policies to mitigate conflict. It should be noted that Pakistan in particular, as a nuclear state, has strong potential to act as a stabilising force for this new system, which is another reason that WANA could prove to be an alternative option to the current rivalry. Finally, Pakistan and Turkey are part of the region and are there to stay. Unlike the US presence in the region, which is dependent on military bases, Turkey and Pakistan have the sustainability factor to achieve a more balanced regional security order.

Any successful attempt to rebalance the regional order will have to address the security concerns of both Iran and Saudi Arabia. Security is a need rather than a passing interest for Riyadh and Tehran, and it will have to be adequately satisfied for any balanced regional order to maintain itself in the future. Jane Kinninmont of The Elders (an independent group of global leaders) argues that a rapprochement between the parties will have to 'address mutual concerns . . . For Saudi Arabia the chief preoccupation is that its sovereignty is being undermined through the stoking of internal dissent and the risk of being encircled by pro-Iran forces.'[24] In addition, 'Iran also fears encirclement, both by U.S. bases and by jihadi groups that it regards as proxies of Gulf states'.[25]

Any arrangement to rebalance the regional order, be it a US-led security architecture, a Gulf system or WANA, will have to address the underlying security needs of both Iran and Saudi Arabia. Iran must assure its neighbours it does not aspire to play a hegemonic role in the region. Merely dismissing Saudi security concerns as if they are not credible or (as is usually argued by Iranians), suggesting that the true problem is internal Saudi issues, will not resolve the issue – neither will it bring about the security satisfaction that Iran legitimately seeks. In this regard, Seyed Hossein Mousavian, Head of the Foreign Relations Committee of Iran's National Security Council (1997–2005), agrees Iran needs to do more. He explains:

> For its part, Iran needs to acknowledge and take steps to alleviate the legitimate security concerns of the GCC states. Iran also needs to remember that the alternative to House of Saud in Saudi Arabia will be the House Wahhab.[26]

Mousavian also suggests that the two countries need to engage in a serious conversation on security and end the tension between them. He cites a security agreement reached in 1997 between Hasan Rouhani and Emir Nayef and the role he himself played in producing this agreement. Indeed, the agreement addressed the security concerns of both sides and can potentially be used as a starting point for further conversation between Riyadh and Tehran.[27] Even on the most difficult challenge to Iran's security, the US military bases, Mousavian concedes that this issue can be resolved by agreeing on the departure of all foreign troops within fifteen years, after Iran and Saudi Arabia have developed enough trust and integrated security and economic systems.[28] Another view put forward in a track two workshop by an Iranian policy advisor was that the presence of foreign powers in the Gulf was in fact important for the security arrangements of the region to work. In his words,

> [a]t least for the foreseeable future, the presence of the foreign powers will be necessary to make countries like Bahrain and even Saudi Arabia feel more comfortable to collaborate on building more stable security arrangements. It is something that we – in Iran – will say publicly that we are against it and we don't like it; however, in reality the foreign powers will be there to assure some Gulf countries about their security.[29]

Trading concessions of equal value can serve as a mechanism to meeting the security needs of both parties and subsequently guide resolution on the security level. For Iran, this will mean scaling back on arming militias in the region and fighting proxy wars, while for Saudi Arabia it will require taking serious steps to 'integrate the Islamic Republic into the region's political and economic structures rather than trying to keep it out'.[30] Given the lack of trust between Riyadh and Tehran, the two tracks will have to proceed simultaneously; progress on one track will provide a mechanism to trigger progress on the other.

The integration of Iran is likely to yield a more stable regional order, which is a core security interest for Saudi Arabia. Integration stipulates abiding by the rules and offers the possibility of containment, while keeping parties outside the system allows them to play by their own rules. For example, Bill Clinton invested serious efforts to admit China to the World Trade Organization (WTO) to ensure that China trades by the rules and thus remains contained. Saudi Arabia, then, may have a better chance at rebalancing the regional order by integrating Iran rather than building alliances to confront Tehran and keep it outside the regional system.

Reforming Conflict Strategies

Both Iran and Saudi Arabia have pursued counterproductive strategies to achieve their national objectives, further complicating the conflict rather than resolving it. If they continue in this vein, the two parties will lose out in the long run, despite the ability of one or both parties to achieve some limited gains in one of the region's conflict zones.

Both Iran and Saudi Arabia are locked into a zero-sum conflict, with each party's strategy characterised by contentious tactics that aim to defeat the other militarily. Saudi Arabia's primary focus is balancing the security architecture of the Arab world, keeping Iran contained within its own geographical borders. Iran, on the other hand, has adopted a security strategy of expansion in the Arab region, with the primary tool used to achieve this goal the building up of armed militias that have the ability to destabilise the region. The very essence of both strategies is security competition in the traditional form of an arms race, building up alliances, maximising hard power, and overwhelming the other rival. While maximising hard power does help in various stages of conflict and negotiation, limiting conflict strategies to such approaches will only lock Iran and Saudi Arabia into a vicious cycle that will ultimately drain both countries' resources and create a protracted stalemate with a clear absence of both peace and war.

However, both parties can achieve their objectives – mutual security and acceptance in the region – by introducing significant revisions to their strategies, especially in the following areas.

Sectarian policy reform

Sunni–Shia sectarianism is generally viewed as being at the heart of this Iran–Saudi rivalry. Regardless of the role it has played in motivating this conflict, it is reasonable to argue that sectarianism has been used by both Iran and Saudi Arabia to advance their own interests and secure legitimacy for regime survival. By raising sectarian tension and polarisation, both regimes secure their legitimacy and popular support among their own citizenry for the protection they provide. In Saudi Arabia, for example, the 'Shia threat' is used in times of crisis 'to rally the rest of the population, most of whom are Sunnis of different persuasions, around the ruling family', according to Toby Matthiesen.[31] Justin Gengler further explains that,

> the extreme sense of anxiety permeating the Gulf region means that governments enjoy a reservoir of popular support and legitimacy simply for their provision of security in an insecure region, affording them the freedom to renegotiate their tacit social contracts with citizens more or less unilaterally.

However, this logic of playing on sectarian tension can backfire.[32] For example, as Gengler explains,

> having convinced Sunnis of the existential threat posed by Iran and its Shia agents in Bahrain, the authorities found it impossible to quiet their own supporters, who began pressing for an even harsher security response to continued protests, thus quickening the spiral of violence and repression that has characterized the post-2011 period. Some Sunni activists even dared to criticize senior royals, including King Hamad bin Isa Al Khalifa himself, for their perceived weakness.[33]

Iran, on the other hand, has historically justified its intervention in Syria, Iraq and elsewhere in the Arab world to its own domestic constituency as necessary to its efforts to fight Sunni jihadist terrorists abroad, so that they do not become a threat to Iran at home. The Iranian government is therefore marketing its policy of arming militias in the region to its citizenry as defending national security and fighting a sectarian war that is imposed by Saudi Wahhabism-driven extremists of Sunni ideology like ISIS and Al-Qaida.

Therefore, a starting point to halt the escalation of this conflict and take steps towards resolution would be for both parties to significantly reform their conflict strategies, in particular the sectarian segments.

Despite its strong denial of sectarianism as a driver of its foreign policy, Iran has heavily relied on sectarianism as a tool to expand influence in the region. Its claim to merely be 'supporting the oppressed' does not explain why Iran supports revolutions in Bahrain and Yemen, yet when it comes to Syria and its Alawite leaders, the revolution becomes 'an external conspiracy'.[34] How can a strategy of 'supporting the oppressed' be at work in Yemen and Bahrain – as Iran supports the Shia faction in each case – while a policy of supporting the oppressor is put in place in Syria? To build credibility within the region, Iran needs to remove the sectarian component of its foreign policy and instead take a principled approach that will convince the public that it is not pursuing a sectarian agenda. The hypocritical sectarian strategy that it has been following easily allows not only their main rival Saudi Arabia to insist on the sectarian nature of Iran's foreign policy but also allows others in the region to argue against Iranian foreign policy in this way as well. This polarisation helps Sunni extremists in recruitment against Tehran's actions; Iran should not be surprised that radical Sunni groups are targeting its interests. By adhering to a non-sectarian line in its foreign policy, Iran will prevent Saudi Arabia from using a sectarian argument against it. Riyadh may even be convinced that Iran is not truly advancing Shiism in the region, which could lead to de-escalation on Riyadh's part.

Iran's reform of its sectarian strategy should also include outreach to the Sunni community within its own borders. In so doing, Iran would strengthen its own internal front in this conflict and send the right messages to the Arab world that it is genuinely interested in building non-sectarian relations with its neighbours, something many would warmly welcome.

One major aspect that Iran needs to focus on is its relationship with the Shia communities of the Arab world. Iran should refrain from presenting itself as the guardian of the interests of Shia communities in Bahrain, Kuwait, Yemen, and elsewhere. Shia Muslims throughout the Arab world are part of their own societies, and as such, their loyalties tend to go first and foremost to their own countries, not to another country that happens to share a sectarian affiliation. By presenting itself as the protector of their respective agendas, Iran has hindered rather than helped the legitimate cause of equal citizenship rights that Shia citizens have sought abroad. Iranian interventions have indeed damaged the relations of Shia communities with their fellow citizens of Sunni backgrounds, disrupting the social fabric of the broader societies where they live.

For instance, sectarianism on a large scale did not exist in Yemen before the 2014 Houthi coup. However, when Iran began to politicise the Houthi cause, broader Yemeni society started to see the Houthis only as proxies of Iran, and Sunni–Shia sectarianism became the core of the conflict. Iranian intervention in the internal affairs of Shia communities has also given Saudi Arabia an excuse to justify its repressive policies against the Shias in the eastern part of their country. A genuine reform of the relationship with the Shia communities in the Arab world should include a complete separation of politics and religion. Only through this separation will Iran be able to discredit any attempt to label its foreign policy as sectarian-based with the goal of spreading Shiism – an objective Iran appears to be strongly pursuing.

Iran has also suffered from instability inside its own borders due to sectarianism, and a solution should focus on addressing sectarianism – internally and externally – rather than denying its existence. For example, 'the Sunni separatist group, Jundullah in Baluchistan has corroborated with Al-Qaida in its attacks on the Iranian regime'.[35] One way to address sectarianism internally would be by allowing Sunni Iranians to have more prominent mosques in Tehran – and for Shia communities in the Arab region to have their own *Hussainiyas*.[36] Since Iran is diverse in terms of ethnicity and religious sect, a rise in internal sectarianism could inspire other ethnic groups to also escalate tension with the state. For example, tension is generally the norm between Arabs and the government in the Khuzestan province, where Arabs form 70 per cent of the three million inhabitants.[37] Sometimes this takes on an international dimension, with activists wishing to show the world the plight of the Arabs in the region.[38] The main demand of Arab inhabitants of the province is for 'cultural space and equality'.[39] In addition, they are driven by fears of government plans to conduct 'ethnic redistribution across the region'.[40] In other words, these ethnic groups have their own causes, and any significant escalation in sectarian tension could easily spill over to them, which makes it more challenging for Iran to maintain internal stability.

Saudi Arabia, on the other hand, should be careful of the potential 'self-fulfilling prophecy' of mistreating its own Shia communities. Perceiving Shia Saudis as fifth columnists loyal to Iran, and treating them as such, may lead them to actually turn to Iran, or at least be sympathetic to its message. Riyadh insists that its Shia community receives full rights as equal citizens. While this may apply in many areas, there are still some senior government positions that they are not eligible to occupy, especially high ranks in the military. Discrimination against the Shia in Saudi Arabia is much deeper, according to Toby Matthiesen: 'Shia in Saudi Arabia are confronted with a religious establishment that promotes the Wahhabi interpretation of Islam, the religious police, and a state apparatus from which they are often barred.'[41] In addition, Shias are not allowed to build their own shrines in the country, which emphasises their Shia identity (and its potential association with Iran) at the expense of their own national identity.

In this regard, Jamal Khashoggi explained that the Wahhabi clergy in Saudi Arabia have been increasingly alienating the Shia with their rhetoric.[42]

Furthermore, educational curricula that follow the Sunni Hanbali school of jurisprudence alienates Shia students, who have to learn these views in order to pass a grade. This arrangement creates frustration within the Shia community and causes them to interpret any injustice that befalls them along sectarian lines.[43]

It is very possible that exaggerations, misperceptions and stereotyping do exist and colour the relationship between the government in Riyadh and its Shia minority. For this reason, Saudi Arabia needs to engage with its Shia community in a genuine dialogue that truly addresses their social, political, economic and religious grievances. Saudi Arabia could then fully guarantee that the loyalty of their Shia community was pledged to their own country rather than the idea of *Velayat-e Faqih*.[44] Religious minorities in general, not just Saudi Shias, will also need to understand that they must solve their issues within their own states. Allying with a foreign country, be it Iran or any other, will not provide the solution, no matter what happens inside their own countries. A commitment to non-violence and a granting of political voice to these minorities within a national framework will help them achieve their rights, rather than giving their loyalties to foreign countries.

A Shia population that is loyal and committed to their own country will significantly strengthen Saudi Arabia's internal front, especially as it relates to Iran. A solidly built internal front is as important for Riyadh's conflict strategy as is the arms race for Iran's.

No matter how one looks at it, sectarianism has been at the core of the conflict for both Iran and Saudi Arabia. Originally, sectarianism was used as a tool to advance agendas on both sides of the rivalry and subsequently became a cause for further escalation of the conflict. Reforming conflict strategies requires both parties to neutralise sectarianism as a factor and, if this is successful, the conflict will be significantly downgraded, making it easier to manage and resolve. In terms of how to neutralise sectarianism, Simon Mabon suggests that both parties adhere to a wider acceptance and tolerance of doctrinal differences within Islam. He explains that 'increasing tolerance will reduce the severity of internal security dilemmas driven by religious differences' and 'remove an important degree of competition from the rivalry'.[45] While he agrees on removing sectarianism as a factor to resolve this conflict,

Vali Nasr adds that this can only happen once the unequal distribution of power and resources along sectarian lines in domestic situations is addressed. He considers the roots of sectarian conflict to lie in 'the lopsided distribution of resources and power that have benefited one sect at the cost of the other'.[46] Resolution, then, can only be reached 'if the distribution of power and resources reflects the demographic realities of the region', something which authoritarian leaderships have been unsuccessful in doing thus far.[47] By addressing the root causes of sectarian differences, he contends, governments will be able to manage these divisions: 'As is the case with all disputes involving a religion or ethnicity, loyalties die hard, but they are less likely to command bloodshed if they are divorced from social, economic, and political injustices.'[48]

This strategy gives hope for both parties that sectarianism, as bad as it might appear at present, might still be nullified by addressing the grievances of Sunni and Shia communities on both sides simply by allowing them their full citizenship rights: access to senior government positions, equal government investment in their own territories, and the right to exercise their religious beliefs.

Domestic reform

Sectarianism is only one challenge to national unity and social cohesion in Iran and Saudi Arabia. In fact, both countries experience several other domestic problems – social, political and economic – that present a serious threat to their future stability from within. Prioritising solutions to domestic problems on both sides will strongly improve the chances for a fair resolution of the conflict between them. It is because of these domestic drivers that the two regimes resort to escalation, polarisation and externalisation of internal conflicts. As in many cases, externalising conflicts helps regimes justify their existence and silence domestic criticism of their leadership. Members of internal opposition groups are generally accused of betraying the country or being agents of a rival state if they criticise or question leadership during times of conflict.

In his 2013 book on the Saudi–Iranian rivalry, Simon Mabon listed a number of areas that need to be addressed in order to improve the nature of Saudi–Iranian relations.[49] At the top of this list is the resolution of domestic problems within Iran and Saudi Arabia. Accordingly, increased internal stability would reduce 'the perception that groups are manipulated by external powers'.[50]

For Saudi Arabia, one of the changes that is imperative to counter Iranian intervention in the region is deep political and constitutional reform. The current political structure of the Kingdom does not support playing a powerful role to strategically balance the regional order with Iran. A Saudi columnist in *al-Hayat*, Khaled Al Dakheel, in an interview on Al Jazeera TV's programme 'Fi Al-Umq' (In Depth), spoke of redefining Saudi Arabia's role as a powerful party in the Gulf by reforming politically, constitutionally, military and economically. Politically, Al Dakheel specified that the Kingdom needs to 'revisit the relationship between the state and society'.[51] In other words, Saudi Arabia needs a new social contract that rebuilds trust between the state and the citizen. Currently, there is a serious problem in the way the state understands its relationship with Saudi society. According to Anas Altikriti, CEO of the London-based Cordoba Foundation, the government sees this relationship as a one-way street, where the government distributes funds and services to the people and the latter should be happy for what they are receiving and therefore remain loyal. In his words, 'a senior Saudi government official told me: our people love us, why would not they? We gave them schools, hospitals, roads, etc. Why wouldn't they be happy?'[52]

For the government to genuinely believe that these services are 'favours' is problematic. The government needs to understand that a desire for political voice is legitimate within Saudi society, where the people have the right to have a say in running their country. Domestic reforms that will enable Saudi Arabia to counter Iranian expansion can be achieved mainly by building a genuine and solid partnership between the state and Saudi society. Such a partnership requires accountability and transparency from both parties. The Saudi people do not need to 'be given' these services, as these are their rights, but rather need to be accepted as partners in running affairs. According to a Gulf expert at Qatar University, Professor Mahjoub Zweri, 'Saudi Arabia cannot confront Iran's intervention in the region as it attempts to do now unless it achieves national harmony on the basis of citizenship.'[53]

Saudi Arabia missed an opportunity to counter Iranian intervention by standing against political reform, not only at home but in other countries affected by the Arab Spring as well. It has very publicly chosen to support counter-revolutions that have kept the region vulnerable to Iranian influence. The largest investment was in Egypt, where Abdel-Fattah el-Sisi essentially blackmailed Saudi Arabia for aid by hinting that he might ally with Iran in Syria and refuse to fight with Saudi Arabia in Yemen if he did not receive support. Sisi's regime has become a financial burden on Saudi Arabia, rather than the powerful ally against Iran that Riyadh wanted.

Political reform in this region would have stopped Iranian intervention strategically and structurally, as it would not have left people with the decision of either allying with Iran or remaining in the hands of an autocratic dictator like Egypt's Sisi, Yemen's Saleh or Syria's Assad. Arab youth did not revolt against dictatorships to embrace an Iranian theocracy; not one Arab Spring uprising lifted the flag of Iran or called for any Iranian help. Successful Arab uprisings, therefore, could have built democratic systems that conflict ideologically with Iranian theocracy. For example, due to its robust civil society and power-sharing system built after the Arab Spring, Tunisia has become immune to Iranian expansionism. It is important to note here that Iran has only been successful in building alliances in the region with dictatorships like Syria's Assad and Iraq's Maliki. A successful democratic system in Egypt would have formed a shield against Iran's expansion, not only in Cairo but across the entire region. Instead, Egypt's Sisi made many gestures supporting dictators like Syria's Assad, sent messages accommodating Iran in Syria, and blackmailed Saudi Arabia for more financial aid.

Addressing the domestic economic challenges that the two countries face will encourage them to engage in political reforms. In this regard, Frederic Wehrey argues,

> a more likely driver of foreign-policy shifts may be domestic economic factors rather than leadership changes: Looming strains on the welfare state and bottom-up demographic pressures from the increasingly youthful populace are likely to shift the focus of Saudi energies inward in the years ahead. This may in turn bring some curtailment and realignment of the Kingdom's policies toward Arab transitional states, policies that have thus far been harmful to the growth of political pluralism and reform.[54]

Iran's domestic economic challenges and links to political reform and conflict resolution with Saudi Arabia are equally important and require prioritisation as well. For many years, Iranians were told that the American imposition of sanctions against Tehran was the cause of their difficult economic situation. The sanctions suited the regime's agenda and gave them an excuse to ignore the economic pressure the country was facing. However, signing the nuclear agreement with the P5+1 in 2015 left the regime exposed to public scrutiny and held it more accountable for delivering on the economic level. It was no surprise that the Islamic Republic experienced a wave of protests in dozens of Iranian cities in December 2017 and January 2018, mainly on economic grounds – 35 per cent of educated youths are unemployed in Iran.[55] It was also unsurprising that protests driven by economic grievances eventually became political, with slogans used against both the Supreme Leader and the President, as well as in opposition to Iran's activist (and expensive) foreign policy in the region. Dozens were killed in the protests, and Iran was on the verge of an uprising similar to those of the Arab Spring. The Iranian government should take these protests seriously and shift its focus from building armed militias in neighbouring countries to building up its own economy and delivering for unemployed Iranian youth.

With the arrival of Donald Trump to power, cancelation of the nuclear deal and imposition of the harshest sanctions ever against Iran in November 2018, the economic challenge for Tehran has become much greater, and it is unclear whether the domestic population will continue to accept sanctions as an excuse for failing to deliver on jobs and improving their livelihoods. Obviously, purely economic solutions are difficult to envision, given the strict sanctions that have been imposed on the country, which demonstrates the need for a political solution first. At the heart of Iran's challenges is the conflict with Saudi Arabia, meaning that credible change in Iran's foreign policy towards the region could be a starting point. Even modest changes to the Iranian policy of arming militias in Iraq and Yemen, which Riyadh considers a fundamental threat to its national security, could lead to credible reform from Saudi Arabia, as it would then be under pressure to reciprocate in terms of outreach to Tehran on the issues driving the conflict.

The fact remains, however, that no significant changes in Iran's foreign policy have been detected, either after the signing of the deal during Obama's times or after the re-imposition of the sanctions in November 2018 by Donald Trump. Pursuing a military strategy at the expense of building an effective domestic economic strategy is reminiscent of the USSR's policies: Moscow focused on an arms race and military industry while ignoring the domestic need for economic prosperity. In the end, its collapse was primarily economically driven rather than due to its strategy of confronting the West. Iran should draw lessons from the past and not fall into the same trap, especially after its economically driven protests of 2017–8. It goes without saying that bleeding funds for many years in a brutal civil war in Afghanistan also played a significant role in the collapse of the Soviet Union; Iran has replicated this experience as well in Syria and Yemen.

One of the biggest challenges to Iran's reform of its conflict strategy is the fact that the country is still being run with a revolutionary mindset. As Parsi explains, '[t]he political elite in Tehran is slowly and reluctantly coming to grips with being a post-revolutionary state. The society has been way ahead of it for quite some time.'[56] The Iranian leadership has not evolved away from its revolutionary thinking, which has curtailed not only political and economic reforms in the country but has had a major impact on exacerbating the security situation in the region and intensified the conflict with Saudi Arabia.

Political reforms are needed as much as economic reforms in Iran, which would also lead to significant improvement in the likelihood of a resolution of the conflict with Saudi Arabia. The struggle between the factions termed 'reformists' and 'conservatives' has not had any major positive impact on the conflict. Even as a 'reformist', Hassan Rouhani has not been able to make any major breakthrough in rapprochement with Iran's Gulf neighbours. It is interesting to notice that the Iran–Saudi relationship improved significantly and reached a place of relative rapprochement under ultraconservative Iranian president Mahmoud Ahmadinejad, yet reached one of its worst levels during the era of reformer Hassan Rouhani. Ahmadinejad met several times with Saudi King Abdullah, while Rouhani's meetings have been limited to his traditional Gulf contacts, mainly in Kuwait and Oman.

Soft power strategy reform

Soft power, a concept developed by Joseph Nye in the 1990, represents a 'constructivist/neoliberal vision of influence that is in contradistinction of the realist vision of power [that sees] influence as a direct function of material resources'[57] such as an army, natural resources, territory, people and technological advancement. 'Rather than coercing compliance through physical assets, soft power constitutes the "cultivation" of compliance through the creation of goodwill in the international community. The goodwill is essentially cultivated by building a positive image.'[58] Goodwill is definitely a factor absent in the conflict between Iran and Saudi Arabia.

In fact, both countries have failed to a large extent to generate robust soft power to help them achieve their objectives out of this conflict; instead, they have invested heavily in an aggressive hard power arms race and a zero-sum conflict. To advance conflict resolution, both countries need to invest in developing soft power strategies that will help them decrease their dependency on classical conflict strategies (e.g. the arms race, building armed militias) that generally push conflict towards escalation and war.

Building armed militias does not help Iran be accepted in the Arab world; nor does it make it a partner, an objective that Tehran has traditionally attempted to achieve. Iran's image in the Arab countries has never been worse – one major reason for this is the association of Iran with the brutal civil war in Syria. A poll of elite Arab television commentators by the Al Jazeera Center for Studies found that nearly 90 per cent of respondents viewed political relations between Iran and the Arab world as 'bad' or 'very bad', with fewer than one-third expecting any improvement over the next five years.[59] As the main backer of the Assad regime – and having boots on the ground in Syria – Iran is largely seen as equally responsible for the atrocities committed by the regime and the militias supported by Iran, with over 2,000 Iranian and other Shia militia casualties in Syria since 2012.[60]

When the Iranian revolution broke out back in 1979 and raised notions of justice, freedom for Palestine, and standing up against unfair American foreign policy – especially its bias towards backing Israel – Iran found public support all over the Arab world with ordinary citizens. Today, however, Khamenei's pictures, for instance, are raised only by the armed militias in Syria, Iraq and Southern Lebanon. Iran must understand that it cannot pursue a partnership with the Arab world by force or with this type of image. The Iranian model is not appealing to the Arab world today. As Middle East commentator Rami Khouri put it, 'if you ask any Arab youth where he would like to go, they will all tell you they want to go to Dubai. No one wants to go to Tehran.'[61]

Furthermore, during my extensive analysis of Arab uprisings since 2011, I was frequently asked by the international media whether those uprisings were leading to a 'Turkish democracy' model but was never asked if Arab youth were demanding an 'Iranian democracy'.

The Iranian involvement in the war in Syria has significantly damaged Iran's image in the region and in the world. The cost in terms of soft power has been incredibly high, and it will therefore take Iran serious work to recover its image. A major factor that positioned Iran to gain sympathy in the region and the rest of the world was Saddam Hussein's use of chemical weapons against them during the 1980–8 war between the two countries. Iran can no longer play the role of victim of chemical weapons after being the primary ally and backer of the Assad regime, which massacred its own people with exactly the same chemical weapons that Iran suffered from during its war with Saddam Hussein.[62]

A chief reason for Iran's failure to build successful soft power in the Arab world is the mixed messages it sends to the region. Some of its rhetoric calls for peace and dialogue with the Arab countries, yet other times there are calls for taking pride in claiming Iran to be in control of four Arab capitals. These mixed messages have undermined Iranian credibility in the region and significantly damaged its soft power. While Iran's foreign minister, Javad Zarif, has advocated dialogue and understanding in *The New York Times*, other Iranian officials speak of control and dominance in the region. Zarif says,

> The establishment of a collective forum for dialogue in the Persian region, to facilitate engagement, is long overdue . . . regional dialogue should be based on generally recognized principles and shared objectives, notably respect for sovereignty, territorial integrity and political independence of all states; inviolability of international boundaries; non-interference in internal affairs; peaceful settlement of disputes; impermissibility of threat or use of force; and promotion of peace, stability, progress and prosperity in the region.[63]

On the other hand, Ali Reza Zakani, Tehran city representative in the Iranian parliament, commented after the Shia Houthis gained control of the Yemeni capital, Sanaa, that four Arab capitals were ruled by Iran. He said '[t]hree Arab capitals have today ended up in the hands of Iran and belong to the Islamic Iranian revolution'.[64] He went on to state that '[t]he Yemeni revolution will not be confined to Yemen alone. It will extend, following its success, into Saudi territories. The Yemeni-Saudi vast borders will help accelerate its reach into the depths of Saudi land.'[65] Furthermore, Ali Younesi, top advisor to President Hassan Rouhani, was quoted making a similar statement – regarding the Iraqi capital this time – proclaiming that 'Baghdad is our capital, the centre of our culture and identity – today as in the past.'[66] In addition, Iran's Major General Mohammad Hossein Baqeri said, as cited by the Iranian Tasnim news agency, 'One day, we may need bases on the coasts of Yemen and Syria, and we need the necessary infrastructures for it under the international maritime law.'[67]

Contradictory rhetoric can seriously damage a country's credibility in the international arena. In fact, such statements help Iran's rival, Saudi Arabia, whose leadership maintains that 'we don't know who we talk to in Iran', implying that talks are ineffective and harmful to peace and dialogue between the two parties.

Partnerships with regional actors are not made by building armed militias or spreading chaos in the region. Iran has the full legitimate right to aspire to be a regional power, but this can only be achieved by partnerships, not by creating instability. In fact, Iran could lose control of its own borders if instability in the neighbouring countries becomes entrenched. Conflicts always have the potential to spill over into neighbouring areas, and Iran is not immune.

Unfortunately, Iran's mixed messages seem to reflect a structural division within Iran itself, which makes dialogue and accommodation with the region quite challenging. In this regard, Afshin Molavi argues that Rouhani

> hails from the Rafsanjani camp that believes in pragmatic engagement with Gulf Arab states, not confrontation. But the powerful IRGC is less interested in rapprochement with GCC states. This view is seemingly shared by Iran's most powerful figure, Supreme Leader Ayatollah Ali Khamenei.[68]

This seems to suggest that the change should come from either the conservative and powerful Supreme Leader or the IRGC or, preferably, both actors.

Saudi Arabia is equally in need of reforming its soft power strategy if it wants to contain Iranian intervention and find a constructive resolution to the conflict. Saudi Arabia cannot counter Iranian influence in the region only by building hard power and fighting proxy wars. The confrontational strategy that Riyadh adopts towards Iran needs that global factor, which can be achieved by mastering the role of soft power. Gallarotti and Al-Filali make the argument that

> historically, a principal and the most consistent source of Saudi power at the domestic, regional and global levels has not been revenues from oil, but the cultural power that inheres in a nation that is both the capital of the Muslim and Arab worlds.[69]

To develop an effective soft power strategy, Saudi Arabia needs to rid itself of the enormous burden that it carries globally, which is the brand of Wahhabism. Whether Riyadh agrees and regardless of how this has developed, Wahhabism has been linked globally to terrorism, and Saudi Arabia will not be able to gain world sympathy or the support it needs to counter Iran as long as this association of Wahhabism and terrorism exists. This link is explained by former Saudi intelligence chief, Prince Turki Al Faisal, as follows:

> cancers cells, where do they come from? They come from healthy cells in the body, but the rest of the body is healthy. So, yes, ISIS [Islamic State in Iraq and Sham] does some of the things that can be pointed to as being similar to what we do, but we have a judicial system.[70]

Reforming the role of the clergy in politics can be one significant way of addressing this association and building a different soft power brand. In fact, Saudi Crown Prince Mohammed Bin Salman (MBS) did exactly that in 2017, as he curbed the religious police, sacked thousands of imams and launched a new centre for moderation to censor 'fake and extremist texts'.[71] As he explained to foreign investors, '[w]e are only returning to what we used to be, to moderate Islam, open to the world and all religions'.[72] Despite these moves to moderate and limit the influence of radical clergy, MBS has failed to convince many observers that the measures were taken for the right reason; instead, they have been seen merely as a step to consolidate his power. Admittedly, MBS's measures targeted not only the radical clergy but also the moderates who – if the reform was done for the right reason – would have been his natural allies to limit the influence of the radical clerics. Only three months after becoming crown prince, MBS arrested moderate and very popular clerics like Sheikh Salman Al Ouda, Awad al-Qarni, and more than a dozen others. According to Human Rights Watch, the arrests were 'politically motivated' and are 'another sign that Mohammad bin Salman has no real interest in improving his country's record on free speech and the rule of law'.[73] Furthermore, their Middle East director, Sarah Leah Whitson said, 'Saudis' alleged efforts to tackle extremism are all for show if all the government does is jail people for their political views'.[74] *The Economist* made a similar argument claiming that 'Arab leaders are acting much like Kemal Ataturk, Turkey's dictator in the early 20th century, who abolished the caliphate and sharia, and banned traditional garb, all while consolidating his own power.'[75]

Lifting the ban on women driving in Saudi Arabia was another attempt by the Crown Prince to appear as a reformer and consolidate his power. Allowing women to drive in Saudi Arabia should not be mistaken for democracy or genuine political reform. In the words of Stéphane Lacroix, '[t]hough mostly popular, the modernizing reforms have little to do with empowering civil society or promoting democratic governance. They are better understood as a bid to make the Saudi leadership yet another "modernizing autocrat" in the region.'[76] Allowing women to drive and to a attend the wider variety of entertainment options now available in the Kingdom is by no means a substitute for the provision of political rights.

There are still other ways that Saudi Arabia can break its association with terrorism, such as by examining its foreign aid policies and what is taught in the religious schools inside the Kingdom and those it supports abroad. Ultimately, Saudi Arabia needs to come up with a convincing strategy that completely and clearly distinguishes it from terrorism. In the words of one Iranian participant in a track two workshop, '[t]he world should be allying with us not Saudi Arabia; we allow our citizens to vote, we truly fight terrorism, and definitely allow our women to drive'.[77]

Genuinely reforming Saudi Arabia's soft power requires the Kingdom to crack down on the rampant corruption that has exhausted its bureaucracy, deepened mistrust between the public and their government, and made it difficult for Riyadh to market itself abroad. Regimes cannot fight wars without the solid support of their own publics. It should be noted that there are some 10,000[78] princes in the ruling family, which raises serious concerns over the legitimacy of that family and deepens the mistrust of the people for their government, since members of the ruling family tend to receive state payments. Therefore, Riyadh does not seem to have many options but to fight corruption first. Understanding this need, MBS again launched one of Saudi's biggest campaigns in decades to 'fight corruption'. In November 2017, MBS arrested dozens of Saudi princes and ex-ministers in the Ritz-Carlton hotel in Riyadh. Among those arrested was Saudi billionaire Prince Al-Waleed Bin Talal and Prince Miteb Bin Abdullah, the head of the National Guard.[79]

This massive purge was seen by many independent analysts as a 'consolidation of power by Crown Prince Mohammed bin Salman, who seems to be systematically removing potential challengers to his power before his succession to the throne'.[80] According to Gulf affairs expert Bruce Riedel,

> the decision by Saudi King Salman bin Abdul-Aziz Al Saud to sack Minister of National Guard Prince Mutaib bin Abdullah, the favorite son of the late King Abdullah, is intended to remove a potential power rival of his own favorite son, Crown Prince Mohammed bin Salman.[81]

Fighting corruption has historically been used as a convenient excuse to consolidate power and marginalise rivals. For example, 'President Xi Jinping has used a similar anti-corruption theme to replace a generation of party and military leaders and to alter the collective leadership style adopted by recent Chinese rulers'.[82] It could be fairly argued that MBS's anti-corruption campaign was anything but fighting corruption – at least this was how it came across to many observers of the Saudi political scene. To settle the corruption charges against the princes, MBS negotiated individually with each one of them the amount they had to pay to be released – some reports claim that Al-Waleed bin Talal alone was requested to pay $6 billion. The fact that the charges were negotiated this way, rather than via an institutional and judicial approach, is likely to cause more damage to Saudi Arabia's soft power. MBS's campaign and the way he is treating powerful individuals within the Kingdom is in fact creating enemies internally that could negatively affect Saudi's policy to confront Iran.

To make things worse for MBS, in the midst of this anti-corruption campaign *The Wall Street Journal* reported that the Crown Prince was 'identified as the buyer of record-breaking da Vinci'. The Crown Prince has arguably 'used a proxy to purchase the 500-year-old "Salvator Mundi"' for $450.3 million.[83] Furthermore, *The New York Times* reported at a similar time that the Crown Prince was the buyer of the most expensive house in the world, the Chateau Louis XIV in France: 'A $300 million chateau is one of a string of extravagant purchases for a prince who is cracking down on ill-gotten wealth and preaching fiscal austerity.'[84]

This is certainly not the most effective or fairest way for Saudi Arabia to fight corruption, enact meaningful reforms, or strengthen its soft power to counter Iranian expansion. Riyadh must engage in a genuine and utterly sincere fight against corruption, no matter where it exists, in order to win the minds and hearts not only of the Saudi public but globally as well.

Since the 11 September attacks in the United States, Saudi Arabia had not faced an event more damaging to its image abroad as the murder of Saudi journalist and *Washington Post* columnist Jamal Khashoggi in the Saudi consulate in Istanbul in October 2018. It is rare to find the international community so united in the way it responded to the heinous crime of killing a journalist inside a diplomatic mission, which is supposed to serve its citizens rather than assist in their murder. It will take Saudi Arabia's soft power years if not decades to recover from the damage this crime has caused.

Another area Saudi Arabia will need to address to strengthen its efforts to contain Iran is how it manages relationships with its allies. It has developed a reputation for expecting its allies to fully adopt whatever strategy it develops to manage the conflict with Iran or other foes – essentially a principle of being 'either with us or against us'. This expected conformity with Riyadh's position does not leave a margin for allies to manage their own national priorities. Saudi Arabia also expects a similar level of escalation to be taken by allies once Riyadh decides to escalate a situation.

Saudi Arabia should avoid using this approach and try instead to build its own 'coalition of the willing' when alliances need to be built. Leaving a margin for allies to take on independent policies suitable for their own agendas and national priorities will encourage them to join these coalitions. By not allowing allies to adopt independent positions in this way, Saudi Arabia almost lost Oman to Iran when Riyadh cut relations with Tehran in 2016 and asked its allies to follow suit. In the 2017 Gulf crisis, Morocco – an ally in the Saudi-led war in Yemen – refused to cut diplomatic relations with Qatar when asked to do so by Saudi Arabia and the blockading-countries coalition (UAE, Egypt and Bahrain); Morocco actually went on providing Qatar with some food supplies.[85]

Finally, political reform (as discussed earlier in this chapter) will certainly boost Saudi Arabia's soft power if it is done correctly, especially with regards to forging a new social contract that allows for political participation, good governance, transparency and equal rights to all on the basis of citizenship.

Formal Track One Government Mediation

Since neither Iran nor Saudi Arabia has been able to make a breakthrough towards any kind of reconciliation in recent years, particularly since the US invasion of Iraq in 2003, it would be fair to argue that a third-party intervention is needed at this stage. Even if such an intervention cannot resolve the conflict outright, it could at least jar the present impasse and restart the process of seeking a resolution at least by one side. Because this is an inter-state conflict and because the decision-making process ultimately lies with government officials on both sides, formal track one diplomacy is an obvious candidate for such an intervention.

Track one diplomacy is defined as mediation between states, or 'a process whereby communications from one government go directly to the decision-making apparatus of another'.[86] Furthermore, according to De Magalhaes, official diplomacy is '[a]n instrument of foreign policy for the establishment and development of contacts between the governments of different states through the use of intermediaries mutually recognized by the respective parties'.[87] Such mediation is thus distinct from track two in 'its formal application at the state-to-state level. It follows a certain protocol to which every state is a signatory.'[88]

Due to its capacity to enforce agreements, at least in some cases, track one diplomacy 'is usually considered to be the primary peacemaking tool of a state's foreign policy. It is carried out by diplomats, high-ranking government officials, and heads of states and is aimed at influencing the structures of political power.'[89] The activities of regional and global organisations like the United Nations are also included in track one diplomacy.

The strength of track one diplomacy is primarily its 'ability to use political power to influence the direction of negotiations and outcomes', either through military means or international treaties.[90] Official mediation also has the advantage of access to 'material and financial resources that give high leverage and flexibility in negotiations'.[91] In addition, track one efforts benefit from official resources like intelligence gathering and technocratic know-how,[92] as well as clear knowledge of state foreign policies.[93] There are major benefits to pursuing official mediation efforts. Indeed,

> [t]he reason for working with top leadership is that these actors believe that problems emanating from a faulty political structure can best be resolved if those in political power are involved at the negotiation table. It is those people at the highest political level that have the power and authority to change the political structures and bring peace to the nation.[94]

The Iran–Saudi conflict could also benefit from what is called track 'one-and-a-half' which falls between official diplomacy and unofficial negotiations. This is described as 'diplomatic initiatives that are facilitated by unofficial bodies, but directly involve officials from the conflict in question'.[95] While the parties are official representatives, non-officials like private individuals or non-governmental organisations (NGOs) convene the meetings.[96] As a result, 'diplomatic agility and nonpartisanship are some of the main strengths of track one and a half diplomacy'.[97] With the combination of official and unofficial participation, track one-and-a-half diplomacy 'draws on the strengths of track-one diplomacy (the authority and resources) and the strengths of track-two diplomacy (the creativity of unofficial discussions)'.[98]

Track one mediation between Iran and Saudi Arabia has historically been limited for a number of reasons. Primarily, those who are capable of mediating (e.g. Western states like the US and Europe) are not doing so at present; in addition, the parties themselves have not indicated that they are interested in meaningful mediation, as they continue to see the conflict as a zero-sum game. Nevertheless, successful mediation remains a serious possibility, provided that the right mediator can pursue the right strategy at the right time.

This conflict, like any other in the world, is not immune to resolution and successful mediation. The potential mediators can be categorised into three different groups, outlined below.

The West

The interests of Western countries – especially those of the United States[99] – do not necessitate an urgent resolution to this conflict unless it is resolved on the West's own terms. The US is already a primary party to the conflict with Iran, and it is therefore interested in keeping Saudi Arabia as part of an alliance to counter Iran, rather than making peace with Iran. Under the Nixon administration in the 1970s, the 'Twin Pillars' strategy guided US interactions with Iran and Saudi Arabia: strengthening each country with arms sales while encouraging coordination to limit Soviet expansion in the region.[100] Since the removal of the Shah from power in 1979, US strategy has shifted between confrontation and containment of the Iranian regime, while Saudi Arabia has become increasingly important as a stable American ally in a region wracked by conflict.

Any intervention in the region by the US or other Western countries like the United Kingdom and France is generally perceived with a high level of suspicion, which seriously complicates potential mediation led by these actors. Their colonial history in the region undermines any trust of mediation outcomes, due to suspicions that each may be pursuing its own goals by managing the process. Jane Kinninmont of The Elders suggests that Scandinavian countries – who have no colonial history in the region – and other world powers could better serve as mediators in the Iran–Saudi conflict. She explains,

> the process could potentially be facilitated by northern European (e.g. Nordic) countries that have less historical 'baggage' in the region, are seen as neutral brokers and are not involved in the nuclear talks; or it could be facilitated in partnership with non-aligned rising powers, such as Brazil or South Africa.[101]

The United States and other Western countries are unlikely to play much of a role in promoting mediation and conflict resolution between Iran and Saudi Arabia until the West's own conflict with Iran is resolved. The United

States gave at least tepid encouragement for Saudi Arabian outreach to Iran following the nuclear deal with Iran, after which President Obama suggested that regional conflicts 'require us to say to our friends as well as to the Iranians that they need to find an effective way to share the neighborhood and institute some sort of cold peace'.[102] Even here, though, the onus in President Obama's statement is entirely on the Saudi side to come up with some sort of diplomatic initiative.

One of the few exceptions to the position of the West on this conflict has been Germany, which has invested significant diplomatic energy in reducing tensions and promoting mediation between Riyadh and Tehran. Germany's leadership believes that the Iran–Saudi rivalry emboldens terrorists, and the resolution of the conflict could help address one of the root causes of terrorism. In 2015, German Foreign Minister Frank-Walter Steinmeier met with Ayatollah Ali Akbar Hashemi Rafsanjani – one of the founding fathers of the Islamic Republic, the fourth Iranian president, and the man tasked with improving the Republic's relationship with Saudi Arabia after the Iran–Iraq war. In this meeting, Steinmeier pledged to mediate between Iran and Saudi Arabia to reduce the tension between the two countries. When asked about the reason for his intervention, he said, 'Political differences between Iran and Saudi Arabia have resulted in strengthening terrorists in the region, and if these two Islamic countries cooperate, other Islamic countries will also put aside their differences.'[103]

The German position on this conflict exposes the fallacy of the current Western approach of trying to isolate and respond only, rather than being proactive in attempting to resolve the Middle East 'cold war' – one of the primary drivers of terrorism in the Middle East has actually *been* the Iran–Saudi conflict. First, it contributes to the deterioration of security in the region, providing an enabling environment for terrorism in places like Syria, Iraq and Yemen. Second, Iranian expansion in the region was perceived by some fundamentalist groups as a spread of Shia Islam, which triggered violent responses by Sunni extremists. Third, Saudi Arabia found an effective strategy to counter Iranian expansion in advocating Wahhabi ideology, which many considered a catalyst to violent extremism in the region. All this suggests that a tolerant Western attitude towards an Iranian–Saudi conflict constitutes a self-defeating policy for fighting terrorism in the region.

Small-state mediation

In general, small-state mediation can be influential in brokering peace agreements in international conflicts. It proved successful in making breakthroughs in cases like the Israeli–Palestinian conflict, when Norway brokered the Oslo agreement between the two parties in 1993. Despite the shortcomings of the Oslo Accords and the unsuccessful implementation of the agreement on the ground, the achievement of an initial agreement still demonstrated that a small state can be trusted as an effective neutral mediator and thus produce helpful agreements.[104] Furthermore, Qatar's intervention in the 2008 Lebanese conflict prevented a looming civil war: the conflict had already begun to unfold when Qatar invited all factions to Doha and mediated constantly for ten days. In the end, all parties signed an agreement before returning to Beirut, de-escalating the tension.[105] Despite the general sense of instability in Lebanon, the 2008 agreement – brokered by a small neutral state – prevented a violent clash between the different parties.

In the case of the Iran–Saudi conflict, scholars believe there is room for small-state mediation. Steven Wright, a Gulf Studies expert at Hamad Bin Khalifa University, suggests that Oman would be ideal to play this role, as Oman is a GCC member and maintains good relations with Iran.[106] Furthermore, Peter Alsis *et al.* suggest that Oman's independent foreign policy is an additional advantage to enabling it to mediate between Iran and Saudi Arabia.

> Oman has a unique role in the region. It is generally accommodating towards Iran, has tensions with Saudi Arabia, close ties to the UK, and serves as a major strategic ally for U.S. military and diplomatic interests. As a result, it often plays the role of intermediary and has some diplomatic leverage over Iran.[107]

Qatar could have been a candidate for small-state mediation before the start of its own crisis with Saudi Arabia, which led to a Saudi-led blockade of the country in June 2017. In fact, Emir of Qatar Sheikh Tamim bin Hamad al Thani called for better relations between GCC members states and Iran during a speech before the United Nations General Assembly in September 2015. Importantly, he suggested Qatar as the mediator for future talks between Iran and Saudi Arabia.[108] Soon after that, Iranian foreign minister Jawad Zarif echoed the Qatari Emir's proposal.[109]

In light of the GCC crisis, Kuwait is positioned to play this role and mediate between Iran and Saudi Arabia. In fact, Kuwait has played a critical mediation role between Qatar and Saudi Arabia, the UAE and Bahrain during the ongoing Gulf crisis and helped to successfully resolve the previous crisis between these states in 2013–14. Kuwait emerged as the only credible candidate for mediation in the first few months of the ongoing dispute, with all parties warmly welcoming the role of Emir Sabah Al Sabah. Kuwait is a GCC member and maintains strong relations with Saudi Arabia; at the same time, due to its sizable Shia minority of around 30 per cent of the population, as well as its geographic position, it also maintains special relations with Iran.[110] This positions Kuwait to play an intermediary role between Riyadh and Tehran.

Additionally, all three of these potential mediators benefit from having regional legitimacy. All three are GCC members and share geography, history and culture with both Iran and Saudi Arabia. In other words, they are stakeholders in the regional system, and peace, stability and mutual collaboration lie at the heart of their national interests.

Despite these encouraging signs about the potential for effective small-state mediation, there are nevertheless limitations to this approach. For small-state mediation to be effective, the parties themselves must be ready to talk. They must come to understand that prolonging or even escalating conflict is not helping their ultimate objectives. The conflict itself needs to exact enough of a cost for the parties to be willing and interested in talking. In his argument about 'ripeness' and the best timing for mediation, Zartman suggests that it is when the parties reach what he called a 'mutually hurting stalemate' that offering an enticing opportunity for a cost-reducing agreement can be most effective.[111] Conflict ripeness would provide suitable conditions for countries like Kuwait, Oman and Qatar to intervene and mediate.

In this case, small states could be the most suited to pursuing a facilitation strategy that does not intervene in the decision making directly, but rather limits its role to making mediation logistically and administratively possible.[112] While small states can attempt to mediate in situations where parties to the conflict do not see the advantage of talking, it is obviously more challenging for them to succeed if the powerful parties refuse to move from their original positions.

Regional powers mediation

As one Saudi official explained, '[w]e need a powerful mediator who can oversee the dialogue and guarantee the implementation of the results if mediation is to work with Iran'.[113] When talking about 'powerful mediators', the West and particularly the United States tend to be mentioned, as was the case in the quote above. They can certainly play a role in mediation, but there are limitations to their abilities (as discussed earlier), which makes it unlikely at the present time while the existing structure of this conflict persists that they would be seen as suitable mediators. However, potential mediating countries that are powerful and are from the region – as suggested by Mehran Kamrava – include Turkey and Pakistan.[114]

Turkey

Though Turkey operates a different foreign policy from both Iran and Saudi Arabia, it still shares a *strategic interest* with both countries that cannot easily be ignored. It is a fate of geography that Turkey lies within their spheres of influence, which makes the national interest of all three parties overlap in several areas including security, economics and energy. In February 2016, Turkish Prime Minister Ahmet Davotuglu visited Tehran and stated,

> [w]e may have different views but we cannot change our history or our geography . . . It is extremely important for Turkey and Iran to develop some common perspectives in order to end our region's fight among brothers, to stop the ethnic and sectarian conflicts.[115]

The interests in common of the three countries places successful mediation by Turkey within its own national interest: to help instigate an environment of peace, security and collaboration rather than one of instability, war and violence.

In addition to their common interests, Turkey overall enjoyed good relations with both Iran and Saudi Arabia, which further qualifies it to mediate in this conflict. In December 2015, Turkey and Saudi Arabia agreed on the need to set up a 'strategic cooperation council' to strengthen military, economic and investment cooperation between the two countries.[116] The relationship between Turkey and Saudi Arabia suffered a serious setback with the murder of Saudi journalist Jamal Khashoggi in the Saudi consulate in Istanbul but this is unlikely to have a strategic impact on the future relationship between Ankara and Riyadh. In August 2017, Iran's army chief visited Turkey, and, together with Turkish President Tayyip Erdogan, both parties announced an agreement to 'boost military cooperation'.[117] Among other things, the two parties also agreed to 'increase counter-terrorism intelligence sharing'.[118]

In a mediation role between Iran and Saudi Arabia, Turkey would also benefit from knowledge of the region and the specifics of conflict, culture and political systems contained within. Ellen Laipson, president emeritus of the Stimson Center, writes that Turkey benefits from knowledge of the 'deeper dynamics at work',[119] which enables Ankara to take on this role. Moreover, Laipson suggests that Turkey could also benefit from pairing with Iraq – whose Prime Minister has offered his services as mediator – to make the case for mediation between Iran and Saudi Arabia even stronger. With Erdogan being Sunni and Abadi a Shia, they could complement each other. A major benefit of this pairing or alliance of mediators would be ownership of the conflict resolution. As Laipson explains, 'Turkey and Iraq's efforts represents a desirable long-term goal: regional states taking greater responsibility for regional problems.'[120]

Last but not least, a mediator such as Turkey could help rebalance the regional order, which was shifted to Iran's advantage following the American invasion of Iraq and Baghdad moving towards Iran's position. With Turkey part of the final arrangement, it is an equally powerful player to help balance the relationship in a way that serves peace and stability in the region. Turkey's foreign policy in the past few years seems to suggest that Ankara is in fact attempting to balance the regional order, which could provide the foundation for a new understanding between Tehran and Riyadh. As Turkish political analyst Pinar Tremblay explains, 'for now, Ankara is more interested in balancing Saudi Arabia and Iran against each other rather than in mediating between them'.[121] The biggest advantage of a balance is in curbing polarisation in the region; reaching a solution in an asymmetric power conflict is difficult as the more powerful party becomes less incentivised to make concessions or collaborate to reach solutions.

Pakistan

Pakistan was the first and possibly the only country to intervene between Iran and Saudi Arabia after the diplomatic crisis that followed the Saudi execution of Shia Sheikh Nimr al-Nimr in January 2016 and the Iranian burning of the Saudi embassy in Tehran. Shortly after Pakistani intervention, Iran's Supreme Leader, Ayatollah Khameini, publicly condemned the attacks against the Saudi embassy for the first time, a gesture interpreted as resulting from Pakistani mediation.[122] With its nuclear capabilities, Pakistani involvement would significantly change the balance of power between Iran and Saudi Arabia if it decided to join any future confrontation, and for this reason the effect of a potential Pakistani role in mediation cannot be ignored in both times of war and times of peace in the Middle East.

It would be difficult to understand the Iran–Saudi conflict without examining Pakistan's position. When General Pervez Musharaf toppled Pakistani President Nawaz Sharif in a coup in 1999, the latter was later flown in a Saudi royal plane along with his family members to his exile in Jeddah in Saudi Arabia.[123] Furthermore, 'Pakistan deployed thousands of soldiers in Saudi Arabia in the 1980s to deter any aggression by Iran against the Kingdom, for example, and Saudi Arabian money has helped bankroll Pakistan's nuclear weapons program.'[124] Though the Pakistani parliament voted against joining Riyadh in the war in Yemen, the text that parliament voted on still promised to 'stand shoulder to shoulder' with Saudi Arabia in the event of an invasion or any threat to Islam's holiest sites in Mecca and Medina.[125]

Pakistan takes Saudi peace and security seriously, as the political stability of a reliable and trusted ally directly affects the stability of Islamabad. Saudi Arabia hosts 2.2 million Pakistani expatriates[126] and is Pakistan's single largest source of remittances.[127] Further strengthening this relationship, as Arif Rafiq puts it,

[i]n times of difficulty, Saudi Arabia has come to Pakistan's aid – for example, by providing oil on deferred payment when Islamabad was hit by U.S. sanctions after conducting nuclear tests in 1998. A severe, existential crisis in Saudi Arabia would shock the Pakistani economy and result in the potential loss of a strategic security partner. From the perspective of an ally, Islamabad sees Riyadh's escalating conflict with Tehran as injurious to Saudi interests.[128]

In addition, '[p]ost-revolution Iran has been closer to India than Pakistan. And in the 1990s, Iran and Pakistan were on opposite sides of a proxy war in Afghanistan'.[129]

Despite the close and historic ties between Pakistan and Saudi Arabia, Islamabad remains careful not to escalate conflict with Iran, as there is much at stake for Pakistan's national interests if the Iran–Saudi conflict escalates to war. Indeed, 10–15 per cent of its population are Shia,[130] and any sectarian Iran–Saudi confrontation could reflect itself on already very tense Sunni–Shia relations in Pakistan. When Saudi Arabia executed Shia cleric Shaikh Nimr al-Nimr in January 2016, prominent Tehran-backed Shia groups protested against the execution, even as a Saudi-backed segment within Pakistan's Sunni community supported it.[131] The last thing that Pakistan wants to do is become a sectarian Sunni–Shia battleground.

Furthermore, Pakistan shares a 909 kilometre-long border[132] with Iran, meaning that instability along this border could cause a serious threat to Pakistan's national interests. Instead, then, Pakistan sees a real possibility of living as 'good neighbours' with Iran.[133] Pakistan has also proposed a 'free trade agreement'[134] with Tehran, as the government sees serious business potential there, especially after the lifting of major sanctions with the advent of the Iran nuclear deal.[135]

Given its interdependencies with Iran and Saudi Arabia, Pakistan will have to make every effort to avoid having to pick one party over the other. It has a vested interest in not allowing this conflict to escalate, so that it does not find itself a battleground for Iran–Saudi or Sunni–Shia conflict. Thus, mediation and a peaceful resolution to the Iran–Saudi conflict lies at the heart of Pakistan's national interest. In addition, successful mediation of this conflict will ensure that Pakistan is not distracted from its primary rival, India.

In line with this policy of non-alignment, Pakistan turned down a request from Saudi Arabia in April 2015 to join the fighting in Yemen. Pakistani lawmakers voted unanimously in favour of a resolution that 'Pakistan should maintain neutrality' in the Yemeni conflict so as 'to be able to play a proactive diplomatic role to end the crisis'.[136] Pakistan could also play a significant role in any future peacekeeping forces whether in Yemen or any other Iran–Saudi related conflict. In fact, 'Pakistan has a long history of providing excellent forces to United Nations peacekeeping missions'[137] and is seen as being 'experienced in managing Sunni–Shia sectarian tensions, which will be crucial to any peace process in Yemen',[138] or in any other conflict involving sectarian divisions.

Track Two

Despite being the official channel to resolve international conflicts, track one diplomacy is limited in what it can achieve in intractable conflicts like that of Iran and Saudi Arabia. Indeed, official foreign policy can be disconnected from some parties to the conflict, often failing to represent less powerful segments of the country in question since foreign policy decisions tend to be made from the top down rather than being based in grassroots support.[139] Furthermore, direct track one diplomacy cannot take place unless relations exist between the governments in conflict.[140] Official actors are also sometimes constrained by government positions and thus cannot seek the more creative solutions to conflicts characteristic of track two efforts.[141] Additionally, track one diplomacy is influenced by electoral cycles and so cannot always provide long-term solutions.[142] To compensate for these shortcomings, track two emerges with an indispensable role in the overall management of international conflicts. Track two approaches complement rather than replace track one efforts and could contribute to better management and resolution of the Iran–Saudi conflict.

Track two diplomacy was first defined, in a 1981 *Foreign Policy* article by American diplomat Joseph Montville, as

> unofficial, non-structured interaction. It is always open-minded, often altruistic . . . strategically optimistic, based on best case analysis. Its underlying assumption is that actual or potential conflict can be resolved or eased by appealing to common human capabilities to respond to good will and reasonableness.[143]

Montville later expanded this definition to describe track two diplomacy as

> an unofficial, informal interaction between members of adversary groups or nations that aims to develop strategies, influence public opinion, and organize human and material resources in ways that might help resolve their conflict. It must be understood that track two diplomacy is in no way a substitute for official, formal, 'track one' government-to-government or leader-to-leader

relationships. Rather, track two activity is designed to assist official leaders by compensating for the constraints imposed upon them by the psychologically understandable need for leaders to be – or at least to be seen to be – strong, wary, and indomitable in the face of the enemy.[144]

The original organisers of track two diplomacy were primarily 'university-based "scholar-practitioners" who in the 1960s sought to better manage violent intergroup conflicts by applying new theories of inter-group relations to their transformation'.[145] Track two diplomacy has since developed, however, to involve many participants outside of academia with a view to influencing government policy. As a result, '[t]his second generation of practitioners is more applied than theoretical and, as a result, a gap between evolving social-psychological research on inter-group conflict and the practice of track two diplomacy has emerged'.[146]

There are several types of track two activities that are designed to affect intractable conflicts. However, three types seem to have been practiced widely in dealing with Middle East conflicts:[147]

1. *Complementary negotiation activities*: A small group meets in a similar fashion to official negotiations. This group engages in discussions that track one actors cannot for a variety of reasons. The parties explore options that governments cannot or will not – perhaps being unwilling to show signs of weakness or to communicate through official channels with the other side. This type of negotiation activity is not a replacement for track one negotiation but complementary to it.
2. *Educational and exploratory activities*: Large groups, sometimes numbering thirty or forty individuals, meet with the objective of exchanging views and exploring similarities and commonalities. The participants are not negotiating but rather exploring options and educating themselves about the other party's priorities and red lines.
3. *Networking and social activities*: The objective of this type of track two activity is primarily to give the participants a chance to meet each other and develop social relationships, since their conflict zones do not allow them to do so. Networking and personal relationships may provide a framework for impact on a grassroot level and the development of conflict resolution ideas.

Track two diplomacy has differentiated itself from other types of conflict resolution models by developing its own models, dynamics and resolution mechanisms. Perhaps at the most basic level, track two diplomacy differs from official, or track one, efforts at conflict resolution because it assumes that 'protracted social conflicts cannot be resolved without paying attention to the inter-societal dimensions and social identity needs of the conflicting parties'.[148]

Track two diplomacy can further be distinguished from track one due to its focus on process rather than outcome.[149] Though track two dialogues rarely resolve conflicts, they serve to create new relationships among warring factions, as well as to build trust and understanding at both the grassroots and elite levels.[150] Making progress even at the unofficial level would be a great achievement for track two work between Iran and Saudi Arabia, yet would not necessarily fully resolve the conflict.

Because track two dialogues are not as public as track one efforts, they allow officials to explore potential solutions without taking political risks.[151] Track two diplomacy is thus in many ways more flexible than track one:

> among the varied goals of track two are to provide a safe, off-the-record venue for dialogue; to create the conditions necessary for formal agreements to 'take hold'; increase communication, understanding and trust among polarized groups; break-down the stereotypes and dehumanizing cognitions that permit the partisans to wage the conflict destructively; and to develop consensus-based proposals that can be transferred to the track one processes.[152]

In fact, Çuhadar and Dayton divide track two diplomacy into 'outcome-focused' and 'process-focused' initiatives:

> While the former is designed to generate proposals that can be used or adopted in official policymaking and negotiation processes, the latter type has a priority to build relationships, trust, empathy, and mutual understanding among adversaries in order to prepare the groundwork for a widely supported peace to take hold.[153]

Although there is some overlap between these approaches, track two efforts differ in their potential to address social and psychological issues beyond official policy.

Montville describes track two diplomacy as involving 'three interdependent processes'.[154] The first comprises small workshops bringing together representatives from varying factions with the hope of developing new relationships, enhancing understanding of the conflict, and brainstorming means of conflict resolution.[155] The second process involves influencing public opinion to make an end to hostilities more palatable for people on both sides of the conflict.[156] Finally, joint economic development, though not necessary for ceasing hostilities, provides additional support for continued cooperation across factions.[157]

Track two diplomacy is helpful most often in conflicts considered too intractable to be resolved using traditional diplomatic means.[158] As De Vries and Maoz explain,

> [t]hat is because such conflicts tend to involve not only tangible interests (i.e. economic or territorial issues) that can be negotiated, but rather involve values and basic human needs such as personal security, recognition, identity and political participation, which are non-negotiable.[159]

To help communicate messages to official diplomacy,

> [t]rack two participants are expected to have some communication with government policymakers (many participants are often influential former government officials, active and retired military personnel, think tank specialists, and journalists) so that the ideas discussed in the unofficial setting have the prospect both to reflect and to filter into the thinking of official policy circles.[160]

Considering that the goal of track two efforts is ultimately to influence track one negotiations, the distinction between official and non-official dialogue is often blurred. In fact, track two meetings at times receive government support.[161] When the tracks are mixed and governments become involved, even unofficially, the process is sometimes called track 'one-and-a-half' diplomacy. On some occasions, government officials attend unofficial dialogue without participating; they instead listen to the discussion and perhaps take notes. Susan Allen Nan defines track one-and-a-half diplomacy as, 'unofficial interactions between official representatives of states'.[162] When an NGO serves as a mediator between two state or state-like actors, the NGO facilitates a track one-and-a-half process. Track one-and-a-half diplomacy draws on the strengths of track one diplomacy (the authority and resources) as well as those of track two diplomacy (the creativity of unofficial discussions).[163]

Participants in track two dialogues are important instruments of change for popular opinion more broadly. While national and often factional allegiances remain, 'over time some participants have observed that they feel they are now part of a group which thinks differently from those who are outside the process'.[164] Certainly, track two dialogue aids understanding among participants from different backgrounds through two primary means: '1) by allowing participants to get to know each other personally in informal and social settings, helping to break down psychological barriers and stereotypes and 2) by helping individuals better understand their adversaries' threat-perceptions, policies and red-lines'.[165] Although such enhanced understanding will not necessarily lead to resolution of the conflict, it will lead to greater understanding and sensitivity across traditionally adversarial lines.[166] '[D] iplomacy is not just about producing negotiated outcomes but also about influencing how others think'.[167] Changes in policy take time, regardless of whether they come about through track two dialogue efforts,[168] and indeed, '[t]rack two dialogue is a process, not an event'.[169]

However, this rich literature on track two and its role in conflict resolution should be treated carefully when applied in different cultural contexts. The remarkable functionality of track two and its support of track one diplomacy as developed in a Western context may not fully apply to the Iran–Saudi conflict.

For example, Montville argues, 'a principal, if not the principal, role for nongovernmental action is to shape the overall political environment so that leaders might be encouraged to take positive steps toward resolving a conflict'.[170] In both Iran and Saudi Arabia the role of NGOs is extremely limited. Where NGOs exist, they tend to either reflect the government positions or attempt to avoid politics altogether. Both countries have a very centralised, top-down decision-making process wherein NGOs are expected to function in line with this process, rather than outside it. While NGOs might still be able to influence track one diplomacy, they need to have permission from the highest governmental authority first, rather than taking the initiative to influence governments as Western-developed track two literature argues.

Dalia Dassa Kaye describes the impact on participants in the track two dialogue: 'over time some participants have observed that they are now part of a group which thinks differently from those who are outside the process'.[171] This may in fact happen for participants in an Iran–Saudi track two dialogue. However, to state their views and share their perspective publicly could be interpreted as disloyalty to their countries and their leaders, putting them in danger of retaliation. The same limitation applies to Montville's argument about track two dialogue 'influencing public opinion to make an end to hostilities more palatable for people on both sides of the conflict'.[172] In an authoritarian context – as in Iran and Saudi Arabia – the role of public opinion in influencing political decisions is always limited. However, an impact on public opinion can still be relevant when the leadership decides to change policies regarding the conflict. Authoritarian leaders care about the public supporting the decisions they make, as it signals continued loyalty to and support of their leadership. In other words, the impact is felt in supporting conciliatory decisions made by the leadership, not pressing the leadership to make conflict-resolution decisions, which means that track two dialogue is still relevant.

The Iran–Saudi conflict is not a stranger to track two initiatives. Over the past decade, a number of such initiatives have been carried out by different players, from the Gulf region as well as international actors, albeit with limited impact. Below we take stock of the major track two initiatives used in the Iran–Saudi conflict.

The Gulf Research Center

One privately funded major track two dialogue was organised by the Gulf Research Center and its director, Abdulaziz Sager. A steering committee comprising representatives from the GCC, Iran and a Swiss think tank organised eight rounds of discussion, with the first one starting in March 2012.[173] Participants included senior-level non-officials with close ties to policymakers in their respective governments; foreign ministries, at least in the GCC countries, were kept well-informed and were free to send someone to attend in their personal capacities.[174] Two major objectives were outlined: first, identifying disputed issues as well as reaching a better understanding of the national interests of both sides; and second, establishing regular exchanges of views between the two sides to reduce the levels of misperception and uncertainty about each other's intentions.

The Gulf Studies Program at Qatar University

The university organised several track two workshops during the years 2014–17 that involved academics, former diplomats and policy advisors from Iran, Saudi Arabia and the rest of the Gulf countries. One workshop, held in March 2016, was co-sponsored by UK-based think tank Chatham House. A number of participants were formal and informal advisors closely linked to policymakers in Iran and the Arab Gulf countries. Issues discussed included but were not limited to security, sectarianism, proxy wars, rapprochement, and prospects for regional conflict resolution. Meetings were held under the Chatham House rule to give the participants the opportunity to speak freely with no concerns of media attribution of individuals' thoughts, ideas and proposals. The author participated in these workshops and drew his own observations and conclusions.

Center for Regional and International Studies (CIRS), Georgetown University in Qatar

The CIRS held one workshop on an 'Iran–GCC Dialogue',[175] another on the potential for a 'Strategic Security Forum',[176] and one public event on 'Managing the Saudi–Iranian regional rivalry'.[177] Participants were mostly academics, along with former diplomats and Middle East think tank representatives. They came from Iran and several Arab Gulf countries, with each workshop involving approximately twenty participants. Workshops were held under the Chatham House rule to give the participants a relaxing environment in which to talk openly. Issues discussed included conflict causes, dialogue, perceptions, regional and proxy conflicts, and prospects of rapprochement. The author participated in these workshops and drew his own observations on the debate and interaction between the participants.

CAPRO

The Center for Applied Research in Partnership with the Orient (CAPRO) in Germany, in cooperation with the EastWest Institute's Middle East and North Africa department in Brussels, established a track two dialogue in

2015 to exchange perspectives and perceptions between current and former diplomats, policy analysts and security experts. This initiative entails workshops and publications on issues of mutual concerns. In the first year of the project, dialogue meetings were dedicated to 'Iranian and Saudi perspectives on ISIL (Islamic State in Syria and the Levant)', as well as 'Iranian and Saudi perspectives on the refugee crisis'. Consecutive workshops were held on topics such as 'the post-oil economy', 'environmental challenges', 'media and public discourse', 'security threats of 2018', 'grounds of economic cooperation' and 'knowledge production and knowledge exchange'.[178] The author participated in this project and drew his own observations and conclusions.

This track two initiative has deliberately been focused on tackling specific themes rather than dealing with the larger issues of the conflict between Riyadh and Tehran. A very specific contribution like this, though initially small, can help build channels of communication between the two sides and encourage a collaborative relationship on other issues in the future. Successful workshops on this level would reinforce the idea that rapprochement is possible if the right approach is used.

In addition to these four examples, the author also participated in several other track two initiatives including, but not limited to, those held by the Arab Center for Research and Policy Studies in Doha, the European Iran Research Group (EIRG), and the International Institute for Strategic Studies (IISS).

Achievements

The achievements of these types of workshop that have been held between Iran and its Arab Gulf neighbours, including Saudi Arabia, have been modest, given the limitations in this particular context. Nevertheless, holding this type of interaction on a senior level, given the high levels of mistrust and polarisation, was in itself an achievement. Sager says, 'the concept itself [of engaging in dialogue] has not been questioned'.[179] This is especially important, given that foreign ministries (at least those from the GCC) were notified of the dialogue. Secondly, as Sager explained, 'the process has been useful in the assessment of current developments and in gaining a better understanding of how such developments are seen and understood from the other side. The discussions have contributed to more nuanced and differentiated perspectives.'[180]

Coming to a better understanding of the conflict developments was not limited to discussion during the workshop. This educational process continued after the participants returned to their home countries, where they found themselves serving as 'sources of verification' to the conflict developments. As one workshop organiser put it to me, 'we have clearly seen how those we brought together, while sticking to their viewpoints, stayed in contact and saw each other as sources of verification if certain developments were observed in the respective other country'.[181]

Abdullah Baabood, organiser of the Qatar University workshops, argues that the impact of track two workshops at the policymaking level is very difficult to measure and not easily proven; however, given the level of participants and their links to policymakers, one can assume that there is an impact, at least in terms of advice and consultations.[182] In one of the workshops, for example, I had a lengthy discussion with an Iranian participant who later shared with me that he informally advises senior level policymakers.

Some impact was also observed on the participants in the workshops, especially when the discussions focused on specific issues and practical points, as common understanding started to develop and opinion began to converge.[183] The human dimension contributed to easing the tension and allowing an opportunity to interact. One organiser explained to me, 'meetings help to humanize the "other" and his or her conflicting viewpoints. It is one thing to read about certain viewpoints but something else to personally meet someone who holds and presents these views.'[184] In some cases, communication started to develop between participants at the workshops and afterwards (observed by both the organisers and the author). This could have a significant impact, especially in the long term; these personal communications could help improve management of the conflict if the individuals involved rise to positions of power in their respective countries. As Jamal Khashoggi explained,

> there is something to be said about the potential benefits of track two diplomacy between the two countries. Track two is great for public relations and won't cost the government anything. Who knows, it might sow the seeds for some real change in the future.[185]

In line with Khashoggi's views, another organiser described his/her observation with regards the impact on personal relationships as follows,

> what we have always observed is that during workshop sessions, discussions can be at times heated. But all get back to proper socializing mode during joint dinners and conversations on the sidelines. These kind of arguably unintended side-effects must be given room to happen in any meaningful initiative.[186]

Changing public opinion, at least in a modest way, could be another area of potential impact of these workshops. Jamal Khashoggi, as a highly influential columnist in the Arab world and participant in a number of track two workshops with Iranians, wrote a piece in the mainstream Saudi-published Arabic outlet *al-Hayat* to introduce the concept to the public, and discussed the potential improvement of conflict management and limitations. In his words,

> It was an encouraging start for track two between Saudi Arabia and Iran, but it requires patience and an understanding that it is a long journey between older than three thousand year-old neighbours. So why not try it even during the confrontation between our countries?[187]

Limitations

Despite the modest progress, limitations to track two work in this context remain great. One main reason for the limited impact on the overall conflict is, according to one of the organisers, because of the nature of the track two activities. The organiser says,

> in the short and medium term, we do not expect to see meaningful change in the tensions which could be traced back to our project. However, this long-term effect can happen once the political environment allows participants to spread the word about the need to seek dialogue and an exchange of views in order to be able to build bridges with adversaries rather than accentuating conflict.[188]

However, the organiser also alerts us that 'such dialogue meetings can make the situation even worse, should participants come together and simply reiterate the official line without any willingness to think "outside the box"'.[189]

The biggest hurdle to impactful track two work is the authoritarian nature of the political system on both sides of the conflict. Centralisation of decision making and the firm grip of the political regimes in both countries leave little room for non-governmental initiatives like track two to work and prosper. Though held in a territory outside of Iran and Saudi Arabia, the presence of the state was clear during the proceedings of track two meetings in Doha, Qatar, as per the author's observations of the dynamics in the workshops. Saudi participants rarely accepted invitations to join these meetings, as their government generally rejected dialogue and other types of interaction with Iranians. Participants feared repercussions back home if they participated on their own. Iranians, on the other hand, were generally eager to participate, yet tended to come to the dialogue with one position across the board, which was closely linked to the government line.[190] When I asked about this alignment with the Iranian government's position, they generally replied that this is the way they see the conflict. However, some scholars told me that Iranian participants were concerned about what they might face back home, as the government watches what they say.[191] Nevertheless, as time went by and trust started to develop in these workshops, some participants began to open up and engage in discussing tough issues.

Abdullah Baabood confirms similar concerns regarding Iranian participants, explaining 'they are fearful of any backlash from their own governments of what they can say at such forums and they tend to largely stick to the official line'.[192] Mehran Kamrava also agrees that such concerns make track two work in this context particularly difficult. He explains, 'these are academics, essayists, etc., who have no real transformative or executive powers and are essentially already under pressure in their own respective countries'.[193]

In addition to state control on both sides, some participants argue that rapprochement between Iran and its Arab neighbours is vetoed by the 'superpowers', and thus track two does not have a chance of making a real difference. An Iranian journalist and researcher on Middle East affairs[194] who participated in one of the track two workshops organised by Georgetown University in Qatar, noted,

> [w]e organized a large number of track two meetings in the late 1990s between Arabs and Iranians, and we were hopeful that such meetings would lead to further collaboration and better understanding between the two

sides. We established an Arab–Iranian friendship society in order to insti-
tutionalize the activities and make them more sustainable. We also tried to
have an Arab–Iranian–Turkish gathering since they are presently the major
three components of this region. We met over 100 intellectuals in Doha's
Sheraton Hotel from Iran and the Arab region for one week, for example.
Unfortunately, the encounters did not last for a long time and no concrete
results were produced.[195]

The same Iranian researcher provided two major reasons for the failure of the
large-scale encounters to produce results:

> An Arab–Iranian understanding is not allowed by the super powers. In addi-
> tion, the meetings were politicized with a high level of state intervention.
> They were not truly track two because of state intervention in the talks.
> Among the participants were intelligence agents, especially those related to
> the Iraqi Baath party.[196]

In addition to the political problems hindering the effectiveness of track
two dialogue, Abdullah Baabood points to other technical and organisational
challenges that prevented the workshops from reaching their full potential.
In his words,

> [s]uch forums tend to be short in terms of days and much time is devoted to
> delivering speeches or papers, resulting in less time being available for discus-
> sions and getting to know each other. Some participants tend to go on speak-
> ing for a long time, regurgitating previously held positions and official lines.
> Presentations and papers tend to be general and not focused on the issues in
> question.[197]

Another challenge the workshops faced was the dynamics that sometimes
drove the debate, such as 'us' against 'them'. During my conversation with one
of the Iranian participants, he mentioned a perception that the 'other side'
hailed from different Arab Gulf countries, all attacking the Iranian position,
leaving him no choice but to defend those positions. This perception pushed
the Iranian participants to remain 'united' in their views, especially given
that the discussion was happening in one of those Gulf countries (Qatar). It

would be useful for the organisers to invite scholars from outside the conflict parties to break up this particular dynamic.

Recommendations

Almost all interviewed workshop organisers of track two dialogues between Iran and Saudi Arabia recognise the limitations of the model and its inability to produce concrete results that could affect the conflict. Sager concedes that no concrete impact was made, and thus suggests that further adjustment to the model is necessary. In particular, he suggests, track two initiatives will need to be upgraded to track one-and-a-half to have a greater impact. In addition, the two parties will need to have more direct and open discussions in order to facilitate the necessary steps to move towards track one-and-a-half.[198] 'When all key issues have been identified and understood by both parties, the dialogue will then need to move to the next level, track one-and-a-half,' he added.

Seyed Hossein Mousavian agrees that there is a need to upgrade the dialogue from track two to track one-and-a-half. To this end, a group of experts along with some official policymakers could work together in meetings to define mechanisms of regional collaboration such as terrorism, security, Saudi concerns, Iran's concerns, Iran's expansion, and economic cooperation. Such talks could find solutions even to the most difficult issues, like the American bases in the Gulf that have historically been seen as a threat to Iran. For example, an agreement could be put forward for the American bases to leave in ten to fifteen years after trust has been established, Mousavian added.[199]

Another improvement to the model could involve the parties revising their current approach, which starts with soft issues to build trust and then moves on to central disagreements. Instead, track two could try to deal with the core issues facing the parties first. Any progress that could be made on this level would be treated as significant, unlike discussions of only minor issues where the parties could find themselves stuck. Mehran Kamrava reflects on his experience of organising track two workshops saying, 'in hindsight, I would not have tackled "soft" issues of popular perceptions, cultural commonalities, and dialogue per se, but "hard" issues of security, mutual threats directed at one another, state-sponsored terrorism, and the like'.[200] Furthermore,

Kamrava seems in agreement with Sager and Baabood that for track two to work, at least in this context, it will have to be linked somehow to track one. He explains,

> Also, these and other experiences have shown me that track two diplomacy is likely to be pointless unless you have participants in actual positions of power that, in private and behind closed doors, can openly and frankly discuss contentious issues and solutions for them. But then I guess that won't be considered track two anymore.[201]

In fact, it would be what his colleagues called track 'one-and-a-half'.

In addition to these revisions, technical adaptation to the model itself will be required. During my participation in these workshops I observed that the ground rules as well as the programmes were relaxed. For example, not all participants were present at the start time. On other occasions, some participants left the workshop in the middle of the day and other new ones joined. While I see the benefits of unstructured or semi-structured workshops, sometimes structured management could be needed in order to produce results. Abdullah Baabood agrees that some technical adaptation to the model to increase impact is needed.[202] His suggestions include:

- invoking the Chatham House rule
- avoiding media coverage
- selecting participants in terms of their impact on policies of their respective countries and their ability to speak their mind
- prior availability of presentations and papers as well as laying out expectations
- strict moderation and chairing of sessions to avoid wasting valuable time
- moving the debate along by posing searching questions
- allowing more time for networking and getting to know each other
- follow-up mechanisms to keep the discussions and the debates going through social media
- inviting some participants who can speak on other similar conflicts and how they were finally resolved
- mixing the participants in terms of background and affiliation such as mixing academics, researchers and practitioners.

Other Approaches

Intractable conflicts can never be resolved using a single strategy, approach, or mediator. The complexity of such conflicts requires a systematic and encompassing approach that is able to mobilise every potential and benefit from any possible opportunity to build peace and reduce the chances of escalation. Track one, track two or third-party mediation alone is unlikely to transform the Iran–Saudi conflict, and for this reason all three approaches are needed, while pursuing all other complementary courses of action that could help. Track three potential actions that will be examined here are people-to-people programmes, outreach to Arab Shias, and gestures of conciliation.

Introducing people-to-people programmes

People-to-people approaches are particularly important for long-term and sustainable peace, because their grassroots-level focus supports a bottom-up approach to peacebuilding. They are especially important given that track one approaches have been unable to make progress between the governments of Riyadh and Tehran. Successful people-to-people programmes can form a kind of social incubator for any future government-brokered solutions in this type of environment. Once there is a strong social bond between the two peoples, the contentious issues of the conflict can dissolve. Building the potential for peace at the grassroots level sends a strong message to governments that their own people are eager to live in peace and harmony, rather than in conflict and confrontation. Official track one peacemaking cannot build a long-term and sustainable peace, unless people of both parties can join and engage in transformation of their conflictual relationships.

Unfortunately, people-to-people peacebuilding in the Iran–Saudi conflict is almost non-existent, raising further concerns about future prospects for conflict resolution. In the six GCC countries, only one or two think tanks specialise in Iranian Studies and thus can focus on understanding the 'foe' and providing recommendations about responding to their policies in a constructive way. Faculty and student exchange programmes between Gulf and Iranian universities are almost entirely absent. No scholarship programmes are available for students or specialised professionals. Given these not very encouraging indicators of how much the people on each side know about each other, and given their almost non-existent interaction, the entire peace project between the two nations is in stagnation.

Peace between Iran and Saudi Arabia must grow among people of both sides to help in resolving through official track one negotiations between the two governments. Analysts watching this conflict express their concern about the lack of grassroots interaction between the two sides. Luciano Zaccara, Gulf Studies professor at Qatar University's Gulf Studies Program, suggests that track one negotiation is not possible at this stage due to the huge gap in trust between the two countries. What is needed at this point is more people-to-people interaction, including student and cultural exchanges, along with other social activities that could change stereotypes and build bonds between the two sides, Zaccara adds.[203] Furthermore, Mehran Kamrava argues that the two governments should send Saudis to Tehran and Iranians to Jeddah to initiate confidence-building measures and give week-long courses as a prelude to student exchange programmes, although first steps should entail getting the foreign ministers to talk.[204]

Alireza Nourizadeh, Director of the Center of Arab and Iranian Studies in London, has another take on the region's need for people-to-people interactions, claiming that Arabs and Iranians did not choose their region but that dialogue happens between people. He claims to oppose the Iranian government, yet still wants to see people engage in dialogue. In his words,

> [t]here is not one Arab newspaper published in Persian language for the people of Iran. Is there one book in Arabic about Persian poetry! I need Arabs to reciprocate as there is plenty of literature in Iran written in Arabic for the Gulf and in Persian for the Iranian people.[205]

There is no doubt that people-to-people exchanges are challenging and have the potential to backfire. If done incorrectly, people-to-people programmes may reinforce stereotypes rather than break them. However, specialised research centres as well as non-governmental organisations could help mitigate the risks of backlash as they are trained to deal with public awareness campaigns and grassroots peacebuilding. Such programmes cannot completely eliminate negative sentiments but can contain them to a certain extent. Opinion articles, film festivals and translated television programmes can all contribute to successful people-to-people peacebuilding.

At the core of bottom-up peacebuilding in the Gulf should be altering school curricula to include education about tolerance, coexistence and de-confliction. Schools and universities should take this need into consideration. The effect of such education programmes might only materialise in the long run, maybe after five or ten years, or even a generation, especially as such programmes are almost non-existent in Iran and Saudi Arabia at the moment. The delay in producing visible results may minimise political incentives to actively foster conflict-sensitive education, but its need is inevitable if former war zones are to be stabilised and conflict meaningfully resolved.[206]

Unlocking the potential of Arab Shias

It is no secret that the shift of Iraq's position to the Iranian camp – now that it is controlled primarily by Arab Shia parties – has unbalanced the regional order and helped launch the Iran–Saudi cold war. By the same token, a more balanced position among Arab Shias can significantly affect the conflict and contribute to its resolution. This is not to suggest that Arab Shias must cut off relations with Iran and side with Saudi Arabia. On the contrary, the good relations they enjoy with Iran and the presence they have in several Arab countries position them strongly to connect the two worlds and affect both at the same time. The interests of Arab Shias overlap with those of Iran and Saudi Arabia, and for this reason they can become the point where all parties meet. The change of Iraq's position in 2003, after the American invasion, exacerbated the conflict between the two sides. Ensuring Iraq's independence from both sides will address one major cause of this conflict, helping restore stability and possibly peace.

There is no doubt that Arab Shia populations have traditionally suffered, socially and politically, in almost all Arab countries where they have existed, and Arab governments have tended to impose certain restrictions on their religious and social practices as well as preventing them from access to senior-government-level positions. This social, political and economic discrimination has contributed to increasing the gap between them and the wider society where they live. In some places, wider society treats them with suspicion – accusations of loyalties to Iran have left some Arab Shias feeling they are perceived as Iranian proxies and has led to a self-fulfilling prophecy. As such, some Arab Shias find association with identities outside their home countries – particularly Iranian Shias – a coping mechanism to respond to the marginalisation they experience in their home countries. However, not all the Shia links with Iran are solely because of the way they are treated in their home countries; some Arab Shias have pledged loyalty to Iran strictly on ideological grounds.

However, no matter how strong the relationship between the Arab Shia and Iran, it will never provide a substitute for their relationship with their home Arab societies. They are linked to their societies on many social, political and economic levels. One should keep in mind that the suffering they have experienced in their home countries has stemmed mainly from dictatorships, which exercised their ruthless brutality not only against the Arab Shias but against Arab Sunnis as well. Arab Sunnis in Iraq, for example, suffered from Saddam Hussein's repression equally if not even more than Arab Shias in some respects; Saddam used chemical weapons against Sunni Kurds. This does not mean that they should pledge loyalty to other Arab Sunni majority states, such as Jordan or Saudi Arabia, because their regime is oppressing them. Regime repression does not legitimise pledging loyalty to external countries – at least not when this regime has been removed from power, as is the case in Iraq now. Arab dictatorships cared only about their survival and thus tended to manipulate a variety of ethnic and sectarian communities in ways that served their own agenda. Thus, both Arab Shias and Sunnis shared similar grievances under the same dictatorships, and that should be a uniting factor for the future of their countries.

That Arab Shias undeniably have relationships with their own Arab societies does not make it impossible for them to also have a good relationship with Iran. They overlap with Iran in terms of ideology and with their surrounding Arab neighbours in terms of nationalism and homeland. This status is in fact what positions them to be able to play a significant role in conflict resolution between the two worlds. Arab Shias could potentially change this status from a 'threat' – as it is seen presently – to an 'opportunity', by playing a conciliatory role between the two sides of the conflict.

As testimony to their ability to influence policies in Tehran, Naser Hadian argues that Iraq has considerable sway in Iran and that Iraqi Shia leader Muqtada al-Sadr, for example, can get meetings with Iran's Supreme Leader, Khamenei, much more easily than many Iranian officials. Hadian has also suggested that the same is true for Lebanon's Hezbollah leader, Hassan Nasrallah.[207] Furthermore, Reza Eslami, a conflict resolution expert from Iran, suggests that to resolve the conflict between Iran and neighbouring Arab states, there has to be better treatment of the Arab Shia in their home countries, especially in Saudi Arabia and Bahrain.[208]

The strength of the Arab Shia population, especially in Iraq, is in its own independence – not being subordinate either to Iran or to Saudi Arabia. The moment that the Shia majority government in Iraq sides with Tehran, they will lose influence in the Arab countries; they will neither be able to play a conciliatory role in this conflict nor will they be able to preserve their interests in Arab countries. Iran will resist Iraqi independence, Azmi Bishara argues. He says that Iran pursues a relationship with a weak Iraq – not a strong Iraq – by influencing parties of 'political Shiasim' that are either partially or fully loyal to Tehran. In both cases, Iran's primary interest is in the 'sectarian fragmentation' of Iraq that contradicts its Arab identity.[209]

Iraq's independence from the influence of Iran – not that this entails an alliance with Saudi Arabia – is in line with its core interest so that it does not lose the privilege of being able to mediate and influence both sides. Siding with Iran means the conflict continuing, which is not what Baghdad needs at this stage – Iraq needs stability in order to embark on a long-term reconstruction process that will take decades. Any continuation of the conflict will cause further delay.

Siding with Iran would have a serious impact on Iraq's own internal stability as well, beyond merely losing leverage to influence neighbouring Arab countries. Iraq will be a stronger country with a government truly representative of all its segments: Shia, Sunni and others. Marginalisation of Arab Sunnis could push them to seek other countries to be loyal to, exactly as Arab Shia are perceived to do by their societies, being more loyal to Iran than their own countries. The same logic applies to Saudi Arabia: it must stop treating its Shia community with suspicion that its members are loyal to Iran. Instead, Riyadh should engage them in all parts of state and society, including in senior government positions. Saudi Arabia will be stronger when its Shia community strongly identifies with the state, instead of feeling as though they are the targets of state security.

Moreover, Arab Shias should realise that Iranian intervention in their affairs has exacerbated their own plight, worsening their relationships with their own home countries. Presenting itself as the leader of Shia in the world suggests, for some, a manipulation of their own legitimate grievances about Iran's own political agenda. Abbas Kadhim, senior fellow and director of the Atlantic Council's Iraq Initiative and a prominent Iraqi Shia figure, explains that Iran wants the Arab Shia to serve as 'sandbags'[210] in a regional battle. What matters to Iran first and foremost is the stability and security of the regime. Protecting 'Velayat-e Faqih' is the primary objective and everything can be used to protect this objective.[211]

Turning the Arab Shia role in this conflict from a perceived threat – due to manipulation and suspicions of external loyalties – to an opportunity requires removing the grievances they have with their home countries on one hand and on them fulfilling their own independence from both sides of the conflict. Iraq is especially capable of playing this role though it needs the political will to do so.

Launching gestures of conciliation

Gestures can play a significant de-escalatory role in international conflict.[212] The Iran–Saudi conflict has matured – approaching a mutually damaging stalemate– to the extent that genuine gestures could yield a powerful impact towards conflict de-escalation. Effective gestures could include, but are not limited to: Iran launching credible peace plans in one or more of the regional proxy conflicts such as Yemen and Lebanon; Iran or Saudi Arabia taking on-the-ground measures to de-escalate one or more conflict zones; Iran or Saudi leaders making a visit similar to Richard Nixon's 1972 visit to China (that allowed a normalization of relations between Washington and Beijing); or even, in such a tense environment, a phone call from Saudi

Arabia's King or Iran's Supreme Leader to his counterpart. For his part, Iranian Foreign Minister Jawad Zarif wrote multiple articles in *The New York Times*[215] and *The New Arab*[214] offering dialogue. Unfortunately, though, these articles were ignored and elicited almost no response.

One reason that Zarif's gestures failed could be that the overture came from the foreign minister, rather than from the top rank of Iranian leadership such as the Supreme Leader, the President, or even the head of the Revolutionary Guards. Zarif is considered relatively moderate, and so doubts tend to be raised as to the extent to which he represents the position of the Iranian leadership. In other words, gestures need to come from powerful leaders to maximise chances of success. Returning to the example of Richard Nixon, he was both a strong Republican leader and the President of the United States when he went to China; had he sent his secretary of state, the impact likely would not have been as great.

Another major reason that Zarif's articles did not produce results is the deep mistrust that engulfs the relationship between Iran and Saudi Arabia. There is a lack of credibility when any initiative is taken on either side of the conflict. Articles like those of Zarif are usually received with high levels of suspicion about the real motive behind them. Saudis usually interpret these articles as an attempt to (a) legitimise an Iranian role in the Arab region, or (b) buy time to cover for further expansion of influence in the region, especially through the support of armed militias like Hezbollah in Lebanon and the Houthis in Yemen. The US and China faced a similar trust deficit in the past, but Washington did not need to visit to 'legitimise' its role in world conflict; an established superpower needed no recognition from China that it could influence world politics.

Articles in *The New York Times* will not help de-escalate the present conflict. To the contrary, they are seen as an Iranian move to win international support and isolate Saudi Arabia. If Iran is genuinely interested in de-escalation and resolution, gestures like launching a credible peace plan for any of the regional conflicts in which it is involved will shatter mistrust and pave the way for meaningful dialogue. People need to see action, rather than just rhetoric, and it is for this reason that the real impact of Zarif's articles is in exacerbating mistrust and worsening the conditions for resolution.

Unfortunately, when Iran launched a peace plan in the early days of the war in Yemen, the outcome only made things worse for Iran and the Houthis, rather than bringing about change to the course of the conflict. The plan called for an 'immediate ceasefire and end to all foreign military attacks, humanitarian assistance, a resumption of broad national dialogue' and the 'establishment of an inclusive national unity government'.[215] The major shortcoming of such a plan is that, while it called on Saudi Arabia to stop its military campaign, it failed to call on the Houthis to make any concessions on their side. When one reads the plan carefully, it translates as legitimising the Houthi coup and continued Houthi control of state institutions, while allowing them to keep forces in all areas of Yemen that they captured by force. The plan, in other words, attempted to normalise the Houthis–Saleh coup rather than provide a genuine approach to resolve the conflict. Furthermore, putting the parties into 'national dialogue' while the Houthis are in control of territories and state institutions means that the dialogue is being held under the auspices of sympathetic foreign powers. The unsurprising result of such an initiative was that no one took it seriously – neither the Saudis nor the international community. It should be mentioned that Iran submitted the plan to the United Nations, which likewise showed no interest in it.

It is extremely important for Iran to change its image of deliberately destabilising the region; one effective way to do this is through the launch of credible, meaningful and operationalised peace plans. Iran has an opportunity to be a part of the solution, not the conflict. Iran's ultimate objective of playing a role as a regional power can be achieved by facilitating solutions, not creating conflicts and building armed militias. Iran helping to contain the Houthis in Yemen would invite other parties to come to Iran's aid in other areas like Iraq, Lebanon and Syria. That is how Iran can earn the recognition of its key regional role. Iran is an important country and it can never be separated from the region; it should take the role it deserves by being the party that is able to produce solutions.

Credible gestures of conciliation can be particularly effective when the target is an utterly centralised political system like that of Saudi Arabia. In a system where the royal family makes nearly all policy decisions, a gesture that earns the trust of the monarch can facilitate many areas of conflict resolution activities, such as dialogue, negotiation and mediation. As Abdullah Baabood explains, 'If the Iranians are able to send a message that touches the heart of the King of Saudi Arabia, you will see an entire conflict resolution process taking place.'[216]

Notes

1. Dina A. Zinnes, 'An analytical study of the balance of power theories', *Journal of Peace Research* 4, 2 (1967): 270–88, p. 272.

2. Partha Chatterjee, 'The classical balance of power theory', *Journal of Peace Research* 9, 1 (1972): 51–61, p. 51.

3. Morton A. Kaplan, 'Balance of power, bipolarity and other models of international systems', *The American Political Science Review* 51, 3 (1957): 684–95, p. 690.

4. D. Scott Bennett, 'Balance of power dynamics and war: a competing risks model of escalation', p. 3, http://www.personal.psu.edu/dsb10/papers/BOP%20Escalation%202-06.pdf.

5. Walter Korpi, 'Conflict and the balance of power', *Acta Sociologica* 17, 2 (1974): 99–114, p. 113.

6. Bennett, 'Balance of power dynamics and war', p. 1.

7. Kaplan, 'Balance of power', p. 689.

8. Ibid. p. 689.

9. Ibid. p. 689.

10. Ibid. p. 689.

11. Robert Pear, 'Khomeini accepts "poison" of ending the war with Iraq; U.N. sending mission', *New York Times*, 21 July 1988, http://www.nytimes.com/1988/07/21/us/khomeini-accepts-poison-of-ending-the-war-with-iraq-un-sending-mission.html.

12. Robin Wright and Peter Baker, 'Iraq: Jordan see threat to election from Iran', *Washington Post*, 8 December 2004, http://www.washingtonpost.com/wp-dyn/articles/A43980-2004Dec7.html.

13. Author's interview and discussion, Doha, June 2015.

14. Keynoush, *Saudi Arabia and Iran*, p. 178.

15. Abdullah Al-Thuweini, 'Tehran Official: Baghdad is capital of new Persian empire', *The New Arab*, 10 March 2015, https://www.alaraby.co.uk/english/news/2015/3/10/tehran-official-baghdad-is-capital-of-new-persian-empire.

16. Author's interview and discussion, Doha, November 2015.

17. Author's interview and discussion, Doha, November 2015.

18. Email exchange with the author, March 2016.

19. Hillary Clinton, 'America's Pacific century', *Foreign Policy*, 10 October 2011, http://foreignpolicy.com/2011/10/11/americas-pacific-century/.

20. Susa Heavey, 'Saudi Arabia, Iran must shape "cold peace", Obama says', *Reuters*, 20 March 2016, http://www.reuters.com/article/us-mideast-crisis-obama-idUSKCN 0WC23A.

21. Abdullah Al Shayji, Doha Forum, author's moderation of an Arab–Iranian panel, 22 May 2016.

22. Ibid.

23. Jane Kinninmont, 'Iran and the GCC: unnecessary insecurity', *Chatham House*, July 2017, https://www.chathamhouse.org/sites/files/chathamhouse/field/field_document/20150703IranGCCKinninmont.pdf.

24. Ibid.

25. Ibid.

26. Mousavian, 'Saudi Arabia is Iran's new national security threat'.

27. Author's interview and discussion, Doha, May 2016.

28. Author's interview and discussion, Doha, May 2016.

29. Author's participation in an Iran–Gulf track two workshop organised by The European Iran Research Group, Montreux, Switzerland, 12–13 December 2017. Identities of participants are not publicly revealed as the workshop was held under the Chatham House rule; however, thoughts can be cited.

30. Riza Marashi, 'Ending the Iranian–Saudi cold war', *National Iranian Council*, https://www.niacouncil.org/ending-the-iranian-saudi-cold-war/.

31. Matthiesen, *The Other Saudis*, p. 1.

32. Justin Gengler, 'Sectarian backfire? Assessing Gulf political strategy five years after the Arab uprisings', *Middle East Institute*, 17 November 2015, https://www.mei.edu/publications/sectarian-backfire-assessing-gulf-political-strategy-five-years-after-arab-uprisings.

33. Justin Gengler, 'Bahrain's Sunni awakening', *Middle East Research and Information Project*, 17 January 2012, https://merip.org/mero/mero011712.

34. The Alawites were originally a breakaway sect from Twelver Shia Islam in the ninth century, and – despite being a minority within newly independent Syria – rose to prominence on the basis of their strong presence within the country's armed forces and on Hafez al-Assad (himself an Alawite) seizing power in 1970.

Leon Goldsmith, 'Alawites for Assad: why the Syrian sect backs the regime', *Foreign Affairs*, 16 April 2012, https://www.foreignaffairs.com/articles/middle-east/2012-04-16/alawites-assad.

35. Peter Alsis, Marissa Allison and Anthony H. Cordesman, 'US and Iranian strategic competition in the Gulf States and Yemen', *Center for Strategic and International Studies (CSIS)*, 16 November 2011, pp. 16–17, https://goo.gl/ZJY5Ka (last accessed 1 January 2019).

36. A *Hussainiya* – named for Hussain bin Ali, third Imam of Shia Muslims – is a congregation hall for Shia meetings and religious ceremonies.

37. Human Rights Watch, *Iran, Religious and Ethnic Minorities: Discrimination in Law and Practice*, available at https://www.hrw.org/legacy/reports/1997/iran/Iran-06.htm#P397_84566 (last accessed 13 October 2018).

38. Ali Ansari, *Modern Iran Since 1921* (London: Pearson Education, 2003), p. 231.

39. Mabon, *Saudi Arabia and Iran*, p. 164.

40. Rasmus C. Elling, 'State of mind, state of order: reactions to either unrest in the Islamic Republic of Iran', *Studies in Ethnicity and Nationalism* 8, 3 (2008): 481–501, p. 486.

41. Matthiesen, *The Other Saudis*, p. 1.

42. Author's interview and discussion, Doha, November 2015.

43. Author's interview and discussion, Doha, November 2015.

44. *Velayat-e Faqih*, or 'guardianship of the Islamic jurist', is a theory within Shia Islam that gives an Islamic jurist custodianship over the people until the return of the Imam.

45. Mabon, *Saudi Arabia and Iran*, pp. 219–21.

46. Nasr, *The Shia Revival*, p. 252.

47. Ibid. p. 252.

48. Ibid. p. 253.

49. Mabon, *Saudi Arabia and Iran*, pp. 219–21.

50. Ibid. pp. 219–21.

51. Khaled Al Dakheel, interview with Al Jazeera TV channel, 26 September 2016.

52. Author's discussion with Altakriti in an Iran–Saudi track two workshop held in Vienna, Austria, November 2017. Altakriti gave permission to disclose his name but not that of the Saudi official.

53. Author's interview and discussion, Doha, May 2015.

54. Frederic Wehrey, 'Saudi Arabia's anxious autocrats', *Journal of Democracy* 26, 2 (April 2015): 71–85, p. 84.

55. Asef Bayat, 'The fire that fueled the Iran protests', *The Atlantic*, 27 January 2018, https://www.theatlantic.com/international/archive/2018/01/iran-protest-mashaad-green-class-labor-economy/551690/.

56. Parsi, 'The elusive project of common security', p. 13.

57. Giulio Gallarotti and Isam Yahia Al-Filali, 'Saudi Arabia's soft power', *International Studies* 49, 3&4 (2012): 233–61, p. 235.

58. Ibid. p. 236.

59. Fatima al-Smadi, 'Opinion poll: Arab elites' attitudes toward Arab–Iranian relations and Iran's role in the region', *Al Jazeera Center for Studies*, 19 January 2016, http://studies.aljazeera.net/en/reports/2016/01/2016118124555639612.html.

60. Ali Alfoneh, 'Iraqi Shia fighters in Syria', *Atlantic Council*, 4 May 2017, http://www.atlanticcouncil.org/blogs/syriasource/iraqi-shia-fighters-in-syria.

61. Author's conversation with Khouri in Washington, DC, September 2017.

62. Daryl Kimball, 'Timeline of Syrian chemical weapons activity, 2012–2018', *Arms Control Association*, November 2018, https://www.armscontrol.org/factsheets/Timeline-of-Syrian-Chemical-Weapons-Activity (last accessed 22 February 2019).

63. Zarif, 'A message from Iran'.

64. The other three capitals are Baghdad, Damascus and Beirut. Mamoon Abbasi, 'Iran continues to boast of its regional reach', *Middle East Eye*, 10 March 2015, http://www.middleeasteye.net/news/iran-continues-boast-regional-reach-944755422.

65. Ibid.

66. Ibid.

67. 'Ten times more effective than nukes: Iran weighs creation of naval bases in Syria, Yemen', *Russia Today*, 26 November 2016, https://www.rt.com/news/368306-iran-bases-syria-yemen/.

68. Afshin Molavi, 'Iran and the Gulf States', *United States Institute of Peace*, http://iranprimer.usip.org/resource/iran-and-gulf-states.

69. Gallarotti and Al-Filali, 'Saudi Arabia's soft power', p. 233.

70. Interview with Turki Al Faisal, former Saudi intelligence chief, 'Inside the awkward US–Saudi alliance against ISIS', *Frontline*, https://www.youtube.com/watch?v=9UDLxkkXPnc (last accessed 10 April 2017).

71. 'Despots are pushing the Arab world to become more secular', *The Economist*, 2 November 2017, https://www.economist.com/news/middle-east-and-africa/21730899-they-are-consolidating-their-own-power-process-despots-are-pushing.

72. Ibid.

73. 'Saudi Arabia: prominent clerics arrested, coordinated crackdown on dissent', *Human Rights Watch*, 15 September 2017, https://www.hrw.org/news/2017/09/15/saudi-arabia-prominent-clerics-arrested.

74. Ibid.

75. 'Despots are pushing the Arab world to become more secular'.

76. Stéphane Lacroix, 'Saudi Arabia just let women drive, don't mistake it for democracy', *The Washington Post*, 5 October 2017, https://www.washingtonpost.com/news/monkey-cage/wp/2017/10/05/saudi-arabia-finally-let-women-drive-dont-mistake-it-for-democratic-reform/?utm_term=.0abf3b63bdcc.

77. Track two workshop organised by the Gulf Studies Program at Qatar University and co-sponsored by Chatham House in London. The workshop was held under the Chatham House rule where discussions can be cited for publication but identities of participants remain undisclosed. Doha, March 2016.

78. John E. Peterson, *Saudi Arabia and the Illusion of Security* (Oxford: Oxford University Press for the International Institute for Strategic Studies, 2002), p. 48.

79. Stephen Kalin and Katie Paul, 'Future Saudi King tightens grip on power with arrests including Prince Al-Waleed', *Reuters*, 4 November 2017, https://www.reuters.com/article/us-saudi-arrests/future-saudi-king-tightens-grip-on-power-with-arrests-including-prince-alwaleed-idUSKBN1D506P.

80. Marc Lynch, 'What Saudi Arabia's purge means for the Middle East', *Washington Post*, 6 November 2017, https://www.washingtonpost.com/news/monkey-cage/wp/2017/11/06/what-saudi-arabias-purge-means-for-the-middle-east/?utm_term=.18d2f4629a67.

81. Bruce Riedel, 'High stakes as Saudi Crown Prince tries to remove opponents', *Al-Monitor*, 4 November 2017, https://www.al-monitor.com/pulse/originals/2017/11/saudi-arabia-crown-prince-remove-opponents-national-guard.html.

82. David Ignatius, 'The Saudi Crown Prince just made a very risky power play', *The Washington Post*, 5 November 2017, https://www.washingtonpost.com/opinions/global-opinions/the-saudi-crown-princes-risky-power-play/2017/11/05/4b12fcf0-c272-11e7-afe9-4f60b5a6c4a0_story.html?utm_term=.a76dc5e1b5dc.

83. Shane Harris, Kelly Crow and Summer Said, 'Saudi Arabia's Crown Prince identified as buyer of record-breaking da Vinci', *Wall Street Journal*, 7 December 2017, https://www.wsj.com/articles/saudi-arabias-crown-prince-identified-as-buyer-of-record-breaking-da-vinci-1512674099.

84. Nicholas Kulish and Michael Forsythe, 'World's most expensive home another bauble for a Saudi prince', *The New York Times*, 16 December 2017, https://

mobile.nytimes.com/2017/12/16/world/middleeast/saudi-prince-chateau.
html?_r=0&referer=https://www.google.com/.

85. 'Morocco says will send food to Qatar after Gulf states cut ties', *Reuters*, 13 June 2017, https://www.reuters.com/article/us-gulf-qatar-morocco/morocco-says-will-send-food-to-qatar-after-gulf-states-cut-ties-idUSKBN1940RD.

86. A. S. Said, C. O. Lerche Jr and C. O. Lerche III, *Concepts of International Politics in Global Perspective* (Englewood Cliffs: Prentice Hall, 1995), p. 69.

87. Jeffrey Mapendere, 'Track one and a half diplomacy and the complementarity of tracks', *Culture of Peace Online Journal* 2, 1 (2005): 66–81, p. 66.

88. Ibid. p. 67.

89. Ibid. p. 67.

90. Ibid. p. 67.

91. Ibid. p. 67.

92. Ibid. p. 67

93. Ibid. pp. 67–8.

94. Ibid. p. 76.

95. Susan Allen Nan, 'Track one-and-a-half diplomacy: contributions to Georgia–South Ossetian peacemaking', in R. J. Fisher (ed.), *Paving the Way: Contributions of Interactive Conflict Resolution to Peacemaking* (New York: Lexington, 2005), p. 165.

96. Mapendere, 'Track one and a half diplomacy', p. 69.

97. Ibid. p. 77.

98. Nan, 'Track one-and-a-half diplomacy', p. 165.

99. The role of the United States in this conflict and whether it can play a stabilising role is discussed in detail in the section of this chapter entitled 'Restoring the Regional Order's Balance of Power'.

100. Gause, *The International Relations of the Persian Gulf*, pp. 16–44.

101. Kinninmont, 'Iran and the GCC'.

102. Jeffrey Goldberg, 'The Obama doctrine', *The Atlantic*, April 2016, https://www.theatlantic.com/magazine/archive/2016/04/the-obama-doctrine/471525/.

103. Arash Karami, 'German FM: Iran, Saudi tensions strengthen terrorists', *Al-Monitor*, 19 October 2015, http://www.al-monitor.com/pulse/originals/2015/10/iran-saudi-germany-foreign-minsiter.html.

104. 'Oslo Accords: declaration of principles on interim self-government arrangements', 1993, http://cis.uchicago.edu/oldsite/sites/cis.uchicago.edu/files/resources/CIS-090213-israelpalestine_38-1993DeclarationofPrinciples_OsloAccords.pdf.

105. United Nations, Security Council, *Doha Agreement on the outcome of the meeting of the Lebanese National Dialogue*, S/2008/392, 10 June 2008, http://www.securitycouncilreport.org/atf/cf/%7B65BFCF9B-6D27-4E9C-8CD3-CF6E4FF96FF9%7D/Lebanon%20S2008392.pdf.

106. Author's interview and discussion, Doha, May 2016.

107. Alsis *et al.*, 'US and Iranian strategic competition', p. 17.

108. Peter Kovessy, 'Emir offers to host "meaningful dialogue" to ease Arab–Iranian tensions', *Doha News*, 29 September 2015, http://dohanews.co/emir-offers-to-host-meaningful-dialogue-to-ease-arab-iranian-tensions/.

109. Hassan Ahmadian, 'Iranian olive branch offers diplomatic paradigm shift', *Al-Monitor*, 4 November 2015, http://www.al-monitor.com/pulse/originals/2015/11/iran-new-regional-paradigm.html.

110. Ibrahim al-Marashi, 'Shattering the myths about Kuwaiti Shia', *Al Jazeera*, 30 June 2015, http://www.aljazeera.com/indepth/opinion/2015/06/shattering-myths-kuwaiti-shia-150629081723864.html1.

111. William Zartman, *Ripe for Resolution: Conflict and Intervention in Africa* (Oxford: Oxford University Press, 1985).

112. For more on facilitation or what he calls 'communications strategy' in mediation, see Jacob Bercovitch and Richard Jackson, *Conflict Resolution in the Twenty-First Century: Principles, Methods, and Approaches* (Ann Arbor: University of Michigan Press, 2009), pp. 33–46.

113. Author's interview and discussion, January 2017.

114. Author's interview and discussion, Doha, June 2015.

115. Ayla Jean Yackley and Bozorgmehr Sharafedin, 'Rivals Turkey and Iran seek to "manage differences"', *Reuters*, 5 March 2016, http://www.reuters.com/article/us-iran-turkey-visit-idUSKCN0W70DB.

116. 'Saudi Arabia, Turkey to set up "strategic cooperation council" – Saudi FM', *Reuters*, 29 December 2015, http://uk.reuters.com/article/uk-saudi-turkey-idUKKBN0UC1GX20151229.

117. 'Turkey to boost military cooperation with Iran after army chief's visit', *Reuters*, 17 August 2017, https://www.reuters.com/article/us-turkey-iran-military-idUSKCN1AX1AK.

118. Ibid.

119. Ellen Laipson, 'Can regional powers mediate the Saudi–Iran conflict?', *World Politics Review*, 12 January 2016, http://www.worldpoliticsreview.com/articles/17648/can-regional-powers-mediate-the-saudi-iran-conflict.

120. Ibid.

121. Pinar Tremblay, 'Could Iran–Saudi conflict provide Turkey "graceful exit" from Syria?', *Al-Monitor*, 11 January 2016, http://www.al-monitor.com/pulse/originals/2016/01/turkey-saudi-arabia-iran-strife-opportunities-and-perils.html.

122. 'Khamenei condemns Saudi embassy attack', *Reuters*, 20 January 2016, http://english.alarabiya.net/en/News/middle-east/2016/01/20/Khamenei-condemns-attack-on-Saudi-embassy-in-Tehran.html.

123. Luke Harding, 'Pakistan frees Sharif to exile in Saudi Arabia', *The Guardian*, 10 December 2000, https://www.theguardian.com/world/2000/dec/11/pakistan.saudiarabia.

124. Bruce Riedel, 'Pakistan and Saudi Arabia reconcile after rift over Yemen war', *Markaz* blog, *Brookings Institution*, 8 November 2015, http://www.brookings.edu/blogs/markaz/posts/2015/11/08-saudi-pakistan-reconciliation-yemen-peacekeeping-riedel.

125. Jon Boone and Saeed Kamali Dehgan, 'Pakistan's parliament votes against entering Yemen conflict', *The Guardian*, 10 April 2015, https://www.theguardian.com/world/2015/apr/10/pakistans-parliament-votes-against-entering-yemen-conflict.

126. Shah Faisal Kakar, 'KSA–Pakistan ties touch new heights', *Arab News*, 14 August 2015, http://www.arabnews.com/saudi-arabia/news/790986.

127. 'Country-wise workers' remittances', *State Bank of Pakistan*, http://www.sbp.org.pk/ecodata/Homeremit.pdf (last accessed 8 February 2018).

128. Arif Rafiq, 'Can Pakistan broker an Iran–Saudi détente?', *The National Interest*, 21 January 2016, http://nationalinterest.org/feature/can-pakistan-broker-iran-saudi-d%C3%A9tente-14972?page=show.

129. Ibid.

130. 'Pakistan', *CIA World Factbook*, https://www.cia.gov/library/publications/the-world-factbook/geos/pk.html (last accessed 8 February 2018).

131. Rafiq, 'Can Pakistan broker an Iran–Saudi détente?'

132. 'Geography', *Pakistan Tourism Development Corporation*, http://www.tourism.gov.pk/geography_pakistan.htm (last accessed 8 February 2018).

133. Rafiq, 'Can Pakistan broker an Iran–Saudi détente?'

134. Mubarak Zeb Khan, 'Pakistan eyes free trade pact with Iran', *Dawn*, 20 January 2016, https://www.dawn.com/news/1234061.

135. Rafiq, 'Can Pakistan broker an Iran–Saudi détente?'

136. 'Yemen conflict: Pakistan rebuffs Saudi coalition call', *BBC*, 10 April 2015, http://www.bbc.com/news/world-asia-32246547.

137. 'UN chief hails Pakistan's leading role in peacekeeping operations', *UN News Center*, 13 August 2013, http://www.un.org/apps/news/story.asp?NewsID=45613#.WarNa4VOLSF.

138. Riedel, 'Pakistan and Saudi reconcile'.

139. Mapendere, 'Track one and a half diplomacy', p. 67.

140. Ibid. p. 67.

141. Ibid. p. 68.

142. Ibid. p. 68.

143. Joseph V. Montville, 'Track two diplomacy: the work of healing history', *The Whitehead Journal of Diplomacy and International Relations* 17, 2 (Summer/Fall 2006): 15–25, p. 16.

144. Joseph V. Montville, 'The arrow and the olive branch: a case for track two diplomacy', in Vamik D. Volkan, Joseph V. Montville and Demetrios A. Julius (eds), *The Psychodynamics of International Relationships*, vol. II (Lexington: Lexington Books, 1991), pp. 162–3.

145. Çuhadar and Dayton, 'The social psychology of identity and inter-group conflict', p. 274.

146. Ibid. p. 274.

147. Author's participation in a track two workshop organised by The European Iran Research Group, Montreux, Switzerland, 12–13 December 2017. Three types of track two activities were adapted from group discussion in the workshop. Identities of participants are not publicly revealed as the workshop was held under the Chatham House rule; however, thoughts can be cited.

148. Esra Çuhadar and Bruce W. Dayton, 'Oslo and its aftermath: lessons learned from track two diplomacy', *Negotiation Journal* 28, 2 (2012): 155–79, p. 157.

149. Ibid. p. 158.

150. Ibid. p. 158.

151. Montville, 'The arrow and the olive branch', p. 163.

152. Çuhadar and Dayton, 'The social psychology of identity and inter-group conflict', p. 282.

153. Ibid. p. 282.

154. Montville, 'The arrow and the olive branch', p. 163.

155. Ibid. p. 163.

156. Ibid. p. 163.

157. Ibid. pp. 163–4.

158. M. De Vries and I. Maoz, 'Tracking for peace: assessing the effectiveness of track two diplomacy in the Israeli–Palestinian conflict', *Dynamics of Asymmetric Conflict* 6, 1–3 (2013): 62–74, p. 63.

159. Ibid. p. 63.

160. Dalia Dassa Kaye, 'Track two diplomacy and regional security in the Middle East', *International Negotiation* (2001): 49–77, p. 52.

161. De Vries and Maoz, 'Tracking for peace', p. 63.

162. Susan Allen Nan, 'Coordination and complementarity of conflict resolution efforts in the conflicts over Abkhazia, South Ossetia, and Transdniestria', Doctoral Dissertation, George Mason University, Fairfax, VA, 1999.

163. Ibid.

164. Kaye, 'Track two diplomacy and regional security', p. 65.

165. Ibid. p. 60.

166. Ibid. p. 60.

167. Dalia Dassa Kaye, *Talking to the Enemy: Track Two Diplomacy in the Middle East and South Asia* (Lanham: National Book Network, 2007), p. 5.

168. Kaye, 'Track two diplomacy and regional security', pp. 59–60.

169. Ibid. p. 60.

170. Montville, 'The arrow and the olive branch', p. 167.

171. Kaye, 'Track two diplomacy and regional security', p. 65.

172. Montville, 'The arrow and the olive branch', p. 163.

173. Author's email and phone correspondence with Abdulaziz Sager, January 2016.

174. Ibid.

175. 13 January 2016, Doha, Qatar.

176. 25 September 2016, Doha, Qatar.

177. 27 October 2015, Doha, Qatar.

178. Author's email discussion with CAPRO's representatives, June 2019.

179. Author's email and phone correspondence with Abdulaziz Sager, January 2016.

180. Ibid.

181. Organiser preferred to remain anonymous.

182. Author's interview and discussion, September 2017.

183. Author's interview and discussion, September 2017.

184. Organiser preferred to remain anonymous.

185. Author's interview and discussion, Doha, November 2015.

186. Organiser preferred to remain anonymous.

187. Jamal Khashoggi, 'The secret Saudi–Iranian track two negotiation', *al-Hayat*, 6 December 2013, http://www.alhayat.com/Details/579415.

188. Organiser preferred to remain anonymous.

189. Organiser preferred to remain anonymous.

190. Author's observations during track two workshops organised by Qatar University's Gulf Studies Program, Doha, March 2016.

191. Author's conversation with Iranian participants in track two workshops, March 2016.

192. Author's email correspondence with Abdullah Baabood, September 2017.

193. Author's email correspondence with Mehran Kamrava, September 2017.

194. Name of speaker is not provided here because the workshop was held under the Chatham House rule.

195. Arab–Iranian dialogue workshop organised by Georgetown University in Qatar, 13 January 2016.

196. Ibid.

197. Author's email correspondence with Abdullah Baabood, September 2017.

198. Author's email and phone correspondence with Abdulaziz Sager, January 2016.

199. Author's interview and discussion, March 2016.

200. Author's email correspondence with Mehran Kamrava, September 2017.

201. Ibid.

202. Author's interview and discussion, Doha, September 2017.

203. Author's interview and discussion, Doha, September 2015.

204. Author's conversation and discussion, June 2015.

205. Alireza Nourizadeh, speaker at the Doha Forum, author's moderation of a Gulf–Iran relations workshop, 22 May 2016.

206. 'Tafahum', a track two workshop organised by CAPRO, 'Security Roadmap for West Asia and the Arabian Peninsula', 29–30 April, Rome, Italy (author's notes).

207. Author's interview and discussion, Doha, April 2016.

208. Author's phone interview and discussion, January 2016.

209. Azmi Bishara and Mahjoub Zweiri, 'Introduction', in Azmi Bishara and Mahjoub Zweiri (eds), *Iran and the Arab World, a Review in History and Politics* (Doha: Arab Center for Research and Policy Studies, 2012), p. 13.

210. Sandbags are bags filled with soil and, among other uses, are used in military fortification in bunkers and trenches. The metaphor is used here to describe how Iran uses the Shia in the Arab countries to protect itself and defend its own national interest.

211. Author's interview and discussion, Washington, DC, September 2015.

212. Christopher Mitchell, *Gestures of Conciliation: Factors Contributing to Successful Olive-Branches* (London: Palgrave Macmillan, 2000).

213. Zarif, 'A message from Iran'.

214. 'Zarif writes for the New Arab: we're willing to collaborate with the countries in the region', *The New Arab*, 20 May 2017, https://goo.gl/GkC6D0.

215. 'Iran submits four-point Yemen peace plan to United Nations', *Reuters*, 17 April 2017, http://www.reuters.com/article/2015/04/17/us-yemen-security-iran-idU SKBN0N823820150417#8kgJHEAdtBzoCiQO.97.

216. Author's interview and discussion, Doha, September 2017.

Conclusion

The debate about the root cause of the Iran–Saudi rivalry is unlikely to end soon; indeed, confusion over the basic issues at stake remains part of the problem. Even more problematic, this confusion is not limited to the general public but extends to top policymakers – even President Obama seemed to indicate that the conflict was about ancient sectarian issues. Sectarianism, domestic political leadership, geopolitical gains, and economic benefits are all contributing causes to the conflict. However, if one seeks to design a pragmatic conflict resolution strategy, a desire for security must be understood as the major underlying cause. Both Iran and Saudi Arabia have legitimate security needs that, one way or another, will have to be addressed. American 'encirclement' of Iran by its military bases in the surrounding countries has contributed to an Iranian 'encirclement' of Saudi Arabia through its armed militias funded in Iraq, Syria, Lebanon and Yemen. The imbalance in the regional order created by the American invasion of Iraq in 2003 facilitated Iranian expansion in the region, which exacerbated the security crisis of Saudi Arabia, leading to Riyadh's nervousness in managing the regional conflict with Tehran. In this aggressive race to satisfy security needs, secure geopolitical gains and lead the Muslim world, Iran and Saudi Arabia have manipulated sectarianism to help them achieve their objectives, which has in turn become a cause for further escalation of hostility between the two countries.

Both countries are taking a counterproductive approach to satisfying their security needs, pushing the conflict into further chaos and making potential resolution more elusive than ever before. In fact, Iran's current foreign policy is exacerbating its security concerns in the region in two ways. First, by 'encircling' Saudi Arabia Tehran has contributed to pushing Riyadh into a tighter alliance with the United States and Israel, the latter of which Tehran considers the primary threat to its national security. Saudi Arabia has entered into a total of $460 billion worth of deals in potential arms sales from the Trump administration, the primary objective of such a collaboration being to counter the perceived Iranian threat. Furthermore, for the first time in its history, Saudi Arabia has entertained suggestions of a certain level of 'normalisation' with Israel, the historic Arab enemy, to foster an alliance against Iran.

Second, by supporting dictatorships as in Syria and other sectarian forces in Yemen and Iraq, Iran's foreign policy is reinforcing the conditions that produced terrorism or 'Sunni radicalism', which Tehran considers another chief threat to its national security. The Iranian government marketed its military support of the Assad regime to its domestic population as a way to fight terrorism. Tehran has instead helped to reinforce the policies of sectarian discrimination that produced ISIS in Iraq, and repression and dictatorship in Syria through the Assad regime that have contributed to Islamic radicalism there. A deteriorating security environment (where terrorism thrives) has resulted from Assad's ruthless policies against his people and Maliki's sectarian policies against Iraqi Sunnis. Iran's foreign policy has come to sustain these conditions and ensure their survival.

Likewise, in its attempt to counter Iranian influence, Saudi Arabia is reproducing the conditions that made its national security strategy vulnerable in the first place. Instead of becoming self-reliant, Saudi Arabia has increased its dependence on external providers of security, namely the United States, leaving its security strategy subject to the changes in US administrations and their foreign policy priorities. Under the Obama administration, Riyadh felt abandoned and vulnerable, while under Trump, it has become a critical US ally in the confrontation of Tehran. It is uncertain who will be in power next in Washington and in what direction the next administration will take the relationship with Saudi Arabia. Secondly, Saudi Arabia has deepened its security dilemma by initiating a confrontational approach or what it called a 'decisive strategy' with Iran. Such a strategy has seriously struggled in Syria, Iraq, Lebanon, and worst of all in Yemen. With losses on multiple fronts, Saudi Arabia is less secure than before this strategy was adopted.

Both Iran and Saudi Arabia must stop the politicisation of sectarian divisions, as this is deepening their crisis rather than helping them bring an end to their cold war. Saudi Arabia 'sectarianising' the conflict to mobilise the broader Sunni world against Iran will be difficult to reverse later. Intense sectarianising is likely to lead to extremism and potentially to terrorism, not just against Iran but even against Saudi Arabia itself. This situation is reminiscent of the American–Saudi 'ideologising' of the Afghanistan war against the Soviet Union by recruiting and funding mujahideen from around the Muslim world to fight a 'holy war' against the 'infidel communists'. When the USSR exited the scene, both the United States and Saudi Arabia had to deal with the rise of Al-Qaida, former mujahideen who had fought the Soviet Union in Afghanistan. Saudi Arabia should keep in mind that it has a sizable minority of Shia Muslims among its own population, and intense sectarianising will directly reflect on the social and domestic harmony of its own society.

By arming Shia militias in the region, especially in Arab countries, Iran is likewise deeply involved in destructive sectarianism, a policy that needs to stop. Iran's armed militias in the region certainly did not help its nuclear negotiation with the West, nor have they been able to derail or change the US administration's policy towards Tehran. Instead, Iran finds itself funding a number of civil wars in Syria, Yemen and Iraq, all at the expense of building a resilient economy for its own people – no wonder protests rooted in economic anxiety broke out in late 2017. One important aspect Iran should consider about this strategy is that militias have the ability to destabilise but not to build strong and stable states, which means protracted Iranian involvement is likely in these unstable zones where armed militias operate. For example, Yemen will never be stable with a minority Iranian-backed Houthi government in power that marginalises other political factions. A Houthi-controlled Yemen will always be a burden on Iran, not an asset.

Equally troubling, Iran's fomenting of sectarianism in the conflict has led to strained relationships between the Shia communities and their surrounding Sunni-majority societies. Polarisation among Sunni–Shia communities has never been more extreme than in recent history, and it will take decades for such a structural rift to be remedied. Shia communities are first and foremost part of the wider society of their home nations, and creating tension among different communal groups cannot be the basis for a stable future in the region.

It is Iran and Saudi Arabia's legitimate right to aspire to lead the Muslim world, but leadership does not come through imposition, pressuring and intimidation. It has become a key component of the cold war to pressure other Muslim majority countries to join their alliance advancing the 'us or them' dynamic. While Iran's main approach has been to build up armed militias in Sunni-majority countries, Saudi Arabia has linked financial assistance to demonstrated political loyalties to Riyadh's position regarding conflicts with Iran and other countries. The Nimr al-Nimr crisis was one clear example of this bargain of money for loyalty. Iran and Saudi Arabia can lead by example but need a model leadership style so that other Muslim majority countries can follow them. Respecting other countries' sovereignty and engaging with them as equal and true partners will position Riyadh and Tehran to lead. Iran and Saudi Arabia can benefit from the European Union's experience in foregoing partnerships between countries of power disparity. For example, Germany's leadership position in the EU does not come through 'building armed militias in the Netherlands' or linking its financial aid to Greece to Athens showing 'political loyalty to Berlin'. Germany leads by being a true partner to the rest of EU member states.

Iran and Saudi Arabia need to realise that they must take ownership of their own conflict, despite the involvement of regional and global powers in their conflict. Particularly with the arrival of Donald Trump in the White House, the US administration and Israel are now playing a key role in determining the trajectory of this conflict; it has been hijacked by Trump and the Israeli government. Obviously, these parties will pursue their own interests, rather than those of the primary parties to the conflict themselves, Iran and Saudi Arabia. It is in the interest of both the US and Israel to keep the conflict in a state of protracted stalemate, as it has been since the removal of Saddam's regime in Iraq. For them, the Iranian threat should not be removed, so that Saudi Arabia continues to rely on the US as their security vendor in the Gulf, making arms purchases and extending concessions to Israel on Palestine. However, Iran will never be allowed to dominate the region, as this will threaten the American and Israeli interest. In other words, Iran and Saudi Arabia are being used to serve the interests of external factors, as determined by the key players the US and Israel. Riyadh and Tehran should realise they are being used and have the necessary courage to claim back their own conflict and end this state of protracted stalemate. The parties to the conflict should be the ones to define a peaceful outcome that brings about stability, prosperity and mutual respect, not only for Iran and Saudi Arabia but also for the entire Gulf region.

Since Iran and Saudi Arabia are unlikely to voluntarily take a different approach to building relationships with other countries in their political spheres in the foreseeable future, these other countries might want to take the lead themselves in reforming their respective relationships with them. This can be called building 'zones of peace' or a 'non-aligned movement' with regards to the Iran–Saudi rivalry. Oman, for instance, has long resisted tremendous pressure from both countries to side with one against the other. Today, other countries have started to see the benefits to Oman of having refused to allow itself to be a battleground for regional rivalry. Kuwait, Morocco, Qatar and Jordan are all increasingly distancing themselves from being pulled into the rivalry. A truly non-aligned movement could not only avoid these states from becoming part of the battleground but could also enable them to play a proactive role in attempting to contain the conflict. This is exactly what Kuwait has recently moved towards by attempting to play an intermediary role between its two powerful neighbours.

A key factor in bringing the Iran–Saudi conflict to an end has a structural dimension, which is the imbalance of the regional order that was created after the American invasion of Iraq in 2003. The imbalance was exacerbated by Iraq subsequently shifting to join the Iranian bloc, Saudi Arabia's inability to bring Syria to its side, and Riyadh's failure to quell the Iran-backed Houthi rebellion in Yemen. The regional order does not tolerate imbalances of power and will always push back to balance itself. This balance is what will ultimately put an end to the escalation of the Iran–Saudi cold war. Given the failure of the Syrian revolution against the Iranian-allied Assad regime, the rebalancing pressure must come from Iraq's full independence from the influence of both Iran and Saudi Arabia. Building an inclusive and truly representative regime of its own people that does not cater to the interests of Iran should be Iraq's core objective and, at the same time, this would address the imbalance in the regional order. In other words, a free, independent and democratic Iraq with an accountable, inclusive and transparent regime in Baghdad would significantly weaken and contain the rivalry between Iran and Saudi Arabia. However, an inability to completely detach itself from the Iran–Saudi rivalry could turn Iraq into a battleground, suffering from protracted instability – similar to the situation in Lebanon, which ended its civil war in the Taef's agreement in 1989 but continued to suffer long-term instability and emerged as a zone of contestation for Riyadh and Tehran. In contrast, Iraq's Shia Arabs could be the uniting factor that brings the Shia Iranians and the Arab Saudis together with Iraq thus emerging as a place for peace and collaboration.

Another way to balance the regional order would be to incorporate equally powerful players in the security architecture of the region, like Turkey and Pakistan. Thinking in terms of a West Asia and North Africa (WANA) grouping should provide a more suitable framework for peace and security than that of the Middle East. Such countries are an integral part of the region, and so its core stability is of interest to them. Conflict escalation between Iran and Saudi Arabia means that at some point they may have to choose one party over the other, which is an option both countries refuse to take at the moment as they have vital interests shared with both Riyadh and Tehran.

Saudi Arabia's attempt to maintain the balance with Iran by outsourcing its security needs to the United States will only exacerbate its security crisis and make the country more vulnerable to other types of threats. The long-term prospects of an American presence in the Middle East are determined by many variables – not only Washington's interest in the region but also domestic factors back home. Building a self-reliant security strategy would give Saudi Arabia the power it needs to protect itself and counter Iranian expansion.

Saudi Arabia's current approach to security independence is mainly an arms race. There is no doubt that hard power helps, yet deep political, constitutional, social and economic reform are very much needed in the Kingdom in order for it to effectively position itself against any Iranian or other types of external influence. Saudi Arabia needs to fight rampant corruption, combat sectarianism on its own soil, and give equal access to resources based on citizenship, not favouritism and nepotism. The Kingdom needs to engage in a national reconciliation process with its own people that leads to a new social contract, one that redefines the relationship between society and state. Fixing these domestic issues will lead to a strong state that is capable of relying on itself to counter Iran's influence. The external allies that Riyadh currently depends on to build its national security strategy will not always be there, but a unified society would always be there to defend the country.

The Crown Prince's campaign for reform in Saudi Arabia, which started in 2016, is definitely a step in the right direction and is proving appealing on the domestic level, especially to the youth. Saudi Arabia's reputation abroad had suffered immensely through its association with terrorism and 'Wahhabism'. However, the way the reforms have been administered – centrally and individually driven – is problematic. For example, the anti-corruption campaign was conducted entirely outside the judicial system, and the charges were settled through a direct bargaining process between regime figures and those individuals accused of corruption. The Saudi regime needs to take an institutional approach to reform to inject credibility into this campaign and not end up just consolidating their power. Reform can never be sustainable if solely linked to individuals.

Reform in Iran is likewise overdue. In particular, Iran needs to have one official foreign policy voice, especially when addressing conflict issues related to Saudi Arabia and the rest of Arab world. Saudi Arabia is right to be concerned about who exactly they should talk to in Iran, as mixed messages come from the different forces in Tehran such as the presidency, Revolutionary Guards, MPs, or even the imam of Friday prayers at the University of Tehran who gives weekly 'foreign policy lectures'. This becomes even more concerning when the Foreign Minister, Javad Zarif, extends an olive branch in his occasional op-eds at the same time as an MP makes statements about Iran's control of four Arab capitals. Sending these mixed messages to neighbouring Arab countries has significantly undermined Iran's credibility and deepened mistrust about the true intention of Tehran among Arabs. It has also raised concerns about whether there is in fact one truly representative party that can engage in peace efforts to resolve the conflict. Nonetheless, the legitimate Saudi concern about Iran's mixed messages does not justify its refusal to talk or engage in dialogue. First, mixed messages are not unique to Iran, as this situation is common in conflict zones where variation in positions between the government and opposition do exist; in Iran the problem is not with the opposition but rather within the government itself. Second, from a tactical perspective, it is in Riyadh's interest to engage in dialogue with moderate voices in the Iranian government to strengthen their position against radical voices.[1]

It is becoming increasingly evident that a resolution to the Iran–Saudi conflict is still an ambitious objective for the very near future. The conflict environment has not fully ripened for resolution yet. Mistrust between the two parties is huge; the conflict is still perceived as zero-sum; and the narrative of the conflict on both sides has become a driving force for further escalation. Therefore, what is urgently needed at this stage is for the parties to agree on a conflict management system that aims to contain the rivalry and insert some rules and policies that regulate the conflict behaviour of both parties. Better-managed conflicts have a better chance of being resolved (for example, the American–USSR Cold War). The Iran–Saudi conflict is not managed well at present, and this leaves the door open for dangerous and uncontrolled escalation. A conflict management system at this stage should include, among other measures, establishing a hotline between Riyadh and Tehran, confidence-building measures, meetings of experts, and dialogue. Installing such procedures does not in any way mean that the parties are making concessions – a price that conflict parties usually try to avoid – yet can alter the dominant and dangerous variables (e.g. mistrust, zero-sum perception, lack of communications) that currently drive the conflict.

It is clear that the stakes for government engagement are high and a move from one party or the other could be understood as a sign of weakness in such a distrustful conflict environment. However, Iran and Saudi Arabia could capitalise on the use of track two diplomacy that does not subject their governments to what could potentially become an embarrassing situation. Track two diplomacy is designed to assist official leaders by compensating for the constraints imposed upon them by the psychologically understandable need for leaders to be – or at least to be seen to be – strong, wary and indomitable in the face of the 'enemy'.[2] This could definitely aid a process of de-escalation in the Gulf. Governments on both sides should unleash the potential of track two diplomacy as community leaders and other mid-level leadership figures are very eager to contribute to helping their countries build peace in the Gulf region. Unfortunately, authoritarian and centralised political systems in both Iran and Saudi Arabia have prevented track two diplomacy from reaching its full potential, but this is the time to change.

Finally, Riyadh and Tehran should keep in mind that government peacemaking cannot build a long-term and sustainable peace unless people on both sides join and engage in a process of transformation of their conflictual relationships. The bottom-up approach to peacebuilding in the Gulf has long been ignored. Given the unencouraging indicators of how little the people on either side know about each other, and given their almost non-existent interaction, the entire peace project between the two nations is in serious doubt. People-to-people interaction is needed in many areas including education, sport, the media, and economy. Developing shared economic enterprises between groups from both countries, as well as education exchange programmes, could be a good starting point. Such activities should provide the foundation for building a sustainable peace between the two countries in the long run. Peace between Iran and Saudi Arabia must grow among the populace of both sides, which will then help their governments proceed with confidence to sign the peace agreements that they all so urgently need.

Notes

1. Author's concluding thoughts on a discussion on this issue in an Iran–Gulf track two workshop organised by The European Iran Research Group, Montreux, Switzerland, 12–13 December 2017. Identities of participants are not publicly revealed as the workshop was held under the Chatham House rule; however, thoughts can be cited.
2. Joseph V. Montville, 'The arrow and the olive branch: a case for track two diplomacy', in Vamik D. Volkan, Joseph V. Montville and Demetrios A. Julius (eds), *The Psychodynamics of International Relationships*, vol. II (Lexington: Lexington Books, 1991), pp. 162–3.

Bibliography

Scholarly Sources

Abadi, Jacob, 'Saudi Arabia's rapprochement with Israel: the national security imperatives', *Middle Eastern Studies* 55, 3 (2019): 1–17.

Akbarzadeh, Shahram, 'Iran and Daesh: the case of a reluctant Shia power', *Middle East Policy* XXII, 3 (Fall 2015): 44–54.

Alfoneh, Ali, 'Iraqi Shia fighters in Syria', *Atlantic Council*, 4 May 2017, http://www.atlanticcouncil.org/blogs/syriasource/iraqi-shia-fighters-in-syria.

Alsis, Peter, Marissa Allison and Anthony H. Cordesman, 'US and Iranian strategic competition in the Gulf States and Yemen', *Center for Strategic and International Studies (CSIS)*, 16 November 2011, https://goo.gl/ZJY5Ka (last accessed 1 January 2019).

Al-Smadi, Fatima, 'Opinion poll: Arab elites' attitudes toward Arab–Iranian relations and Iran's role in the region', *Al Jazeera Center for Studies*, 19 January 2016, http://studies.aljazeera.net/en/reports/2016/01/2016118124555639612.html.

Altoraifi, Adel, 'The rise and demise of Saudi–Iranian rapprochement (1997–2009)', PhD Dissertation, London School of Economics, 2012.

Amiri, Reza Ekhtiari, and Fakhreddin Soltani, 'Iraqi invasion of Kuwait as turning point in Iran–Saudi relationship', *Journal of Politics and Law* 4, 1 (2011): 188–94.

Ansari, Ali, *Modern Iran Since 1921* (London: Pearson Education, 2003).

Ayub, Fatima, 'Introduction', in ECFR Gulf Analysis, *The Gulf and Sectarianism*, November 2013, p. 2, http://www.ecfr.eu/page/-/ECFR91_GULF_ANALYSIS_AW.pdf.

Bercovitch, Jacob, and Richard Jackson, *Conflict Resolution in the Twenty-First Century: Principles, Methods, and Approaches* (Ann Arbor: University of Michigan Press, 2009).

Bilgin, Pinar, *Regional Security in the Middle East A Critical Perspective* (New York: Routledge Curzon, 2005).

Bishara, Azmi, *Sect, Sectarianism, and Imagined Sect* (Doha: Arab Center for Research and Policy Studies, 2018).

Bishara, Azmi, and Mahjoub Zweiri, 'Introduction', in Azmi Bishara and Mahjoub Zweiri (eds), *Iran and the Arab World, a Review in History and Politics* (Doha: Arab Center for Research and Policy Studies, 2012), p. 13.

Bradley, John, 'Al Qaeda and the House of Saud: eternal enemies or secret bedfellows?', *The Washington Quarterly* 28, 4 (2005): 139–52.

Bulloch, John, and Harvey Morris, *The Gulf War: Its Origins, History and Consequences* (London: Methuen, 1989).

Butterfield, Herbert, *History and Human Relations* (London: Collins, 1951).

Bzostek, Rachel, and Allison Rogers, 'Oslo +20: reassessing the role of confidence building measures', *The Social Science Journal* 51, 2 (2014): 250–9.

Cafiero, Giorgio, and Daniel Wagner, 'Iran exposes the myth of GCC unity', *The National Interest*, 7 September 2015, http://nationalinterest.org/feature/iran-exposes-the-myth-gcc-unity-13787.

Chatterjee, Partha, 'The classical balance of power theory', *Journal of Peace Research* 9, 1 (1972): 51–61.

Chubin, Shahram, and Charles Tripp, *Iran–Saudi Arabia Relations and Regional Order* (Oxford: Oxford University Press for the International Institute for Strategic Studies, 1996).

Clinton, Hillary, 'America's Pacific century', *Foreign Policy*, 10 October 2011, http://foreignpolicy.com/2011/10/11/americas-pacific-century/.

Cordesman, Anthony H., *Saudi Arabia: Guarding the Desert Kingdom* (Oxford: Oxford University Press, 1997).

Çuhadar, Esra, and Bruce W. Dayton, 'Oslo and its aftermath: lessons learned from track two diplomacy', *Negotiation Journal* 28, 2 (2012): 155–79.

Çuhadar, Esra, and Bruce Dayton, 'The social psychology of identity and inter-group conflict: from theory to practice', *International Studies Perspectives* 12 (2011): 273–93.

Curtis, Peter Theo, 'A militia, a madrassa, and the story behind a siege in Yemen', *New Republic*, 30 January 2012, https://newrepublic.com/article/100214/yemen-shia-militia-sunni-madrassa?page=0%2C1.

Daigle, Craig, 'The era of détente', in Artemy M. Kalinovsky and Craig Daigle (eds), *The Routledge Handbook of the Cold War* (New York: Routledge, 2014), pp. 195–208.

Darwich, May, and Tamirace Fakhoury, 'Casting the Other as an existential threat: the securitisation of sectarianism in the international relations of the Syria crisis', *Global Discourse* 6, 4 (2017): 712–32.

Das, M. N., *The Political Philosophy of Jawaharlal Nehru* (New York: John Day, 1961).

De Vries, M., and I. Maoz, 'Tracking for peace: assessing the effectiveness of track two diplomacy in the Israeli–Palestinian conflict', *Dynamics of Asymmetric Conflict* 6, 1–3 (2013): 62–74.

Dixon, Paul, 'Beyond sectarianism in the Middle East? Comparative perspectives on group conflicts', in Frederic Wehrey (ed.), *Beyond Sunni and Shia: The Roots of Sectarianism in a Changing Middle East* (London: C. Hurst & Co., 2017), pp. 11–38.

Dodge, Toby, 'Seeking to understand the rise of sectarianism in the Middle East: the case study of Iraq', *Project on Middle East Political Science*, 19 March 2014, http://pomeps.org/2014/03/19/seeking-to-explain-the-rise-of-sectarianism-in-the-middle-east-the-case-study-of-iraq/.

Ehteshami, Anoushiravan, 'The foreign policy of Iran', in Raymond Hinnebusch and Anoushiravan Ehteshami (eds), *The Middle East in the International System* (London: Lynne Rienner Publishers, 2002).

Ehteshami, Anoushiravan, 'Iran and its immediate neighborhood', in Anoushiravan Ehteshami and Mahjoub Zweiri (eds), *Iran's Foreign Policy from Khatami to Ahmadinejad* (Reading: Ithaca Press, 2008), pp. 129–30

Elling, Rasmus C., 'State of mind, state of order: reactions to either unrest in the Islamic Republic of Iran', *Studies in Ethnicity and Nationalism* 8, 3 (2008): 481–501.

Fraihat, Ibrahim, 'Keeping Iran and Saudi Arabia from war', *Foreign Affairs*, 30 May 2016, https://www.foreignaffairs.com/articles/iran/2016-05-30/keeping-iran-and-saudi-arabia-war.

Fraihat, Ibrahim, 'Room for containment: the Iran deal and the neighboring Arab states', in Payam Mohseni (ed.), *Iran and the Arab World After the Nuclear Deal* (Cambridge, MA: Harvard Kennedy School, 2015), pp. 44–6, http://belfercenter.ksg.harvard.edu/files/Impact%20on%20Arab%20World%20-%20Web.pdf.

Fraihat, Ibrahim, 'Managing the Saudi–Iranian regional rivalry', a public lecture delivered at Georgetown University on 8 November 2015, https://www.youtube.com/watch?v=snqUvvBEhzE (last accessed 18 June 2019).

Fürtig, Henner, 'Conflict and cooperation in the Persian Gulf: the interregional order and US policy', *The Middle East Journal* 61, 4 (2007): 627–40.

Fürtig, Henner, *Iran's Rivalry with Saudi Arabia between the Gulf Wars* (Reading: Ithaca Press, 2006).

Gallarotti, Giulio, and Isam Yahia Al-Filali, 'Saudi Arabia's soft power', *International Studies* 49, 3&4 (2012): 233–61.

Gause, F. Gregory III, *Beyond Sectarianism: The New Middle East Cold War*, Analysis paper no. 11 (Doha: Brookings Doha Center, 2014), https://www.brookings.edu/wp-content/uploads/2016/06/English-PDF-1.pdf.

Gause, F. Gregory III, *The International Relations of the Persian Gulf* (Cambridge: Cambridge University Press, 2010).

Gause, F. Gregory III, 'Saudi–Iranian rapprochement? The incentives and the obstacles', *Brookings Institution*, 17 March 2014, http://www.brookings.edu/research/articles/2014/03/17-iran-ksa-rapprochement-gause.

Gause, F. Gregory III, 'Sectarianism and the politics of the new Middle East', *Brookings Institution, Up Front* blog, 8 June 2013, http://www.brookings.edu/blogs/up-front/posts/2013/06/08-sectarianism-politics-new-middle-east-gause.

Gengler, Justin, 'Bahrain's Sunni awakening', *Middle East Research and Information Project*, 17 January 2012, https://merip.org/mero/mero011712.

Gengler, Justin, 'The political economy of sectarianism: how Gulf regimes exploit identity politics as a survival strategy', in Frederic Wehrey (ed.), *Beyond Sunni and Shia: The Roots of Sectarianism in a Changing Middle East* (London: C. Hurst & Co., 2017).

Gengler, Justin, *The Political Economy of Sectarianism in the Gulf* (Washington: Carnegie Endowment for International Peace, 2016).

Gengler, Justin, 'Sectarian backfire? Assessing Gulf political strategy five years after the Arab uprisings', *Middle East Institute*, 17 November 2015, https://www.mei.edu/publications/sectarian-backfire-assessing-gulf-political-strategy-five-years-after-arab-uprisings.

Goldsmith, Leon, 'Alawites for Assad: why the Syrian sect backs the regime', *Foreign Affairs*, 16 April 2012, https://www.foreignaffairs.com/articles/middle-east/2012-04-16/alawites-assad.

Graham Jr, Thomas, and Damien J. LaVera, 'The hotline agreements', in Thomas Graham Jr and Damien J. LaVera (eds), *Cornerstones of Security: Arms Control Treaties in the Nuclear Era* (Seattle: University of Washington Press, 2003).

Haddad, Fanar, *Sectarianism in Iraq: Antagonistic Visions of Unity* (New York: Columbia University Press, 2011).

Halliday, Fred, *Nation and Religion in the Middle East* (Boulder: Lynne Rienner, 2000).

Hammond, Andrew, 'Saudi Arabia: cultivating sectarian spaces', in ECFR Gulf Analysis, *The Gulf and Sectarianism*, November 2013, pp. 7–9, http://www.ecfr.eu/page/-/ECFR91_GULF_ANALYSIS_AW.pdf.

Hecker, Siegfried S., 'Adventures in scientific nuclear diplomacy', *Physics Today* 64, 7 (July 2011): 31–7.

Herz, John, *Political Realism and Political Idealism: A Study in Theories and Realities* (Chicago: University of Chicago Press, 1951).

Hiro, Dilip, *Cold War in the Islamic World: Saudi Arabia, Iran and the Struggle for Supremacy* (Oxford: Oxford University Press, 2019).

Hoffmann, Steven, *India and the China Crisis* (Berkeley: University of California Press, 1990).

Holst, Johan Jorgen, 'Confidence-building measures: a conceptual framework', *Survival* 24, 1 (1983): 2–15.

Ibrahim, Fouad N., *The Shi'is of Saudi Arabia* (London: Saqi, 2006).

Jervis, Robert, 'Cooperation under the security dilemma', *World Politics* 30, 2 (January 1978): 167–214.

Jervis, Robert, *Perception and Misperception in International Politics* (Princeton: Princeton University Press, 1976).

Kaplan, Morton A., 'Balance of power, bipolarity and other models of international systems', *The American Political Science Review* 51, 3 (1957): 684–95.

Kaye, Dalia Dassa, *Talking to the Enemy: Track Two Diplomacy in the Middle East and South Asia* (Lanham: National Book Network, 2007).

Kaye, Dalia Dassa, 'Track two diplomacy and regional security in the Middle East', *International Negotiation* (2001): 49–77.

Kerr, Malcolm, *The Arab Cold War, 1958–1964: A Study of the Ideology in Politics* (Oxford: Oxford University Press, 1965).

Keynoush, Banafsheh, *Saudi Arabia and Iran: Friends or Foes?* (London: Palgrave Macmillan, 2016).

Khadduri, Majid, 'Iran's claim to the sovereignty of Bahrayn', *American Journal of International Law* 45, 4 (October 1951): 631–47.

Khan, Mubarak Zeb, 'Pakistan eyes free trade pact with Iran', *Dawn*, 20 January 2016, https://www.dawn.com/news/1234061.

Kinninmont, Jane, 'Iran and the GCC: unnecessary insecurity', *Chatham House*, July 2017, https://www.chathamhouse.org/sites/files/chathamhouse/field/field_doc ument/20150703IranGCCKinninmont.pdf.

Korpi, Walter, 'Conflict and the balance of power', *Acta Sociologica* 17, 2 (1974): 99–114.

Kriesberg, Louis, *Constructive Conflicts, from Escalation to Resolution* (Lanham: Rowman & Littlefield Publishing, 2007).

Laipson, Ellen, 'Can regional powers mediate the Saudi–Iran conflict?', *World Politics Review*, 12 January 2016, http://www.worldpoliticsreview.com/articles/17648/ can-regional-powers-mediate-the-saudi-iran-conflict.

Lederach, John Paul, *Building Peace, Sustainable Reconciliation in Divided Societies* (Washington: United States Institute of Peace, 1997).

Lynch, Marc, 'The entrepreneurs of cynical sectarianism', in Marc Lynch (ed.), *The Politics of Sectarianism* (Washington: Project on Middle East Political Science, 2013), http://pomeps.org/wp-content/uploads/2014/06/POMEPS_Studies4_Sectarianism.pdf.

Mabon, Simon, 'The battle for Bahrain: Iranian–Saudi rivalry', *Middle East Policy* 19, 2 (Summer 2012): 84–97.

Mabon, Simon, 'Kingdom in crisis? The Arab Spring and instability in Saudi Arabia', *Contemporary Security Policy* 33, 3 (2012): 530–53.

Mabon, Simon, 'Muting the trumpets of sabotage: Saudi Arabia, the US and the quest to securitize Iran', *British Journal of Middle Eastern Studies* 45, 5 (2017): 1–18.

Mabon, Simon, *Saudi Arabia and Iran: Soft Power Rivalry in the Middle East* (London: I. B. Tauris, 2013).

Makdisi, Ussama, 'Reconstructing the nation-state: the modernity of sectarianism in Lebanon', *Middle East Report* 200 (July–September 1996).

Maloney, Suzanne, *Iran's Long Reach: Iran as a Pivotal State in the Muslim World* (Washington: US Institute of Peace Press, 2008).

Mapendere, Jeffrey, 'Track one and a half diplomacy and the complementarity of tracks', *Culture of Peace Online Journal* 2, 1 (2005): 66–81.

Marashi, Riza, 'Ending the Iranian–Saudi cold war', *National Iranian Council*, https://www.niacouncil.org/ending-the-iranian-saudi-cold-war/.

Mason, Robert, *Foreign Policy in Iran and Saudi Arabia, Economics and Diplomacy in the Middle East* (London: I. B. Tauris, 2015).

Mason, Simon J. A., and Matthias Siegfried, 'Confidence building measures (CBMs) in peace processes', in Luc Chounet-Cambas (ed.), *Managing Peace Processes: Process Related Questions. A Handbook for AU Practitioners*, vol. 1 (Addis Ababa: African Union and the Centre for Humanitarian Dialogue, 2013), pp. 57–78.

Matthiesen, Toby, 'Hizballah al-Hijaz: a history of the most radical Saudi Shi'a opposition group', *Middle East Journal* 64, 2 (2010): 179–97.

Matthiesen, Toby, *The Other Saudis: Shiism, Dissent and Sectarianism* (Cambridge: Cambridge University Press, 2014).

Matthiesen, Toby, 'Sectarianism in the Middle East', *Boston University Institute on Culture, Religion & World Affairs*, 20 March 2014, https://www.bu.edu/cura/files/2013/10/Matthiesen.pdf.

Mills, Robin, 'Risky routes: energy transit in the Middle East', Brookings Doha Center, Analysis Paper no. 17, April 2016, https://www.brookings.edu/research/risky-routes-energy-transit-in-the-middle-east/.

Mitchell, Christopher, *Gestures of Conciliation: Factors Contributing to Successful Olive-Branches* (London: Palgrave Macmillan, 2000).

Mitchell, Christopher, *The Structure of International Conflict* (London: Palgrave Macmillan, 1981).

Molavi, Afshin, 'Iran and the Gulf States', *United States Institute of Peace*, August 2015, http://iranprimer.usip.org/resource/iran-and-gulf-states.

Montville, Joseph V., 'The arrow and the olive branch: a case for track two diplomacy', in Vamik D. Volkan, Joseph V. Montville and Demetrios A. Julius (eds), *The Psychodynamics of International Relationships*, vol. II (Lexington: Lexington Books, 1991).

Montville, Joseph V., 'Track two diplomacy: the work of healing history', *The Whitehead Journal of Diplomacy and International Relations* 17, 2 (Summer/Fall 2006): 15–25.

Nan, Susan Allen, 'Coordination and complementarity of conflict resolution efforts in the conflicts over Abkhazia, South Ossetia, and Transdniestria', Doctoral Dissertation, George Mason University, Fairfax, VA, 1999.

Nan, Susan Allen, 'Track one-and-a-half diplomacy: contributions to Georgia–South Ossetian peacemaking', in R. J. Fisher (ed.), *Paving the Way: Contributions of Interactive Conflict Resolution to Peacemaking* (New York: Lexington, 2005).

Nasr, Vali, *The Shia Revival: How Conflicts within Islam Will Shape the Future* (New York: W. W. Norton and Company, 2007).

Nasr, Vali, 'The War for Islam', *Foreign Policy*, 22 January 2016, http://foreignpolicy.com/2016/01/22/the-war-for-islam-sunni-shiite-iraq-syria/.

Obaid, Nawaf, 'The Salman doctrine: the Saudi reply to Obama's weakness', Harvard Kennedy School, *Belfer Center for Science and International Affairs*, 30 March 2016, https://www.belfercenter.org/publication/salman-doctrine-saudi-reply-obamas-weakness.

Parsi, Rouzbeh, 'The Elusive Project of Common Security in the Persian Gulf', *Project on Middle East Political Science*, 17 March 2014, https://pomeps.org/2014/03/24/the-elusive-project-of-common-security-in-the-persian-gulf/.

Peterson, John E., *Saudi Arabia and the Illusion of Security* (Oxford: Oxford University Press for the International Institute for Strategic Studies, 2002).

'POMEPS Conversations 28 with Toby Matthiesen', *Project on Middle East Political Science*, 1 November 2013, http://pomeps.org/2013/11/01/pomeps-conversation-28-with-toby-matthiesen-1112013/.

Potter, Lawrence G., 'Introduction', in Lawrence G. Potter (ed.), *Sectarian Politics in the Persian Gulf* (Oxford: Oxford University Press, 2014), pp. 1–31.

Pradhan, Prasanta Kumar, 'The GCC–Iran conflict and its strategic implications for the Gulf region', *Strategic Analysis* 35, 2 (March 2011).

Quandt, William, *Saudi Arabia in the 1980s: Foreign Policy, Security, and Oil* (Washington: Brookings Institution Press, 1981).

Rafiq, Arif, 'Can Pakistan broker an Iran–Saudi détente?', *The National Interest*, 21 January 2016, http://nationalinterest.org/feature/can-pakistan-broker-iran-saudi-d%C3%A9tente-14972?page=show.

Reese, Aaron, 'Sectarian and regional conflict in the Middle East', *Middle East Security Report* 13 (July 2013).

Riedel, Bruce, 'Pakistan and Saudi Arabia reconcile after rift over Yemen war', *Markaz* blog, *Brookings Institution*, 8 November 2015, http://www.brookings.edu/blogs/markaz/posts/2015/11/08-saudi-pakistan-reconciliation-yemen-peacekeeping-riedel.

Ropers, Norbert, 'From resolution to transformation: the role of dialogue projects', Berghof Research Center for Constructive Conflict Management, 2004, http://edoc.vifapol.de/opus/volltexte/2011/2580/pdf/ropers_handbook.pdf.

Ryan, Curtis, 'The new Arab cold war and the struggle for Syria', *Middle East Report* 262 (2012): 28–31.

Ryan, Curtis, 'Regime security and shifting alliances in the Middle East', *Project on Middle East Political Science (POMEPS)*, briefings 31, October 2017, https://pomeps.org/2015/08/20/regime-security-and-shifting-alliances-in-the-middle-east/.

Said, A. S., C. O. Lerche Jr and C. O. Lerche III, *Concepts of International Politics in Global Perspective* (Englewood Cliffs: Prentice Hall, 1995).

Salem, Paul, 'A response to Iranian foreign minister Zarif', *The Middle East Institute*, 30 April 2015, http://www.mei.edu/content/article/irans-arab-policy-change-dialogue.

Shabani, Mohammad Ali, 'Iran: strategist or sectarian', in ECFR Gulf Analysis, *The Gulf and Sectarianism*, November 2013, p. 5, http://www.ecfr.eu/page/-/ECFR91_GULF_ANALYSIS_AW.pdf.

Sharifi-Yazdi, Farzad Cyrus, *Arab–Iranian Rivalry in the Persian Gulf: Territorial Disputes and the Balance of Power in the Middle East* (London: I. B. Tauris, 2015).

Sick, Gary, 'The United States in the Persian Gulf, from twin pillars to dual containment', in David Lesch and Mark Haas (eds), *The Middle East and the United States, History, Politics, and Ideologies* (Boulder: Westview Press, 2005), pp. 327–43.

Smith, Keith, 'Realist foreign policy analysis with a twist: the Persian Gulf security complex and the rise and fall of dual containment', *Foreign Policy Analysis* 12, 3 (2016): 315–33.

Stanford Arms Control Group, 'Agreements and treaties other than SALT and the NPT', in Coit D. Blacker and Gloria Duffy (eds), *International Arms Control* (Palo Alto: Stanford University Press, 1984).

Terrill, W. Andrew, 'The Saudi–Iranian rivalry and the future of Middle East security', *Current Politics and Economics of the Middle East* 3, 4 (2011).

Thacher, Stephen L., 'Crisis communications between super powers', Study Project, US Army War College, 12 February 1990, file:///C:/Users/dinterns/Downloads/ADA222248.pdf.

Ulrichsen, Kristian, 'Palestinians sidelined in Saudi–Emirati rapprochement with Israel', *Journal of Palestine Studies* 47, 4 (2018): 79–89.

United Nations Development Programme (UNDP), 'Why dialogue matters for conflict prevention and peacebuilding', February 2009, http://www.undp.org/content/dam/undp/library/crisis%20prevention/dialogue_conflict.pdf.

United Nations, Security Council, *Doha Agreement on the outcome of the meeting of the Lebanese National Dialogue*, S/2008/392, 10 June 2008, http://www.securitycouncilreport.org/atf/cf/%7B65BFCF9B-6D27-4E9C-8CD3-CF6E4FF96FF9%7D/Lebanon%20S2008392.pdf.

Valbjorn, Morten, and Andre Bank, 'Signs of a new Arab cold war: the 2006 Lebanon war and the Sunni–Shi'i divide', *Middle East Report*, 242 (Spring 2007): 6–11.

Valbjorn, Morten, and Andre Bank, 'The new Arab cold war: rediscovering the Arab dimension of Middle East regional politics', *Review of International Studies* 38, 1 (2012): 3–24.

Valeri, Marc, *Oman: Politics and Society in the Qaboos State* (Oxford: Oxford University Press, 2014).

Vine, David, 'America still has hundreds of military bases worldwide. Have they made us any safer?', *Mother Jones*, 14 November 2014, http://www.motherjones.com/politics/2014/11/america-still-has-hundreds-military-bases-worldwide-have-they-made-us-any-safer.

Walt, Stephen M., *The Origins of Alliances* (Ithaca: Cornell University Press, 1987).

Walt, Stephen M., *Revolution and War* (Ithaca: Cornell University Press, 1996).

Ware, Lewis B., *et al.*, *Low Intensity Conflict in the Third World* (Alabama: Air University Press, 1988).

Warfield, Wallace, 'Moving from civil war to civil society', *Peace Review* 9, 2 (1997): 249–54.

Wehrey, Frederic (ed.), *Beyond Sunni and Shia: The Roots of Sectarianism in a Changing Middle East* (London: C. Hurst & Co., 2017).

Wehrey, Frederic, 'The Roots and Future of Sectarianism in the Gulf', *Project on Middle East Political Science*, 21 March 2014, http://pomeps.org/2014/03/21/the-roots-and-future-of-sectarianism-in-the-gulf/.

Wehrey, Frederic, 'Saudi Arabia's anxious autocrats', *Journal of Democracy* 26, 2 (2015): 71–85.

Wehrey, Frederic, *Sectarian Politics in the Gulf: From the Iraq War to the Arab Uprisings* (New York: Columbia University Press, 2013).

Wehrey, Frederic, 'Uprisings jolt the Saudi–Iranian rivalry', *Current History* 110, 740 (December 2011): 352.

Wehrey, Frederic, Theodore W. Karasik, Alireza Nader, Jeremy J. Ghez, Lydia Hansell and Robert A. Guffey, *Saudi–Iranian Relations Since the Fall of Saddam: Rivalry, Cooperation, and Implications for U.S. Policy* (Santa Monica: RAND Corporation, 2009).

Wright, Robin, *Sacred Rage: The Wrath of Militant Islam* (New York: Simon and Schuster, 2001).

Zarif, Mohammad Javad, 'A message from Iran', *New York Times*, 20 April 2015, http://www.nytimes.com/2015/04/20/opinion/mohammad-javad-zarif-a-message-from-iran.html?_r=1.

Zartman, William, *Ripe for Resolution: Conflict and Intervention in Africa* (Oxford: Oxford University Press, 1985).

Zartman, William, 'Ripening conflict, ripe moment, formula, and mediation', in Diane B. Bendahmane and John W. McDonald (eds), *Perspectives on Negotiation* (Washington: Center for the Study of Foreign Affairs, Foreign Service Institute, US Department of State, 1986).

Zinnes, Dina A., 'An analytical study of the balance of power theories', *Journal of Peace Research* 4, 2 (1967): 270–88.

Author's Interviews

Adib-Moghaddam, Arshin. Chair of Centre for Iranian Studies at the School of Oriental and African Studies (SOAS) in London, March 2016.

Ahmadian, Hassan. Adjunct Professor at the University of Tehran and a senior research fellow at the Center for Strategic Research, email exchange and discussion, May 2016.

Alnajjar, Baqer. Sociology Professor at the University of Bahrain, Doha, May 2015.

Al Shayji, Abdullah. Political Science Professor at Kuwait University, panel discussion, Doha Forum, May 2016.

Al-Smadi, Fatima. Iran expert at *Al Jazeera* Center for Studies in Doha, June 2015.

Altikriti, Anas. CEO of the London-based Cordoba Foundation, Vienna, Austria, November 2017.

Baabood, Abdullah. Director of the Gulf Research Program, Doha, September 2017.

Eslami, Reza. Conflict resolution expert from Iran, phone interview, January 2016.

Faeez, Abdalkader. Director of *Al Jazeera* office in Tehran, June 2019.

Hadian, Naser. Political Science Professor at the University of Tehran, April 2016.

Ibish, Hussein. Expert at Arab Gulf States Institute, Washington, DC, September 2015.

Kamrava, Mehran, Director of the Center for Regional and International Studies at Georgetown University School of Foreign Service in Qatar, Doha, June 2015, September 2015.

Kadhim, Abbas. Senior Fellow and Director of the Atlantic Council's Iraq Initiative, Washington, DC, September 2015.

Khashoggi, Jamal. Opinion leader, journalist, and *Washington Post* columnist, Doha, November 2015, April 2016, May 2016.

Khouri, Rami. Senior Public Policy Fellow at the American University in Beirut and Harvard University, Washington, DC, September 2017.

Mousavian, Seyyed Hossein. Former member of the Iranian Supreme National Security Council. Author's interview and discussion, March 2016 (telephone conversation), May 2016, Doha, Qatar.

Nourizadeh, Alireza. Director of the Centre of Arab and Iranian Studies in London, Doha, May 2016.

Riedel, Bruce. Senior Foreign Policy expert at the Brookings Institution, Washington, DC, April 2016.

Said, Haider. Iraqi expert on Iran and the Gulf, Doha, November 2015.

Sager, Abdulaziz. Director of the Gulf Research Center in Saudi Arabia, email exchange, January 2016.

Saudi official, Riyadh, May 2016.

Wright, Steven. Gulf scholar at Hamad Bin Khalifa University, Doha, May 2015, October 2016.

Vaiz, Ali. Senior Iran analyst at the International Crisis Group, email exchange and discussion, February 2016.

Vatanka, Alex. Iran expert at the Middle East Institute in Washington, DC, January 2016.

Zaccara, Luciano. Iran expert at Qatar University's Gulf Studies Program, Doha, September 2015.

Zweiri, Mahjoob. Iran scholar at Qatar University, Doha, May 2015.

Track Two Workshops

Track two workshops (author's participation – selected):

'Geopolitics, Nuclear Issues and the Middle East', International Institute for Strategic Studies (IISS), Rome, Italy, April 2018.

'Gulf Security', an Iran–Gulf track two workshop organised by the European Iran Research Group, Montreux, Switzerland, December 2017.

'Iran–Arab Relations', Arab Center for Research and Policy Studies, May 2016.

'Iran–GCC Dialogue', Georgetown University's Center for Regional and International Studies in Qatar, January 2016 and September 2016, Doha, Qatar, and a public event in October 2015.

'Iran–Gulf Relations', Gulf Studies Program at Qatar University and co-sponsored by Chatham House in London, Doha, March 2016.

'Security Roadmap for West Asia and the Arabian Peninsula', Center for Applied Research in Partnership with the Orient (CAPRO) in cooperation with the EastWest Institute's Middle East and North Africa department in Brussels, Rome, Italy, April 2019.

News Sources

Abbasi, Mamoon, 'Iran continues to boast of its regional reach', *Middle East Eye*, 10 March 2015, http://www.middleeasteye.net/news/iran-continues-boast-regional-reach-944755422.

Aboulenein, Ahmed, 'Syrian security chief makes public Cairo visit – SANA', *Reuters*, 17 October 2016, http://uk.reuters.com/article/uk-mideast-crisis-syria-egypt-idUKKBN12H2AM.

Ahmadian, Hassan, 'Iranian olive branch offers diplomatic paradigm shift', *Al-Monitor*, 4 November 2015, http://www.al-monitor.com/pulse/originals/2015/11/iran-new-regional-paradigm.html.

'Al-Amiri: Hashid al-Shaabi is the strongest in Iraq', *Al Jazeera*, 1 September 2016, https://goo.gl/YVpoJr.

Al-Bayari, Maen, 'Jordanian opening with Tehran a sign of regional mood', *The New Arab*, 10 March 2015, https://www.alaraby.co.uk/english/comment/2015/3/10/jordanian-opening-with-tehran-a-sign-of-regional-mood.

Al-Buluwi, Abdulmajeed, 'Saudi invitation a first step with Iran', *Al-Monitor*, 16 May 2014, http://www.al-monitor.com/pulse/originals/2014/05/saudi-arabia-iran-region-deescalation.html#ixzz3f1jZ7Vc5.

Al Dakheel, Khaled, interview with *Al Jazeera* TV channel, 26 September 2016.

Al Faisal, Turki, 'Inside the awkward US–Saudi alliance against ISIS', *Frontline*, https://www.youtube.com/watch?v=9UDLxkkXPnc (last accessed 10 April 2017).

Al-Marashi, Ibrahim, 'Shattering the myths about Kuwaiti Shia', *Al Jazeera*, 30 June 2015, http://www.aljazeera.com/indepth/opinion/2015/06/shattering-myths-kuwaiti-shia-150629081723864.html1.

Al-Omran, Ahmed, and Asa Fitch, 'Saudi Arabia forms Muslim anti-terror coalition', *The Wall Street Journal*, 15 December 2015, http://www.wsj.com/articles/saudi-arabia-forms-muslim-anti-terror-coalition-1450191561.

Al-Sakkaf, Nasser, 'Salafis forced to flee Dammaj, government forces unable to protect them, they say', *Yemen Times*, 16 January 2014, http://www.yementimes.com/en/1747/news/3365/Salafis-forced-to-flee-Dammaj-government-forces-unable-to-protect-them-they-say.htm.

Al-Shaibany, Saleh, 'Rouhani meets rulers of Oman and Kuwait to reduce Iran–GCC tensions', *The National*, 15 February 2017, https://www.thenational.ae/world/rouhani-meets-rulers-of-oman-and-kuwait-to-reduce-iran-gcc-tensions-1.52558.

Al-Thuweini, Abdullah, 'Tehran official: Baghdad is capital of new Persian empire', *The New Arab*, 10 March 2015, https://www.alaraby.co.uk/english/news/2015/3/10/tehran-official-baghdad-is-capital-of-new-persian-empire.

Avishai, Bernard, 'Netanyahu's speech', *The New Yorker*, 3 March 2015, https://www.newyorker.com/news/news-desk/netanyahu-speech-congress.

Bayat, Asef, 'The fire that fueled the Iran protests', *The Atlantic*, 27 January 2018, https://www.theatlantic.com/international/archive/2018/01/iran-protest-mashaad-green-class-labor-economy/551690/.

Beauchamp, Zack, 'Iran and Saudi Arabia's cold war is making the Middle East even more dangerous', *Vox*, 30 March 2015, http://www.vox.com/2015/3/30/8314513/saudi-arabia-iran.

Bennett, D. Scott, 'Balance of power dynamics and war: a competing risks model of escalation', http://www.personal.psu.edu/dsb10/papers/BOP%20Escalation%202-06.pdf.

'The black box: Nouri al-Maliki . . . the whole story', *Al Jazeera*, 18 October 2015, https://goo.gl/e6UQeA.

Black, Ian, 'Fear of a Shia full moon', *The Guardian*, 26 January 2007, https://www.theguardian.com/world/2007/jan/26/worlddispatch.ianblack.

Boone, Jon, and Saeed Kamali Dehgan, 'Pakistan's parliament votes against entering Yemen conflict', *The Guardian*, 10 April 2015, https://www.theguardian.com/world/2015/apr/10/pakistans-parliament-votes-against-entering-yemen-conflict.

Browning, Noah, and John Irish, 'Saudi Arabia announces 34-state Islamic military alliance against terrorism', *Reuters*, 15 December 2015, http://www.reuters.com/article/us-saudi-security-idUSKBN0TX2PG20151215.

Castiel, Carol, 'Encounter', *Voice of America*, 15 January 2016, http://www.voanews.com/audio/3126883.html.

Charbonneau, Louis, 'Iran submits four-point Yemen peace plan to United Nations', *Reuters*, 17 April 2017, http://www.reuters.com/article/2015/04/17/us-yemen-security-iran-idUSKBN0N823820150417#8kgJHEAdtBzoCiQO.97.

Chulov, Martin, 'Saudi Arabia cuts diplomatic ties with Iran after execution of cleric', *The Guardian*, 4 January 2016, https://www.theguardian.com/world/2016/jan/03/saudi-arabia-cuts-diplomatic-ties-with-iran-after-nimr-execution.

Comments made at 'Conference: The Arabs and Iran – Problems in the relationship', *Al Jazeera Center for Studies*, 16 February 2016, https://www.youtube.com/watch?v=UoUYA3wysLk.

Cooper, Andrew, speaking at an event hosted by the American–Iranian Council, 8 February 2016, https://www.youtube.com/watch?v=PHcfTvHqcpc.

'Country-wise workers' remittances', *State Bank of Pakistan* http://www.sbp.org.pk/ecodata/Homeremit.pdf (last accessed 8 February 2018).

Dabashi, Hamid, 'Who is the "Great Satan?"', *Al Jazeera*, 20 September 2015, http://www.aljazeera.com/indepth/opinion/2015/09/great-satan-150920072643884.html.

Dehghan, Saeed Kamali, 'Iran's Supreme Leader accuses Saudis of "genocide" in Yemen', *The Guardian*, 9 April 2015, http://www.theguardian.com/world/2015/apr/09/iranian-president-rouhani-yemen-ceasefire.

'Despots are pushing the Arab world to become more secular', *The Economist*, 2 November 2017, https://www.economist.com/news/middle-east-and-africa/21730899-they-are-consolidating-their-own-power-process-despots-are-pushing.

Egan, Matt, 'Saudi Arabia: we're not crashing oil prices to hurt Iran', *CNN Money*, 19 January 2016, http://money.cnn.com/2016/01/19/investing/saudi-arabia-oil-prices-iran/.

Emmott, Robin, and Noah Barkin, 'Iran says ready to put rivalries aside with Saudi Arabia', *Reuters*, 12 February 2016, http://www.reuters.com/article/us-mideast-crisis-iran-saudi-idUSKCN0VL236.

Fattah, Hassan M., 'Saudi–Iran meeting yields little substance', *The New York Times*, 5 March 2007, http://www.nytimes.com/2007/03/05/world/middleeast/05saudi.html.

'Fears in Iraqi government army over Shiite militias' power', *Associated Press*, 21 March 2016, https://www.yahoo.com/news/fears-iraqi-government-army-over-060458082.html?ref=gs.

Filkins, Dexter, 'What we left behind', *New Yorker*, 28 April 2014, http://www.newyorker.com/magazine/2014/04/28/what-we-left-behind.

Fraihat, Ibrahim, 'Iran and Saudi Arabia tensions', *CNN* interview, 7 January 2016, https://www.youtube.com/watch?v=pw9eqNruAto (last accessed 18 June 2019).

Fraihat, Ibrahim, 'Nimr al Nimr: anatomy of a man', *Newsweek*, 13 January 2016, http://newsweekme.com/nimr-al-nimr-anatomy-of-a-man/ (last accessed 27 January 2018).

Gardner, David, 'Trump's "deal of the century" offers nothing good to the Palestinians', *Financial Times*, 5 September 2018, https://www.ft.com/content/40d77344-b04a-11e8-8d14-6f049d06439c (last accessed 6 June 2019).

'Geography', *Pakistan Tourism Development Corporation*, http://www.tourism.gov.pk/geography_pakistan.htm (last accessed 8 February 2018).

Ghattas, Kim, 'The Saudi cold war with Iran heats up', *Foreign Policy*, 15 July 2015, http://foreignpolicy.com/2015/07/15/the-saudi-cold-war-with-iran-heats-up/.

Ghobari, Mohammed, and Mohammed Mukhashaf, 'Saudi-led planes bomb Sanaa airport to stop Iranian plane landing', *Reuters*, 28 April 2015, http://www.reuters.com/article/us-yemen-security-airport-idUSKBN0NJ24120150428.

Goldberg, Jeffrey, 'The Obama doctrine', *The Atlantic*, April 2016, https://www.theatlantic.com/magazine/archive/2016/04/the-obama-doctrine/471525/.

Gordon, Michael R., and Eric Schmitt, 'Tensions flare between Iraq and Saudi Arabia in U.S. coalition', *The New York Times*, 15 April 2015, http://www.nytimes.com/2015/04/16/world/middleeast/iraqi-prime-minister-criticizes-saudi-intervention-in-yemen.html?_r=1.

'Hadi al-Ameri . . . Iran's "General" in Iraq', *Al Jazeera*, 28 February 2016, https://goo.gl/ZgyrEE.

'Hajj stampede: Iran death toll rises to 464', *BBC*, 1 October 2015, http://www.bbc.com/news/world-middle-east-34410484.

Harding, Luke, 'Pakistan frees Sharif to exile in Saudi Arabia', *The Guardian*, 10 December 2000, https://www.theguardian.com/world/2000/dec/11/pakistan.saudiarabia.

Harris, Shane, Kelly Crow and Summer Said, 'Saudi Arabia's Crown Prince identified as buyer of record-breaking da Vinci', *The Wall Street Journal*, 7 December 2017, https://www.wsj.com/articles/saudi-arabias-crown-prince-identified-as-buyer-of-record-breaking-da-vinci-1512674099.

Heavey, Susa, 'Saudi Arabia, Iran must shape "cold peace", Obama says', *Reuters*, 20 March 2016, http://www.reuters.com/article/us-mideast-crisis-obama-idUSKCN0WC23A.

Human Rights Watch, *Iran, Religious and Ethnic Minorities: Discrimination in Law and Practice*, 1997, available at https://www.hrw.org/legacy/reports/1997/iran/Iran-06.htm#P397_84566 (last accessed 13 October 2018).

Ignatius, David, 'The Saudi Crown Prince just made a very risky power play', *The Washington Post*, 5 November 2017, https://www.washingtonpost.com/opinions/global-opinions/the-saudi-crown-princes-risky-power-play/2017/11/05/4b12fcf0-c272-11e7-afe9-4f60b5a6c4a0_story.html?utm_term=.a76dc5e1b5dc.

'Iran calls for "puny Satan" Saudi Arabia to be stripped of Hajj duties', *Middle East Eye*, 5 September 2016, http://www.middleeasteye.net/news/iran-calls-small-and-puny-satan-saudi-arabia-be-stripped-hajj-management-1644348841.

'Iran general warns Bahrain after Shia cleric stripped of citizenship', *BBC News*, 20 June 2016, http://www.bbc.com/news/world-middle-east-36578844.

'Iran suggests Saudi should not run Muslim pilgrimage', *Reuters*, 5 September 2016, https://www.reuters.com/article/saudi-haj-iran/iran-suggests-saudi-should-not-run-muslim-pilgrimage-idUSL8N1BH1DS.

'Iran summons Saudi diplomat over plane interception', *Tehran Times*, 26 April 2015, http://www.tehrantimes.com/index_View.asp?code=246338.

'Iran welcomes old foes to Islamic summit', *CNN*, 8 December 1997, http://edition.cnn.com/WORLD/9712/08/islamic.conference/.

Jafari, Saeid, 'How Iran should approach the GCC', *Al-Monitor*, 3 August 2015, http://www.al-monitor.com/pulse/originals/2015/08/iran-gcc-relations.html.

Jehl, Douglas, 'On trip to mend ties, Iran's President meets Saudi Prince', *The New York Times*, 17 May 1999, http://www.nytimes.com/1999/05/17/world/on-trip-to-mend-ties-iran-s-president-meets-saudi-prince.html.

'Joint statement by EU High Representative Federica Mogherini and Iranian Foreign Minister Javad Zarif', *European Union*, 14 July 2015, http://eeas.europa.eu/statements-eeas/2015/150714_01_en.htm.

Jones, Rory, 'Kuwait charges 26 suspects with plotting attacks against it', *The Wall Street Journal*, 1 September 2015, http://www.wsj.com/articles/kuwait-charges-26-suspects-with-plotting-attacks-against-it-1441132841.

Juneau, Thomas, 'No, Yemen's Houthis actually aren't Iranian puppets', *The Washington Post*, 16 May 2016, https://www.washingtonpost.com/news/monkey-cage/wp/2016/05/16/contrary-to-popular-belief-houthis-arent-iranian-proxies/.

Kakar, Shah Faisal, 'KSA–Pakistan ties touch new heights', *Arab News*, 14 August 2015, http://www.arabnews.com/saudi-arabia/news/790986.

Kalin, Stephen, and Katie Paul, 'Future Saudi King tightens grip on power with arrests including prince Al-Waleed', *Reuters*, 4 November 2017, https://www.reuters.com/article/us-saudi-arrests/future-saudi-king-tightens-grip-on-power-with-arrests-including-prince-alwaleed-idUSKBN1D506P.

Karami, Arash, 'German FM: Iran, Saudi tensions strengthen terrorists', *Al-Monitor*, 19 October 2015, http://www.al-monitor.com/pulse/originals/2015/10/iran-saudi-germany-foreign-minsiter.html.

'Khamenei condemns Saudi embassy attack', *Reuters*, 20 January 2016, http://english.alarabiya.net/en/News/middle-east/2016/01/20/Khamenei-condemns-attack-on-Saudi-embassy-in-Tehran.html.

Khashoggi, Jamal, 'The secret Saudi–Iranian track two negotiation', *al-Hayat*, 6 December 2013, http://www.alhayat.com/Details/579415.

Kimball, Daryl, 'Timeline of Syrian chemical weapons activity, 2012–2018', *Arms Control Association*, November 2018, https://www.armscontrol.org/factsheets/Timeline-of-Syrian-Chemical-Weapons-Activity.

Kovessy, Peter, 'Emir offers to host "meaningful dialogue" to ease Arab–Iranian tensions', *Doha News*, 29 September 2015, http://dohanews.co/emir-offers-to-host-meaningful-dialogue-to-ease-arab-iranian-tensions/.

Kulish, Nicholas, and Michael Forsythe, 'World's most expensive home another bauble for a Saudi prince', *The New York Times*, 16 December 2017, https://mobile.nytimes.com/2017/12/16/world/middleeast/saudi-prince-chateau.html?_r=0&referer=https://www.google.com/.

Lacroix, Stéphane, 'Saudi Arabia just let women drive, don't mistake it for democracy', *The Washington Post*, 5 October 2017, https://www.washingtonpost.com/news/monkey-cage/wp/2017/10/05/saudi-arabia-finally-let-women-drive-dont-mistake-it-for-democratic-reform/?utm_term=.0abf3b63bdcc.

'Landmark Iran–Saudi security deal', *BBC*, 18 April 2001, http://news.bbc.co.uk/2/hi/middle_east/1283010.stm.

'Lebanon's parliament elects ex-general Michel Aoun president', *Deutsche Welle*, 31 October 2016, http://www.dw.com/en/lebanons-parliament-elects-ex-general-michel-aoun-president/a-36211650.

Leonnig, Carol D., 'Iran held liable in Khobar attack', *The Washington Post*, 23 December 2006, http://www.washingtonpost.com/wp-dyn/content/article/2006/12/22/AR2006122200455.html.

'Letter dated 22 May 2008 from the Permanent Observer of the League of Arab States to the United Nations addressed to the President of the Security Council', UN Security Council S/2008/392, 10 June 2008, http://www.securitycouncil-report.org/atf/cf/%7B65BFCF9B-6D27-4E9C-8CD3-CF6E4FF96FF9%7D/Lebanon%20S2008392.pdf.

Lynch, Marc, 'What Saudi Arabia's purge means for the Middle East', *The Washington Post*, 6 November 2017, https://www.washingtonpost.com/news/monkey-cage/wp/2017/11/06/what-saudi-arabias-purge-means-for-the-middle-east/?utm_term=.18d2f4629a67.

Lynch, Marc, 'Why Saudi Arabia escalated the Middle East's sectarian conflict', *The Washington Post*, 4 January 2016, https://www.washingtonpost.com/news/monkey-cage/wp/2016/01/04/why-saudi-arabia-escalated-the-middle-easts-sectarian-conflict/.

McDowall, Angus, 'Saudi King sits next to Iran's Ahmadinejad in goodwill gesture', *Reuters*, 14 August 2012, http://www.reuters.com/article/2012/08/14/us-saudi-iran-syria-summit-idUSBRE87D14H20120814.

'Memorandum of understanding between the United States of America and the Union of Soviet Socialist Republics regarding the establishment of a direct communications link', US Department of State, 20 June 1963, http://www.state.gov/t/isn/4785.htm.

'More countries back Saudi Arabia in Iran dispute', *Al Jazeera*, 6 January 2016, http://www.aljazeera.com/news/2016/01/nations-saudi-arabia-row-iran-160106125405507.html.

'Morocco says will send food to Qatar after Gulf states cut ties', *Reuters*, 13 June 2017, https://www.reuters.com/article/us-gulf-qatar-morocco/morocco-says-will-send-food-to-qatar-after-gulf-states-cut-ties-idUSKBN1940RD.

Mousavian, Seyed Hossein, 'Saudi Arabia is Iran's new national security threat', *Huffington Post*, 3 June 2016, https://www.huffingtonpost.com/seyed-hossein-mousavian/saudi-arabia-iran-threat_b_10282296.html.

Nasr, Vali, 'If the Arab Spring turns ugly', *The New York Times*, 27 August 2011, https://www.nytimes.com/2011/08/28/opinion/sunday/the-dangers-lurking-in-the-arab-spring.html.

Nehme, Dahlia, 'Top Saudi cleric says Iran leaders not Muslims as haj row mounts', *Reuters*, 7 September 2016, http://www.reuters.com/article/us-saudi-iran-mufti-idUSKCN11D0HV.

'Oslo Accords: declaration of principles on interim self-government arrangements', 1993, http://cis.uchicago.edu/oldsite/sites/cis.uchicago.edu/files/resources/CIS-090213-israelpalestine_38-1993DeclarationofPrinciples_OsloAccords.pdf.

'Pakistan', *CIA World Factbook*, https://www.cia.gov/library/publications/the-world-factbook/geos/pk.html (last accessed 8 February 2018).

Pear, Robert, 'Khomeini accepts "poison" of ending the war with Iraq; U.N. sending mission', *The New York Times*, 21 July 1988, http://www.nytimes.com/1988/07/21/us/khomeini-accepts-poison-of-ending-the-war-with-iraq-un-sending-mission.html.

'President Trump compares a phone call with the King to collecting rent', *C-Span*, 28 April 2019, https://www.c-span.org/video/?c4794551/collecting-nyc-tenant (last accessed 4 June 2019).

'Qatar says Gulf Arabs confident region safer with Iran deal', *Reuters*, 3 August 2015, http://www.reuters.com/article/us-iran-nuclear-gcc-qatar-idUSKC-N0Q81Q320150803.

Riedel, Bruce, 'High stakes as Saudi Crown Prince tries to remove opponents', *Al-Monitor*, 4 November 2017, https://www.al-monitor.com/pulse/originals/2017/11/saudi-arabia-crown-prince-remove-opponents-national-guard.html.

Sang-Hun, Choe, 'North Korea reopens border hotline with South', *New York Times*, 3 January 2018, https://www.nytimes.com/2018/01/03/world/asia/north-korea-hotline-south.html.

'Saudi Arabia: prominent clerics arrested, coordinated crackdown on dissent', *Human Rights Watch*, 15 September 2017, https://www.hrw.org/news/2017/09/15/saudi-arabia-prominent-clerics-arrested.

'Saudi Arabia, Turkey to set up "strategic cooperation council"', *Russia Today*, 29 December 2015, https://www.rt.com/news/327391-turkey-saudi-arabia-erdogan-syria/.

'Saudi Arabia, Turkey to set up "strategic cooperation council" – Saudi FM', *Reuters*, 29 December 2015, http://uk.reuters.com/article/uk-saudi-turkey-idUKKBN0UC1GX20151229.

'Saudi Arabia vs Iran: is the cold war heating up?', *UpFront, Al Jazeera*, 16 January 2016, http://www.aljazeera.com/programmes/upfront/2016/01/saudi-arabia-iran-cold-war-heating-160115075435374.html.

'Saudi King Abdullah and Senior Princes on Saudi policy toward Iraq', *Wikileaks*, 20 April 2008, https://wikileaks.org/plusd/cables/08RIYADH649_a.html.

'Ten times more effective than nukes: Iran weighs creation of naval bases in Syria, Yemen', *Russia Today*, 26 November 2016, https://www.rt.com/news/368306-iran-bases-syria-yemen/.

'Text of the basic principles of relations between the United States of America and the Union of Soviet Socialist Republics', *The American Presidency Project*, 29 May 1972, http://www.presidency.ucsb.edu/ws/?pid=3438.

Thompson, Nick, and Inez Torre, 'Yemen: who's joining Saudi Arabia's fight against the Houthis?', *CNN*, 30 March 2015, http://edition.cnn.com/2015/03/27/world/yemen-saudi-coalition-map/.

Tremblay, Pinar, 'Could Iran–Saudi conflict provide Turkey "graceful exit" from Syria?', *Al-Monitor*, 11 January 2016, http://www.al-monitor.com/pulse/originals/2016/01/turkey-saudi-arabia-iran-strife-opportunities-and-perils.html.

'Trump: I told Saudi king he wouldn't last without US support', *Reuters*, 3 October 2018, https://www.reuters.com/article/us-usa-trump-saudi/trump-i-told-saudi-king-he-wouldnt-last-without-u-s-support-idUSKCN1MD066 (last accessed 4 June 2019).

'Turkey to boost military cooperation with Iran after army chief's visit', *Reuters*, 17 August 2017, https://www.reuters.com/article/us-turkey-iran-military-idUSKCN1AX1AK.

'UN chief hails Pakistan's leading role in peacekeeping operations', *UN News Center*, 13 August 2013, http://www.un.org/apps/news/story.asp?NewsID=45613#.WarNa4VOLSF.

'UN condemns attack on Saudi embassy in Iran', *BBC*, 5 January 2016, http://www.bbc.com/news/world-middle-east-35229385.

Vatanka, Alex, interview with *Al Jazeera* TV channel, 17 January 2016.

'Video: Iranian "hero pilot" defies Saudi orders to leave Yemen', *France 24*, 1 May 2015, http://observers.france24.com/en/20150501-video-iranian-pilot-saudi-yemen.

Wintour, Patrick, 'Qatar given 10 days to meet 13 sweeping demands by Saudi Arabia', *The Guardian*, 23 June 2017, https://www.theguardian.com/world/2017/jun/23/close-al-jazeera-saudi-arabia-issues-qatar-with-13-demands-to-end-blockade.

Wright, Robin, and Peter Baker, 'Iraq: Jordan see threat to election from Iran', *Washington Post*, 8 December 2004, http://www.washingtonpost.com/wp-dyn/articles/A43980-2004Dec7.html.

Yackley, Ayla Jean, and Bozorgmehr Sharafedin, 'Rivals Turkey and Iran seek to "manage differences"', *Reuters*, 5 March 2016, http://www.reuters.com/article/us-iran-turkey-visit-idUSKCN0W70DB.

'Yemen conflict: Pakistan rebuffs Saudi coalition call', *BBC*, 10 April 2015, http://www.bbc.com/news/world-asia-32246547.

Zhdannikov, Dmitry, and Alex Lawler, 'Saudi oil policy uncertainty unleashes the conspiracy theorists', *Reuters*, 18 November 2014, http://www.reuters.com/article/opec-idUSL6N0T73VG20141118.

Index